"In this marvelous book, Julius-Kei Kato i
cially students—both Christians who have
Bible and the 'nones'—to the Bible as literature and history and helps them discover their ancestors in Jesus and the writers of the New Testament. I most enthusiastically recommend Kato's book, especially to those who style themselves as atheist and 'none.' They may be surprised to find their ancestors in the Bible!"

—PETER C. PHAN, Georgetown University

"An original, insightful, and accessible book to help us think about why and how we should read the Bible in an age that has often been characterized as 'secular' or 'secularized.' With the metaphor of 'spiritual ancestry,' Kato opens up a way for us to glimpse how we may yet relate to this ancient 'religious' library today—and perhaps even find resonance or relevance in it."

—TAT-SIONG BENNY LIEW, College of the Holy Cross

"Many books on the Bible have been written for Christians. This book is boldly written for secular readers who want to know the spiritual ancestors of the New Testament. Well-written and accessible, this book is a gift and can be used in classrooms, churches, and youth groups. I highly recommend it."

—KWOK PUI-LAN, Candler School of Theology, Emory University

"Julius-Kei Kato invites us on a metaphorical journey to the New Testament village where he presents us to our spiritual ancestors, grand-uncles Mark, Matthew, Luke, John, Paul, and the great founding ancestor Jesus. In a surprisingly compelling way, Kato combines expert biblical scholarship with very accessible storytelling, stirring the attention of professionals as well as students. I highly recommend this inspiring exercise in both decentering biblical studies and challenging our hybrid identities in a multicultural secular age."

—LIEVEN BOEVE, KU Leuven

"Julius-Kei Kato skillfully weaves together his life story, popular culture, and Asian spirituality in his fascinating exploration of biblical texts. His premise that reading the Bible is an act of conversing with our spiritual ancestors in their metaphorical village offers a fresh lens for reading the texts. Deeply insightful, engaging, and accessible."

—RAJ NADELLA, Columbia Theological Seminary

"Addressed to an audience that does not presuppose any religious or faith commitments, *Reading the Bible in a Secular Age* invites the reader into conversation with the major portions of the Christian Scriptures (the historical Jesus, Paul, and the Gospel authors). Julius-Kei Kato maintains the distinctive message of each, whom he calls 'spiritual ancestors,' a term that conveys both the respect due but also the opportunity to disagree with and challenge, rightly putting the responsibility of what to do with this legacy on the reader."

—HENRY W. MORISADA RIETZ, Grinnell College

Reading the Bible in a Secular Age

Reading the Bible in a Secular Age

The New Testament as Spiritual Ancestry

JULIUS-KEI KATO

CASCADE *Books* • Eugene, Oregon

READING THE BIBLE IN A SECULAR AGE
The New Testament as Spiritual Ancestry

Cascade Books
An Imprint of Wipf and Stock Publishers
199 W. 8th Ave., Suite 3
Eugene, OR 97401

www.wipfandstock.com

PAPERBACK ISBN: 978-1-7252-7772-4
HARDCOVER ISBN: 978-1-7252-7773-1
EBOOK ISBN: 978-1-7252-7774-8

Cataloguing-in-Publication data:

Names: Kato, Julius-Kei, author.

Title: Reading the Bible in a secular age : the New Testament as spiritual ancestry / Julius-Kei Kato.

Description: Eugene, OR: Cascade Books, 2023 | Includes bibliographical references and index.

Identifiers: ISBN 978-1-7252-7772-4 (paperback) | ISBN 978-1-7252-7773-1 (hardcover) | ISBN 978-1-7252-7774-8 (ebook)

Subjects: LCSH: Bible, New Testament—Criticism, interpretation, etc. | Bible. New Testament—Hermeneutics. | Secularization (Theology) | Bible—Criticism, interpretation, etc.—Asia

Classification: BS2361.3 K38 2023 (paperback) | BS2361.3 (ebook)

07/19/23

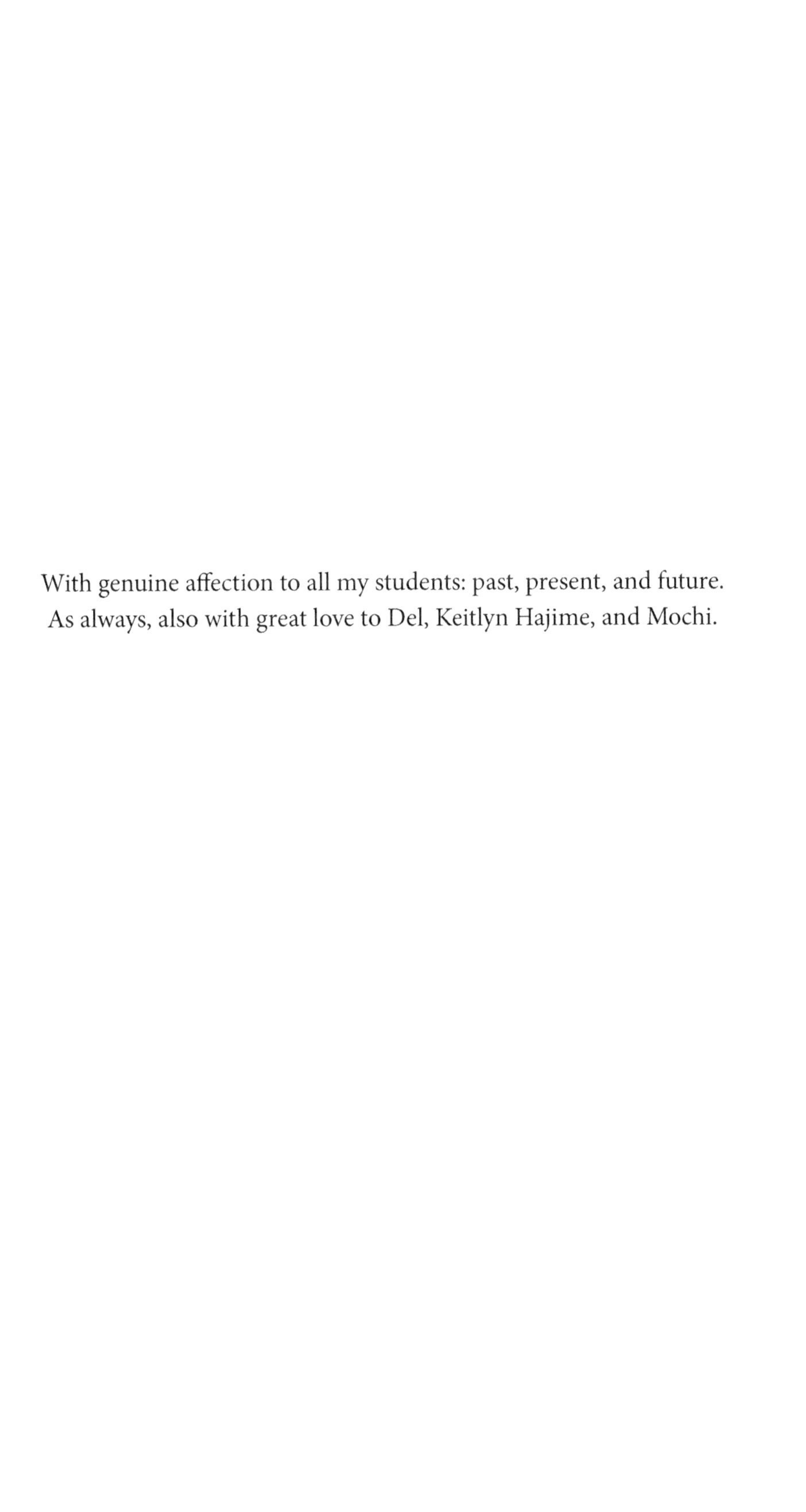

With genuine affection to all my students: past, present, and future.
As always, also with great love to Del, Keitlyn Hajime, and Mochi.

It is very important to make a connection with our ancestors and the future generations. Alienation is a kind of sickness. There are people who don't feel they are connected with anything at all and they suffer from being cut off, from loneliness. There is no understanding. There is no love that can nourish them. Therefore, to practice restoring the connection is very important.

. . . Your ancestors have transmitted to you many positive seeds, but also many negative seeds. It is up to you to practice to develop the positive seeds and to diminish and to transform the negative seeds. The essential is to learn how to do it.

—ZEN BUDDHIST MASTER THICH NHAT HANH,
Dharma Talk: "We are the Continuation of Our Ancestors," July 21, 1997

Contents

Preface

I've been teaching biblical studies at the college/university level for twenty-some years now. I decided to write this book because I feel that it is high time to create a pedagogical resource meant for my students (and other similar learners), as well as those who are in a position of teaching the Bible or other related fields. So here is my humble offering for students and teachers alike. It is based on how I've tried to teach the New Testament, my "bread and butter" course, and the many experiences I've had as a scholar-educator.

One characteristic that has constantly defined the places where I've taught through the years (and which has therefore greatly influenced my teaching) is that I usually could not assume that "religious faith" is a significant factor for a great number of my students. In short, this situation is what we teachers (in religion-related fields) know so well as the secular environment that is increasingly becoming the norm across the Western world, particularly in post-secondary institutions. That is even the case in many institutions that are still affiliated to religious institutions such as my own. Of course, there are notable exceptions, such as places in the Bible-belt in the US.

Since that secular environment has constantly been my context, I have had to exert much effort to make biblical studies relevant through non-theological ways. This factor plays a central role in this book. I repeat: I intentionally *do not use* a theological approach to the Bible here. Rather, I prioritize approaching this collection of writings using primarily literary and historical methods for a very important reason. In this secular age in which we live, I'm becoming more convinced that "theology" (if such an enterprise might even be possible in a context radically marked by diversity in religious belief or lack thereof) can only come *after* we deal first with *the things that commonly bind us all as humans*, hence, the priority of literary and historical approaches. Simply put, one does not need religious faith to study literature and history. Moreover, as a BIPOC scholar, I also employ cross-cultural perspectives as a way of somehow decentering biblical studies from the almost exclusive grip that Western points of view have had on this field until now.

Acknowledgments

EVERY TEACHER HAS PROBABLY heard this saying: If you really want to learn something, teach it! I began teaching in some form in my teens and have continued to do so until today (thirty-some years!) and I can truly attest to the veracity of that saying. The one who learns most from teaching is definitely the very one who teaches!

Here at my academic home, King's University College at Western University (London, Canada), the New Testament has been my "bread and butter" course every single year since 2007. As I look back at the fifteen years I've spent here and at the many students who have studied the New Testament with me, my heart is just overflowing with gratitude: So much learning has happened, especially on my part! I hope I've shared the learning experience with my students as well.

First and foremost, I'd like to thank all my students then—past, present, and even future. There are so many faces and names that come to mind when I say this, that I'm afraid to mention names for fear of forgetting some. Nevertheless, I want to acknowledge some former students who have gone on to help me in my work through the years in special ways, such as engaging me in insightful conversations and providing feedback, being my research assistants, teaching assistants, or even those who have gotten back to me to tell me how they apply the things they learned at my classes. In particular, let me mention: Natalie Pepe, Shannon Marinnan, Chris Emms, Emma MacDonald, Kate Lawson, Andrew Knight-Messenger, LisaLee Newell, Jessica and Gdynia Crave, Adam Moreash, Hannah Waitschies, Mary Ellen Lanou, Daniela and Ariela Dabrowski, Sara Michienzi, Lauren Crawford, Eric Lu, Serena di Cicco, Channelle Robinson, Mia Theocaris, among many others. Most of all, I'd like to thank my most recent research assistants, Christine Atchison, Madeline Bickley, and, particularly, Danielle

Durand, who helped me directly in the preparation of the manuscript of this work: Thank you so much to everyone for your precious service!

A special thank you also to my colleagues at King's: Nigel Joseph, Ruth Yu, and Andrea Di Giovanni, who have helped me in my research in various ways through the years.

I would also like to express my gratitude to the wonderful people at Wipf and Stock who have assisted me in different ways in the process of giving birth to this book. First of all, to Chris Spinks who graciously accepted my proposal and who also encouraged and guided me in various ways as I worked on the book, especially during the tough months of the pandemic. Special thanks also to Stephanie Hough, Mark Stuber, Jorie Chapman, EJ Davila, Matthew Wimer, Savanah N. Landerholm, and George Callihan.

I am so deeply grateful to and humbled by the trust of my colleagues in our guilds of biblical/religious studies and theology who have supported and/or endorsed not only this work but my efforts through the years to advance the disciplines of biblical studies, religious studies, and theology. Your encouragement and endorsement mean the world to me! A grand "thank you" then particularly to: Peter C. Phan, Fumitaka Matsuoka, (the late) Kenan Osborne, Fernando Segovia, Tat-siong Benny Liew, Kwok Pui-Lan, Lieven Boeve, Raj Nadella, Henry Morisada Rietz, Uriah Kim, Joseph Cheah, Grace Ji-Sun Kim, Jin-Young Choi, Chloe Sun, Janette Hur Ok, Monica Jyotsna Melanchthon, Edmund Chia, Gemma Cruz, Christina Astorga, Ruben Habito, Anh Tran, Cristina Lledo Gomez, Catherine Punsalan-Manlimos, Faustino "Tito" Cruz, Min-Ah Cho, Stephanie Wong, and Leo Lefebure.

A very special note of thanks also goes to my colleagues here at King's University College for their unfailing support of me through the years: Steve Lofts, Jonathan Geen, Mark Yenson, Carolyn Chau, Gyongyi Hegedus, Mahdi Tourage, Chaya Halberstam, John Heng, Antonio Calcagno, Robert Ventresca, Allyson Larkin, John Dool and Denis Grecco (of St. Peter's Seminary next door), Hunter Brown, Gilbert Brodie, Phil Mueller, Susan Brown, John Snyder.

Last but not least, I am indebted in a special way to my immediate family, my most precious ones: Del, Keitlyn Hajime, and little Mochi, whose gracious love and support create the environment that continually enables me to work and flourish. I love you all so dearly!

Let me also make special mention of Marianne Larsen and Shoichi Sugano, two dear friends who have supported me as a friend and a scholar all these years.

Introduction

Spiritual Ancestry and Reading the Bible

How They Are Connected

A person without roots cannot be a happy person.

—Thich Nhat Hanh[1]

Our main concern is not to gain pleasure or to avoid pain but rather to see a meaning in our lives.

—Viktor Frankl (paraphrase)[2]

ANCESTRY: MY STORY

"Ancestry" is a theme that has occupied me for practically my whole life. I was born in Manila, the capital of the Philippines, as the second son of a Japanese father from Kyoto, Japan (the ancient capital); and a mother from the Province of Iloilo in the Western Visayas region of Central Philippines. From the time I became aware of myself, my family, and my communities of affiliation, I was always struggling to define who I really was. Although I was born and raised in the Philippines and continue to love my *Inang*

1. Thich Nhat Hanh, quoted in Plum Village, "How to Love and Understand Your Ancestors When You Don't Know Them?," 2:58.

2. The original is: "man's main concern is not to gain pleasure or to avoid pain but rather to see a meaning in his life," from Frankl, *Man's Search for Meaning*, 117.

Bayan (mother country) deeply, as a child, I was always labelled a *"Hapòn"* (a Japanese) because of how I looked and my dead giveaway last name—"Kato." Despite growing up in the capital region, I couldn't speak Tagalog/Filipino straight at first (the language of the region as well as the national language) because my mom spoke to us in her own native language called *Hiligaynon*. English was the common tongue that united my Japanese father and Filipino mother and, hence, we used a lot of English at home.

I distinctly remember that when my grandparents, granduncle and grand-aunt visited us from Japan and spoke amongst themselves or with dad in Japanese, a language I wasn't functional in as a child, I vowed to be able to speak with them one day in that language which I felt was a part of me that had not yet been awakened. When I started to attend school and the teacher would do roll call at the beginning of the year, she would eventually pause when faced with my Japanese surname and ask me, "Are you Filipino?" I remember that I would reply, "I'm Japanese" (meaning: I'm *not only* Filipino *but also* Japanese). There were times when I would sit in agony through social studies sessions on the Second World War as my classmates would glower at me when they learned of the various atrocities committed by—what some of them expressed as—my "brutal" Japanese ancestors during the war.

Experiences such as these left such an indelible mark on me that, at the end of my teens in the mid-1980s, I left my mother's country, the Philippines, where I grew up, and moved to my father's country, Japan. I did that for a number of reasons, a major one of which was because I wanted to search for that part of my ancestry that I did not know very well—my Japanese roots.

Those first years in Japan were tough ones. "Japanese who grew up abroad," the so-called *kikoku-shijo* (literally, "kids returning to the homeland") face a lot of difficulties when they enter a strictly regimented and very different Japanese society from wherever they came from. Besides, the *hāfu* (the half-Japanese or mixed-race kids) had even tougher challenges as they were not well-regarded by many people, given the general tendency to prefer a kind of "Japanese purity" at the time. And I belonged to both groups! Add to that the fact that learning not only to speak but also read and especially write Japanese as a grown-up is nothing short of a gargantuan task. But I was young, idealistic, and on a high stakes search for my Japanese roots. I just gritted my teeth and told myself that, against all those great odds, I would learn the culture and the language well enough to *truly* become Japanese, even if that were the very last thing I would do. The search for my ancestry and roots had a "do or die" importance for me at that point.

After a few years in Japan, I started to feel that I was indeed becoming Japanese with the result that the people and culture that seemed so "other" to me once upon a time were becoming a true part of me. It was at this time that my dad, younger brother, and I had a chance to visit our ancestral tomb in the place where my dad's family originally came from—Akita in Northern Japan. By this time, I could speak, read, and write Japanese with some fluency and conversing first with my dad and with my other relatives in their, or rather, *our* Japanese language jolted me with the realization that I had fulfilled my childhood vow to speak with my family in Japanese!

Moreover, listening to my uncle's hypothesis about our ancestors possibly being *samurai* because of the location of the tomb was also an unforgettably moving experience. I still tell my daughter when things get rough to remember that she is descended from the famed *samurai* of old! Standing in front of our ancestral tomb in Akita—that concrete, material embodiment of our lineage—was a high point in my life. It gave me the shivers! I tangibly felt that I truly and experientially knew now what it meant to be deeply connected also to my Japanese roots and ancestry. Now, I was no longer limping on one foot knowing just one side of my roots (my mother's); I was also tapped onto the other part of my ancestry, my father's Japanese side. This experience finally made me feel whole. Then and there I realized that knowing one's roots and ancestry, as many teachers have reminded us throughout history, is indeed one of the most essential and vital things in life.

SPIRITUAL ANCESTRY AND SPIRITUAL INTELLIGENCE

If our biological ancestry is this important as I've tried to relate in my case, there's another ancestry that is equally, if not more important for our overall well-being. It is what we'll refer to as "spiritual ancestry" and this book will be about it in a major way. The French philosopher, paleontologist, and Jesuit priest Pierre Teilhard de Chardin is often credited (perhaps wrongly!)[3] as having said, "We are not human beings having a spiritual experience. We are spiritual beings having a human experience." Whoever the real provenance of that quote might be, its point is valuable: Spirituality is an essential aspect of being human because, according to this view, it is humanity's primary dimension. What that means is: The deepest longing of the human spirit

3. Although the internet overwhelmingly attributes this quote to Teilhard de Chardin, the website *Quote Investigator* says that this quote should probably be more accurately attributed to the motivational speaker Wayne Dyer. See Dyer, *You'll See It When You Believe It*, 16. See also *Quote Investigator*, "You Are Not a Human Being."

lies in things that are beyond the scope of both conventional science or the glittering material things that media ads continually trot out before us. No, our deepest longings *as humans* actually lie beyond the material realm in the spiritual dimension. It is there where we find the deep drive hardwired in all of us that strongly urges us to seek for *meaning*. How? By a twofold movement of (1) journeying into our inner depths and (2) transcending ourselves for something "bigger" (than our puny egos). Hence, "depth" and "transcendence" are the key words here. That is, by the way, how I define spirituality which is clearly the heart of all religion. Nay, I would even say: It is the heart of *all authentic humanity*.

When I stood before my ancestors' tomb all those years ago, I felt a deep connection to them despite the vast differences in our historical contexts and backgrounds because I finally felt that we shared a common Japanese culture, language, and ethos—things that I had spent a few years actively learning at that point at the cost of blood, sweat, and tears. I learned the valuable lesson that, with some effort on our part, blood and cultural ancestry can give us a deep sense of connectedness and wholeness!

When it comes to spiritual ancestry, it is necessary to realize that, insofar as all of us are "spiritual beings having a human experience," we share a common faculty with our spiritual ancestors despite the wide gaps of historical time and worldviews that separate us from them. Let us call that innate ability "spiritual intelligence." Spiritual intelligence can be described as the powerful drive within humans to seek to understand "the meaning of it all." That in turn leads all humans everywhere and in every historical period to attempt to build big, overarching frameworks that, they hope, could encompass all things—material and spiritual—in the universe—"a theory of everything," if you will. This spiritual intelligence is obviously the origin of our religious worldviews, our spiritualities, our philosophical systems, our ideologies, our visions of the world, our perceptions of reality, and so on. Surprisingly, spiritual intelligence is even the source from which comes the decision of certain people to reject "God" or, more properly expressed, to reject what spiritual intelligence shows to be childish, naïve, and crude ideas about the Ultimate, not to mention dysfunctional forms of religion.

Despite spiritual intelligence producing an irreconcilable diversity of human ideas about the big nature of reality, it is this common drive that pushes us to attempt to figure out "the meaning of it all." Let me go further and say that it is actually this spiritual intelligence that unites us all. It's also known as *the human quest for meaning*, as the Austrian Holocaust survivor and psychoanalyst Viktor Frankl explains in his works.[4]

4. For example, Frankl, *Man's Search for Meaning*.

In the past, that deep drive to seek "the meaning of it all" in the West almost always took place within religion, particularly the Christian religion. But times have changed and nowadays many of us in this secular age try to bracket out religion and God as bygone and irrelevant things. This has unfortunately made us adrift in a spiritual no-man's land, a situation in which we are disconnected from our spiritual roots and unsure how to move forward in the quest for a relevant spirituality for our age.

Despite that, I'm still convinced that what bridges the great divide between the deeply religious world of our ancestors and the secular age in which we find ourselves today is that both they and us still have this common spiritual intelligence that makes us try our best to glimpse "the meaning of it all." And if we can only connect with that common deep desire, we will actually find out that we are very much like our spiritual ancestors in the perennial human quest for meaning. We, like them, somehow know deep within that we will only slake that seemingly unquenchable thirst for meaning if we go deeper into ourselves and transcend ourselves for "something bigger."

The answers we now propose to the "meaning of it all" might be very different from theirs. Some of us may feel for example that they used the concept "God" too easily and uncritically. Many of us consequently react to that by developing a kind of allergic reaction to "God" and religion. But the deep desire to seek meaning through depth and transcendence, in short, the spirituality in our depths is still, I repeat, the one thing that unites us with them. That is the same thing that makes all of us, both us and them, part of species *homo spiritualis.*

What this all comes down to is that *we don't have to reinvent the wheel in the area of trying to discern "the meaning of it all."* Our perennial quest for meaning should neither be performed in a vacuum nor from scratch. Rather, *it should be done first and foremost with a proper acknowledgment of our spiritual roots and ancestry.*

A BROAD DESCRIPTION OF THIS BOOK

This work is a "first step" in a long-term project I have to attempt to propose to people nowadays (I'm thinking particularly of the young people who can potentially be my students) how to develop a relevant spirituality (a "quest for meaning," if you will) for themselves, whether they are religious in the traditional sense or not. And that first step can be solemnly expressed thus: *Thou shalt know thy spiritual roots!* For, as various philosophers remind us, to be rooted, to be connected with one's ancestry, especially in the spiritual realm, is one of our deepest and fundamental needs as humans. To paraphrase Thich Nhat Hanh (see the quote above), without roots, happiness will always elude us.

For us in the West, it is clear from an unchangeable and inescapable history that Christianity and its heart, the Bible, are, for good or ill, the essential components of our spiritual roots for the simple reason that the quest for "the meaning of it all" has been done for most of Western history in serious conversation with, even often controlled by, Christianity and the biblical tradition.

Because of that, I propose here that we get to know our spiritual ancestry by metaphorically standing in front of a concrete and material symbol of the Christian tradition—the book known as the Bible, particularly the part called the New Testament. And then, it's a matter of doing the same thing that was whispered by a divine voice to St. Augustine of Hippo when he was on the verge of a great spiritual breakthrough, "*tolle et lege!*" (Take up and read!).

This book first and foremost will make a case for why it would do us good to take up and read the Bible although we are living in a secular age, which frowns down upon such activities related to "old-time" religion. We should read the Bible even in a secular age because it is one of the best ways to be connected with our spiritual roots and ancestry. I will flesh out my case by suggesting that the New Testament is a kind of a textual village where some of the most important spiritual ancestors that began the Christian tradition continue to live through the texts that either they wrote, were written about them, or were first received by them. The good news is that by learning some strategies to read and interpret the Bible, we can get to know these spiritual ancestors, have relevant conversations with them and thus reconnect with the earliest roots of our spiritual tradition in the West. In this way, we will know where our roots and ancestry lie and with this, we will be better equipped to proceed in our continuous quest for a deeper and bigger meaning in life, whether that involves "God" and established religion *or not*.

There is an (unfortunately fake yet perceptive) Dalai Lama quote that goes like this: "Learn the rules well in order to know how to break them properly."[5] Applied to our spiritual ancestry and roots, this work will insist that, as a first step, we have to encounter our spiritual ancestors in the New Testament and converse with them meaningfully. When we are finally in touch with our roots, we can then more properly discern how to seek for

5. Dalai Lama, "18 Rules for Living." See this website that claims that the 18 Rules are not from the Dalai Lama: https://buddhism-controversy-blog.com/2014/03/01/dalai-lama-fake-quotes/.

meaning in our world and decide what to embrace from our spiritual ancestry, as well as what to revise, resist, or even reject.

AN OVERVIEW OF THE STRUCTURE OF THIS WORK

To go into details, this book will take the following concrete form: It will have two main parts. In part I (chapters 1–5), we will begin by getting an overview of our broad topic and discuss some themes that will prepare us to make a metaphorical journey to the New Testament village to encounter some major "village elders" (spiritual ancestors). That will happen in part II (chapters 6–11). Chapter 12, the conclusion, will bring us from our journey to the New Testament village back home to our Western secularized world and suggest how we can both embrace and struggle with the spiritual ancestry that we have come to know better after our journey.

Let me give a more detailed description of the individual chapters. Chapter 1 will offer broad but key reflections on why we need to read the Bible even in a secular age. Chapter 2 will explain in more detail the nature of the secular age in which we find ourselves in the West today. Chapter 3 will offer a foundational paradigm for viewing the Bible, shifting the focus from a too facile idea of "the Bible as God's word" to the most plain and demonstrable fact—that the Bible contains the words of our spiritual ancestors. It will also discuss some foundational ideas that are linked with the Bible, such as God, faith-as-trust, revelation, belief or unbelief, etc. Chapter 4 will present the main metaphorical image of the Bible, particularly the New Testament as a village where our spiritual ancestors continue to live. It will also suggest some concrete strategies on how to relate with these spiritual ancestors and how to interpret their writings. Chapter 5 will give a general orientation to the New Testament village by giving a "big picture" so that readers could grasp the whole before they enter into details about specific spiritual ancestors in part II. It will also give an important background review of the Old Testament for those who need it.

With that, we will enter part II of the work. Here, we will discuss in detail six important spiritual ancestors who were present at the very beginning of what would eventually become the Christian tradition. They are: Mark, Matthew, Luke, John, Paul, and, of course, Jesus, the great founding ancestor. The intent is to pay a visit to a particularly important spiritual ancestor, encounter them and grasp some, what I will call, "*sine qua non*'s" (Latin for "without which"). By this, I mean some essential characteristics without which we would not understand what "made this particular spiritual ancestor tick" and what is going on in the work attributed to this particular village elder.

After those encounters and conversations with the six spiritual ancestors, we will come back to our present, secular world in chapter 12. The journey will have hopefully given us enough knowledge and insight that would equip us both to embrace and wrestle with our spiritual ancestry. All this is for the purpose of eventually directing us toward constructing a more relevant spirituality here and now that would be effective in aiding us to pursue the depth and transcendence that all of us long for as humans.

There you have it! Does that sound like a plan? Without further ado, let's proceed. The journey begins now . . .

PART I

The Why and How of Reading the Bible in a Secular Age

1

Why Read the Bible in a Secular Age?

An Unapologetic Apologia for the Importance of Biblical Studies Today

To be rooted is perhaps the most important and least recognized need of the human soul.

—Simone Weil[1]

FROM THE TRENCHES OF UNDERGRADUATE TEACHING[2]

I teach biblical and religious studies at King's University College, a liberal arts college in London, Ontario (Canada). King's is a publicly funded Catholic college that is part of a huge public university (of the province of Ontario) next door called Western University. Having a "publicly-funded" Catholic institution of higher learning is a Canadian phenomenon that may not be familiar to our southern neighbors in the US. Unlike in many US Catholic universities, we do not have a mandatory theology requirement for our students. We therefore have to compete with other possible (and

1. Weil, *Need for Roots*, 40.

2. This article originally appeared in a slightly modified version in *The Fourth R: A Journal for Religious Literacy* 33 (2020) 17–20.

generally more attractive) choices to make students interested enough to actually take an elective course on religion. Let me admit it clearly here: nowadays that is really a tough job because religion is becoming more and more a difficult item "to sell." That's what the registrar's office has been telling our department for many years now.

It is an integral part of our job then to devise ways and means to make studying religion, in my particular case, studying the Bible, relevant, significant, and interesting enough so that students might be motivated to take these "unpopular" courses. I usually make my case along the following lines.

By virtue of their location in and/or being raised in a Western[ized] society and civilization, most of my students (and many North Americans in general), without really being conscious of it, live in a society, culture, and civilization in which Christianity (as well as its heart, the Bible) has had such a crucially important cultural role that we could rightly claim the biblical and the Christian heritage as an important part of its roots.[3] This is something that is increasingly being forgotten, neglected, or even repudiated nowadays.

Since Western societies at present have become quite diverse with all sorts of people whose heritages come from various parts of the world, one may rightly ask: Is the original Christian heritage of the West also important for Westerners whose heritage stems from originally non-Western/non-Christian contexts? My reply would still be in the affirmative. Even if one's roots come from originally non-Christian traditions (in fact, I am Japanese on my father's side and my roots there are originally Shinto-Buddhist), I still think that by virtue of their present location in Western societies, they still absorb a significant amount of Christian cultural influence and, hence, the Christian spiritual ancestry of the West still concerns them in a significant manner.

Of course, the biblical-Christian heritage is not the only relevant cultural wellspring for Western civilization; we here in the West are also heirs to many other influences. To name a few, we have the pre-Christian religious mythologies of Europe, the indigenous cultures and traditions of North America, the Greco-Roman cultures, the legacy of the Enlightenment, today's globalized world, the further cultural enrichment that recent immigrants bring to the equation, among many other heritages. We can therefore say that our present identities are actually hybrid in a profound way.[4] However, since I am in the religious studies "business," I try to impress

3. See, for example, Dyas and Hughes, *Bible in Western Culture*; Schippe and Stetson, *Bible and Its Influence*; Beavis and Gilmour, *Dictionary of the Bible and Western Culture*.

4. Many of the things I suggest in this book about "hybridity" is described in more

on my students that neglecting that biblical part of our common Western heritage makes us run the risk of a kind of "rootlessness"[5] that could have unfortunate consequences, such as the rise of totalitarian regimes in the twentieth century or even, arguably, the rise of populism at the present time.

Love it or hate it, for better or for worse, Christianity and its heart, the Bible, have been an integral part of Western civilization for most of its history,[6] hence, an important part of what we may rightly call "our tradition."[7] It would do us well to remember at this point that an essential and crucial part of being human is having a right, healthy, and (ideally speaking) affectionate-yet-critical relationship with one's traditions. Only then will we know where we came from, hence, also who we are (our sense of identity) and, going forward, toward where we should move.

"ROOTS" AND WHY I'M SO KEEN ON THEM

The reason why I am so keen on the need to remain *loyally yet critically* connected with one's roots lies in my BIPOC identity (Black-Indigenous-People of Color) here in North America, particularly as someone who has put down new roots in a new land (Canada-North America), although I am originally from places (the Philippines and Japan in Asia) that are quite distant and very different from where I am now. Let me continue to share a bit of my story for you to understand better where I'm coming from as I write this book.

At present, I live in London, Ontario, Canada. My present home is halfway around the world from my original familial and cultural roots. As mentioned, I was born and raised in Manila, the Philippines, as the son of a Japanese father and a Filipina mother. I've always been fiercely proud of this hybrid identity of mine. In-between the cities of my birth and current home, namely Manila and London, Ontario, I consider myself very fortunate to have the extraordinary experience of having lived, studied, and worked in many other places due to many, shall we say, "accidents" of life

detail in my previous works: *How Immigrant Christians Living in Mixed Cultures Interpret Their Religion*; "Interpretation," 63–75; *Religious Language and Asian American Hybridity*.

5. This theme is going to be described more at length in a later chapter (see chapter 2). For the concept of "rootlessness," see Arendt, *Origins of Totalitarianism* and Weil, *Need for Roots*.

6. For more on this theme, see Holland, *Dominion*; Stark, *For the Glory of God*; Stark, *Victory of Reason*; Ehrman, *Triumph of Christianity*.

7. For an excellent and comprehensive treatment of the notion of tradition, see Valliere, "Tradition," 9267–81.

(better perhaps, "adventures where I've been led in life"). These places span from Tokyo and Jerusalem to Rome, Paris, Munich, Bonn, the Bay Area (in California) and Toronto, among others. In these various places, I've tried to be as open as possible to the local culture and learn whatever I could while never forgetting my roots in Asia. By that I mean: I've always made a serious effort to participate in the local life of people and understand these cultures "from the inside" and not only from a superficial, "outsider's" perspective.

This complex life-journey has made my original ethnic and cultural hybridity richer and more complex, so much so that if someone were to force me now to choose just a single cultural identity, I would simply be unable to do so! In fact, being constrained to choose only one identity would be tantamount to doing violence to the hybridous multiplicity that is present and living within me. As I am now, I describe myself as Filipino-Japanese yes, but also Americanized in significant ways from childhood with a trace of Hispanic culture, all that acquired by growing up in Manila, the Philippines, a past colony of both Spain and the United States. Later, I lived and studied first in Japan for close to twelve years and in Rome for close to six years. My stay in Japan crucially formed me because it made me embrace the Japanese side that was already present genetically and culturally but not clear until I intentionally "became Japanese" in my father's land. My stay in Rome for close to six years made me acquire a bit of "Italian-ness" as well. I spent a truly eye-opening semester as an exchange student in Jerusalem and encountered in an up, close, and personal way the complex contemporary situation of Israel-Palestine while studying the ancient world which spawned the Bible. Moreover, because of wonderful short-term study and immersion opportunities in other countries during the summer months while I was in Europe, I guess I also have bits of German, Austrian, and French "toppings" for good measure. Last but certainly not least, since 2005, I've also been fiercely and proudly Canadian, eh! . . . and what else? Well, I'm a hybrid migrant in a globalized world in which hybridization is happening everywhere, all the time, and in a dizzying array of forms. It is hard to deny that in a globalized world, everyone is becoming in one way or another hybridized. Therefore, even those who are not ethnically and culturally hybrid like me are now in a better position to understand where the discourses and reasoning of ethnic/cultural hybrids are coming from.

More importantly, this hybridity goes even deeper than mere ethnic and cultural identity. It actually touches even my religious identity. By birth, upbringing, and tradition, I am Catholic. However, having lived in Japan for a long time made me not only appreciate the Buddhist tradition profoundly but even resulted in my adopting important aspects of Buddhism as a vital part of how I walk the *michi* (Japanese for "path") of life. Besides, exposure in varying degrees to other religious traditions through experience and study in the course of my life-journey has made me a spiritual hybrid in profound ways. Consequently, I've spent a lot of time studying hybridity and how it impacts our understanding and living of religion and spirituality today. And it seems to me that the spiritual hybridity I find in myself is fast becoming a reflection of the spiritual hybridization that is taking place in the wider world.

And then, there's also this following reason that hits even closer to home. My Filipina wife and I have a daughter, born and raised so far away from our original roots in Asia. From the very start of her life, we've drummed into her the message that she has three countries: Canada, the Philippines, and Japan, and we've tried to teach her to love and be proud of her hybrid and multicultural identity. It is clear to us though that her principal identity is based on where she was born and raised, and that place is clearly Canada. As we observe her growing up, we are often worried though that she would significantly lose her Asian heritages. All we can do is fervently hope that she would remain connected in a significant way to the Asian roots that live in her through her immigrant parents. Hence, my wife and I have always taken advantage of every opportunity to let her be more acquainted with the lands, cultures, languages, and people where we originally came from, halfway around the world from our daughter's "home and native land"[8] of Canada.

Because of these circumstances, I constantly ask questions such as: Who exactly am I now when I have so many worlds present within me? How do I or how does my daughter stay connected to our roots? On the heels of that, I also continuously wonder: What exactly is my daughter's identity? How do we treasure the gems from tradition and reject the dysfunctional elements that are also inevitably found therein? These are just a sampling of the many questions about identity and tradition that I constantly pose.

That's where I'm coming from. That is why I deeply feel that being attached to one's roots, heritage, and ancestry is a very important thing indeed. Roots give one a firm foundation from which to branch out far and wide. This I can attest to by personal experience. For this reason, I am convinced that having firm roots, as the philosopher Simone Weil asserted, is the "most important yet least recognized need of the human soul."[9]

8. Those lines are from the Canadian national anthem, "O Canada."

9. Weil, *Need for Roots*, 40.

THE NEED FOR ROOTS IN OUR TIME

Now that I've affirmed the importance of being connected to one's cultural and even spiritual roots, I will now confess that when I witness the growing reality at the university where I work as a professor of religion that what I have spent a lifetime studying (namely, religion, the Christian tradition and its scriptures) is fast becoming less and less relevant to the young people who come to our institutions of higher learning, I feel a deep sadness. I cannot help but interpret that phenomenon as people losing their cultural and spiritual roots more and more. This is why I urgently feel that making the study of religion and the Bible more relevant (mind you, *even if one is not religious*!) is an important way to help not only my students but most people in the West to be more aware of and connect with their cultural and spiritual roots.

THE NEW TESTAMENT IS A VILLAGE WHERE OUR SPIRITUAL ANCESTORS LIVE

With that intention, let me say here at the outset that at the heart of this book lies a metaphorical image for, what I think, is the urgent task of getting to know our biblical roots and traditions in the West, particularly in our so-called secular age. It is this: I will suggest that the New Testament is, as it were, a village where some of our most important spiritual ancestors continue to live and recount their stories and reflections about life to us today. Moreover, we can even engage these spiritual ancestors in meaningful conversation through a dynamic and creative process of reading and interpreting their writings. This becomes a more exciting task if we keep in mind that these ancestral teacher-storytellers are, in a profound way, the source of many of the key ideas that came to dominate our Western civilization for most of its history. That's why they can be considered by us who are in the West quite correctly as "spiritual ancestors." Hence, getting to know them—their stories and teachings, as well as the circumstances behind the texts they left us—is of utmost importance for us if we are to become more familiar with our spiritual ancestry, an ancestry from which our roots and many of our traditions and ways of thinking are located.

AN ILLUSTRATION FROM ASIAN NORTH AMERICAN LIFE

In my efforts to make my case that biblical and religious studies are worth engaging in as part of one's education, I've gleaned a lot of wisdom from Asian North American (let me use this more inclusive term as I am in Canada) author Amy Tan. Tan is a Chinese-American novelist based in the Bay Area in California. Practically all of her works deal in one way or another with the encounter and mixing of US and Chinese cultures and traditions, and what significance that has for our situation today. In fact, I've realized throughout the years that Tan's numerous novels about the intersections of Asia and North America (something which I also experience on a daily basis) could offer valuable hints to help us understand how cultural studies (in general) and, in my case, critical biblical and religious studies (in particular) could be imagined and approached so as to make them more relevant today to many people here in the West who, I find, identify themselves more and more nowadays as "Spiritual but not Religious" (SBNR), "Multiple Religious Belonging (types)" (MRB), (religious) "Dones" (We're "done" with religion!), or (religious) "Nones" (We have no particular religious affiliation).[10]

At the beginning of this book, I would like to put a bright spotlight on Tan's 2001 novel called *The Bonesetter's Daughter* (henceforward, *TBD*)[11] because it can insightfully illustrate the importance of reading the Bible even in a secular age. A critical correlation between themes in *TBD* with the effort to engage in biblical/religious studies can show that studying one's religious roots (Christianity and the Bible for many of us) is in fact a very relevant activity to engage in as part of one's lifelong education. This could also be applicable in other contexts (such as church settings) in which one is trying to make a case for the relevance of biblical (and/or religious) studies to people who feel more and more that religion in general or the Bible in particular is no longer a relevant matter worthy of one's time and energy.

In *TBD*, we read the story of Ruth, a Chinese-American woman living in San Francisco, who feels the urgency of coming to terms, *now as a grown-up*, with her mother, Chinese immigrant LuLing, who in turn is showing signs of cognitive and emotional deterioration because of age. For Ruth, LuLing is of course the very embodiment of their family's Chinese heritage, an aspect of her Chinese-American hybrid identity with which Ruth has constantly struggled in the course of her life. In her childhood

10. See Drescher, *Choosing Our Religion*; Mercadante, *Belief without Borders*.

11. Tan, *Bonesetter's Daughter*. Cf. also Dong, *Reading Amy Tan*, 47–54. Other Amy Tan novels are also worth consulting because similar themes are dealt with in them, particularly *The Joy Luck Club* and *The Kitchen God's Wife*.

and youth, Ruth was wont to rebel against her mother and the Chinese ways and traditions that LuLing represented and tried to hand on to her daughter. (Note well that "to hand on" is what the word "tradition" means.) Why? As often happens in the case of young, naïve, and immature Asian North Americans with hybrid identities, the ways of the "old world(s)" in Asia do not seem so relevant anymore in a North American context in which they are presently located—a land they would like to be acknowledged as being a part of and not be treated as "perpetual foreigners" just because of their "racial uniform."[12]

Fast forward to the now grown-up Ruth who struggles with multiple issues, such as her job and relationships, and seeks to understand who she really is in the midst of all that. As she sees her mother's condition worsen, Ruth begins to feel acutely the urgency of grappling with her mother's legacy and their family tradition, of which LuLing is the living symbol. The stories and experiences of the past, back in the old country are deeply embedded in the mind, heart, and memory of LuLing, indeed in her very being. But with the onset of early Alzheimer's disease, all that is in danger of being lost without being properly "handed on" to Ruth, her dear US-born daughter. At this very moment, Ruth comes upon a stack of papers LuLing wrote years earlier, stashed in a drawer at home. Ruth immediately realizes that this autobiographical text could be a firm connection with her mother's life story as LuLing's mental condition deteriorates. Moreover, the text is the key to understanding the person who raised Ruth, with all the historical and cultural forces that forged LuLing into the mother and the embodiment of the family tradition that she became.

There is, however, one big obstacle to this tradition being properly received by Ruth: The manuscript is written in Chinese, a language in which Ruth is no longer fluent. Because she realizes how important this task is, Ruth takes pains to find a translator. When she does, she is now finally able to go, as it were, inside her mother's mind and heart *through the text* and recover to some extent the stories and experiences that form a crucial part of the tradition that she, as LuLing's daughter, has to receive and possibly hand on to future generations.

12. For more on this, see, for example, Tuan, *Forever Foreigners or Honorary Whites?*, among many other works.

CORRELATIONS BETWEEN THE BONESETTER'S DAUGHTER AND READING THE BIBLE

There are a number of striking correlations between *TBD* and the situation of our present-day students of the Bible. As mentioned above, although the Bible has been an integral part of the Western civilization and culture in which the majority of our students are immersed, many of them are glaringly unaware of that.[13] The time that they will spend in a college or university program presents an excellent opportunity to put them in a similar frame of mind like *TBD*'s protagonist Ruth. Just as Ruth shifted from hostility/rebellion toward her Chinese heritage to a renewed appreciation of how important a critical appropriation of her roots and tradition is, it would be good if our students could move beyond the apathy and even hostility that now surround "religion," "Christianity," and "the Bible" in many areas of contemporary North American society to a frame of mind in which they could begin to appreciate the importance of digging deeper into the Western tradition, as if, like Ruth, on a quest for their cultural and religious roots.

If they do so, they will undoubtedly encounter the biblical tradition. In other words, for today's students to understand Western society and culture in a more profound way (and thus understand their identities better), it is imperative that they discover in a deeper way the sources of their tradition, of which the Bible is a valuable part. The biblical stories, laws, characters, tropes, themes, plots, teachings, etc., all function like the stack of papers Ruth discovers at home which enables her to delve deeper into her own Chinese roots.

As Ruth faced the barriers of language, history, and culture between her mother's China and her Asian North American world, in her quest to read and understand her mother's text written in Chinese, students of biblical studies also have to grapple with numerous barriers that have to be overcome in order for them to have a deep encounter with the tradition that is contained in the Bible in our vastly different contemporary world.

Contrary to many popular Christian notions, the message of the Bible is often not self-evident. It is not easy to read and understand a text that is separated from us by a gap of two thousand years (some parts of the Bible, even more than that). And then, notwithstanding many theological beliefs about the Bible that emphasize it as God's word, if we look at it in a humanistic way, all the books that make up the Christian scriptures are *first and foremost human constructs*, rooted in specific historical and cultural milieus.

13. For a work on how the modern "secularized" West is actually founded on many Christian principles, see Cupitt, *Meaning of the West*.

Note well that this last statement is the only thing we can demonstrably prove about the Bible. I'm saying that, contrary to how the Bible is often portrayed in Christian circles, there is no demonstrable way to prove that the Bible is divine in origin. Moreover, the texts therein were written in languages that are unintelligible to the vast majority of students, hence the need for competent, responsible, and critical scholarship, similar to Ruth's need of a translator, to mediate between the text and contemporary readers.

RELATING WITH THE BIBLE AS ITS "GROWN-UP CHILD"

In short, what I am trying to do here is to suggest an analogy or metaphor from Asian North American experience and literature to help people realize why there might still be much value in reading and studying the Bible even in our secular age. *TBD* is a story about an Asian North American daughter learning how to relate *as a grown-up* with her aging Asian mother, the epitome of an important part of her roots in Asia. The act of relating with someone boils down to the quality of conversation that these two people have. The nature, style, and quality of conversation between parents and their children are never static. Modes of conversation evolve as both parents and children advance in years and in their relationships with each other. Hence, it is more accurate to describe the parent-child conversation as dynamic and continually developing. For instance, when the child is young and immature, the conversation might be more like a one-way street in which the parents can and often have to impose what they think is best on the child. We can see these dynamics in *TBD* when LuLing tried to impose "Chinese ways" on the young Ruth who often rebelled against those efforts because she wanted to be "more American."

At a later stage in life, the conversation between parent and child (when the former is aging and the latter is already a more mature, grown-up individual) has to be a very different affair. Through the years, the parent-child conversation should develop more and more into a real dialogue, finally maturing in a form of conversation *between two grown-ups* in which each party respects (better even, loves) the other and engages the other in a mutual and respectful exchange of ideas and experiences.[14] That happens of course in an ideal world. The reality is not always so idyllic.

14. I have found many insightful points on the dynamics of the parent-child conversation when the child is already a grown-up in Pittman's *Grow Up! How Taking Responsibility Can Make You a Happy Adult*, particularly "How to Be a Grown-Up Even around Your Own Parents," chapter 5.

In *TBD*, we see the grown-up Ruth re-evaluating the quality of conversation she has had and presently has with her aging mother and does the grown-up thing to do, namely, look once again at her mother and the tradition LuLing embodies more carefully, more critically, with openness and even affection, and *reflect on how that tradition is relevant for herself and the generations that will come after her.* Note that this is not reverting, in a childish sense, to being the "good girl" who docilely obeys everything—the daughter that LuLing wished Ruth could have been growing up. No, Ruth's grown-up revalorizing of her tradition is more like a critical appropriation in which, on the one hand, she now more fully recognizes that the tradition is truly important but, on the other hand, knows better which aspects of it to resist and which aspects of it to retrieve, receive, and adapt to vastly changed circumstances, and also perhaps hand on to the next generation as "the tradition."

A RIGHT RELATIONSHIP WITH ONE'S TRADITION AND ROOTS

That, I contend, could be an appropriate image or metaphor for what should happen when someone embarks on the quest of having a deeper relationship with one's spiritual traditions and roots. Here in the West, one of the best ways to reconnect with one's spiritual ancestry is in effect doing a critical reading and study of the biblical texts. I'm suggesting that, as people located in the West, my students (and anyone else interested) could and should relate with the biblical tradition *as if relating with family and ancestry.* It is a truism of course (one that is nonetheless very true) that we do not choose family; we're just born into it! This could be applied to the legacy of Christianity and its heart, the Bible, vis-à-vis Western civilization. I would say that Christianity and the biblical tradition (because of historical circumstances over which we had no control) is a kind of "parent" of Western civilization. With institutional Christianity in rapid decline in the West, shouldn't we, like Ruth in the face of a deteriorating LuLing, feel a sense of urgency about how to grapple with the legacy of Christianity and the Bible? What do we have to know, remember, retrieve, valorize, and hand on as tradition to the next generation? How do we evaluate this legacy? What do we cherish and treasure? What do we resist and reject? Seeking to answer these questions, I think, is a more mature and responsible way to engage in biblical studies, one that I have and continue to suggest to my students and to anyone who would like to reacquaint themselves with their spiritual ancestry here in the West.

In this continuing effort to retrieve our Western spiritual ancestry, Tan (ironically, someone with part of her roots in faraway Asia like me) and her works could be insightful and helpful. To add a more explicit Asian North American "advertisement" to this enterprise, correlating Tan's novels with biblical studies as done here in North America could also be a way of bringing Asian North American scholarly voices out of the "ghetto" (to which it has often been confined by mainline biblical scholarship) to the forefront of the discipline and educational practice because one can see how some Asian North American experiences can suggest something valuable to our ongoing endeavors to advance biblical and religious studies.[15]

THE GOAL OF THIS WORK

Summing up, what I would like the reader to take away from this book is this: to realize that reading and studying the Bible (particularly the New Testament) is a process that is akin to reconnecting with one's spiritual roots and traditions. That is especially true for people located and living in the West today. That even includes, as mentioned above, people whose ancestry may not be culturally Christian but are in fact living in this cultural milieu that has been irrevocably impacted by the Christian tradition. The effort to connect with ancestry, in turn, is one of the deepest needs of the human soul that could anchor and enable it to discern better how to face the present and future.

To that end, I invite Western readers to treat the Bible, particularly the part of it called the New Testament, as a valuable part of their spiritual ancestry. It follows then that we also treat the characters there as well as the usually unnamed authors and communities that wrote, edited, and received these texts as our spiritual ancestors. Recognizing our ancestry and ancestors[16] is the first baby step to take. But we cannot stop there. We also have to learn how to relate with our ancestry in a mature way as grown-up children of the tradition. That means not only retrieving and cherishing valuable parts of our tradition but also resisting and rejecting its dysfunctional portions.

Now, ancestry, we should not forget, is something that is both significantly connected with us yet, at the same time, separated and distant from us. Our ancestry is where we and our clan ultimately came from but it is located in the past, which, as the English novelist L. P. Hartley insightfully

15. For an important recent work on Asian North American biblical hermeneutics, see Kim and Yang, *T&T Clark Handbook of Asian American Hermeneutics*.

16. A good elaboration of the value of ancestors and ancestry is Hertzel, *Ancestors*.

pointed out, "is like a foreign country: They do things differently there."[17] Our spiritual ancestors are the ones that make up that distant past ancestry. Their worldviews and beliefs created a ripple in the pond of history that touched our civilizations in significant ways in the past and continue to affect us in many ways today. Harking back to the protagonist of *TBD*, Ruth, we can see in her both childish and more mature ways of relating with her tradition and ancestry. An unquestioning, perfectly docile attitude (the attitude that LuLing desired when Ruth was younger) and the rebellious rejection of her mother's Chinese ways (what the young Ruth in fact adopted) would be some immature ways of relating with tradition. When faced, however, with the imminent deterioration of her mother's mind, the now grown-up Ruth seeks to know her mother's background better and critically appropriate it. This, we can say, is the more mature way of dealing with tradition.

In like manner, I would say that our general attitudes toward religion in general, and toward Christianity and its heart the Bible in particular, in the West today often run the gamut from childish, unquestioning docility to adolescent rebelliousness in different forms. We will have to strike a more balanced and more mature attitude. I will reflect on this theme time and again in the course of this book.

17. Hartley, *Go-Between*. This is the first line of the prologue.

2

We've Gone Far from Our Spiritual Roots

Understanding Our "Secular Age"

There is a widespread sense of loss here [in modern secular cities], if not always of God, then at least of meaning.

—Charles Taylor[1]

WE'VE GONE FAR FROM OUR SPIRITUAL ROOTS

I mentioned in the last chapter that, as someone who came from Asia but is now living in North America, I am located in a context that is far removed from where I originally came from. That poses some unique challenges as to how I could maintain a vital connection with my roots while, at the same time, participate fully in the world in which I find myself now. Applying that to our goal of understanding the importance of reading the Bible even in a world where religious belief is fast-diminishing, I would like to suggest that, if I refer specifically to spiritual ancestry, we in the so-called secular West are now living in a context that has been cut and distanced in a significant way from our original roots because those roots were firmly grounded in a worldview in which the spiritual-religious dimension of reality was given

1. Taylor, *Secular Age*, 552.

great importance. We instead find ourselves more and more in an environment in which the default positions on religious and spiritual matters are doubt, skepticism, and unbelief rather than trust and faith which were, generally speaking, the default attitudes of our ancestors. One of the burning questions that confront us then in this chapter is: How did this default attitude change so radically in the space of a few generations?

Despite the secularization of our time, we can still see today in our society the many material and cultural influences of this Christian/biblical past. That is amply demonstrated in architectural structures like churches, as well as in art, literature, songs, and even popular culture, among many other things. This contrast between our religious past, in which people were imbued with Christianity and its biblical tradition, and our present in which people are becoming increasingly disinterested in the Bible and in Christianity—in fact, in all things religious—has created a void which in turn has made many people unaware and ignorant of their connection with their civilization's spiritual ancestry and roots. It is necessary then to remember this important fact: One can never understand one's culture (in this case, the West) as well as one's personal and group identity without understanding one's roots, and I'd like to emphasize here in a special way, our *spiritual* roots. It is undeniable, as I've already said, that those roots in the West are in a major way decidedly *Christian and biblical in nature*. It is an urgent task then to get to know again our spiritual ancestry (presented in this work as the New Testament village) and learn anew that it is the source of the many key ideas on which Western civilization stands.[2]

WE ARE IN A SECULAR AGE

Charles Taylor is a Canadian philosopher who has reflected long and hard on the phenomenon of the secularization of the once very religious Western world. He posits a question at the beginning of his important work, *A Secular Age*, which not only guides the whole work but is also the very same question that we are asking in this chapter: How is it that in the 1500s it was virtually impossible for anyone in the West to doubt the existence of God, whereas now in the 2000s, in the same Western civilization, it has become so difficult for many people to believe in God or in a transcendent being and

2. For a greater elaboration on this theme, I repeat my recommendations of the following works: Holland, *Dominion*; Ehrman, *Triumph of Christianity*; Stark, *Triumph of Christianity*. A work that focuses on the particular contribution of the Catholic Church to Western civilization is Woods, *How the Catholic Church Built Western Civilization*.

dimension?[3] Note that this is a question about—to use Taylor's words—the "conditions of belief."[4] In the past, belief was considered axiomatic: it was a given in the sense that it had high plausibility for most people in the West. People just took for granted that belief in God and the spiritual realm is reasonable while they thought that atheism and agnosticism were strange, even wrong and depraved positions. Now instead, the tables have turned. Belief in God and in a transcendent realm is widely considered to be quite implausible; that is, it is considered to have low plausibility among a substantial number of Westerners.

Taylor's *A Secular Age* is intended as an answer to that question. He tries to do it in the form of a "story"[5] that purports to relate what occurred in Western history, a process that transformed Western civilization into the secularized milieu that we know it to be now. He describes how people try to find meaning in a secular world and what that implies for religion in general. Let me mention just some key ideas from Taylor's work that might aid us to better understand one major concern in this book, namely, what is the present situation with regard to religion that we find ourselves in and what relevance that has and will have for all of us?

WHAT IS A "SECULAR AGE"?

Firstly, what exactly then is a "secular age"? We can say that it is an age in which the following situation is firmly in place: Today, faith in God or maintaining a transcendent worldview (that is, a worldview in which the Transcendent is believed to be real) is largely and constantly contested and challenged in Western societies. In other words, all faith today, even in pockets of the West where people still have religious faith, is nevertheless *fraught with doubt*. We can say then that the "contestability of belief"[6] seems to be the widespread and the general default position of many (most?) people in the West today. If people are believers today, they are, one can say, generally in a socially weaker position (although this can vary considerably according to geographical location) because they are constantly nagged by the open and blatant questioning that contemporary Western society as a whole hurls at them, challenging them to justify why belief in God or in the Transcendent is still reasonable and justifiable. This is also partly the reason for the rise of fundamentalist or even reactionary movements which are

3. Taylor, *Secular Age*, 25.
4. Taylor, *Secular Age*, chapter 1.
5. Taylor, *Secular Age*, 29.
6. Smith, *How (Not) to Be Secular*, 10.

characterized by an emphasis on vigorous apologetics (defence of the faith) in some circles of believers.

However, Taylor also points out that the opposite position also holds true. That is, non-believers and skeptics are at times also caught up in the nostalgic and intriguing possibility that *there might indeed be a God or a transcendent dimension.* Taylor refers to this situation as being "cross-pressured."[7] Therefore, what exactly happened in the West that transformed it from a thoroughly religious to an almost thoroughly secularized civilization in the space of five hundred years or so?

THE "SUBTRACTION THEORY"

The common and popular explanation as what could account for the secularization of the West can be expressed as the "subtraction theory."[8] According to this theory, pre-modern people were (are) "unenlightened" because they did not yet possess the scientific knowledge that began to become dominant in the West since the European Enlightenment from the 1700s onward. Hence, their worldview was encrusted with pre-modern, primitive, mythical, even superstitious beliefs in supernatural beings, fairies, enchantments, magic, spirits, and so on. *Belief in the divine and the spiritual dimension, according to the subtraction theory, is part of this.*

Since the Western Enlightenment though, humans have made giant strides in, what became viewed as, the "real" nature of things based on science (also reason, mathematics, and technology).[9] These modern advancements have sort of taken off or scraped off, if you will, the "enchanted" encrustations in order to reveal the "true" (read: scientific and rational) nature of things. In short, all the enchanted (= mythical) ideas that governed pre-modern humans *were "subtracted" from the equation* (this process can also be called "disenchantment") and what came out of it was *voila!* our secular and "enlightened" world.[10] This is the commonly heard subtraction theory-based way of explaining the emergence of a secular age.

To be noted well though is that Taylor *does not agree* with the subtraction theory; he considers it too simplistic an explanation of the phenomenon

7. This is one meaning of the term among other possible ones. See Taylor, *Secular Age*, chapter 16.

8. Taylor, *Secular Age*, 26.

9. Taylor, *Secular Age*, 273.

10. Taylor, *Secular Age*, 572.

of secularity because it does not do justice to the complexity of how the secular age actually emerged.[11]

THE SECULAR AGE AS AN ACCOMPLISHMENT: EXCLUSIVE HUMANISM[12]

Taylor explains the emergence of the secular age rather as a veritable and impressive post-Enlightenment human accomplishment. From a worldview that was centred on the existence of God and a whole transcendental realm, Westerners, from the Enlightenment onwards, were able to gradually construct a worldview in which the center of gravity shifted from God/Transcendent to Human/Immanent.[13] In gradual stages and with the advancement of the empirical disciplines as well as philosophies based on human reason and consciousness (i.e., those exhibited by Descartes, Kant, etc.,), humans no longer felt the need to invoke the Transcendent (whether that be God or the spiritual realm) in order to find meaning. They began to find meaning in the here and now, in the immanent realm. Take note that this was not merely a poor, measly kind of "life-meaning." Post-enlightenment Westerners have actually constructed meaning (of life) based on immanent realities, on the here and now, on humanistic values divorced from any divine, transcendent, and spiritual dimension and they (many/most? people) are perfectly happy with that; they feel no need to have recourse to a "higher" realm.

The secular age then is the rise of a civilization in which people began to have, what Taylor describes as, "exclusive humanism"[14] as the default "social imaginary" (another Taylor-coined word) which means "the way that we collectively imagine, even pre-theoretically, our social life in the contemporary Western world."[15] Taylor's description and analysis of key moments and movements that effected this change in Western society is, we can say, the heart of his 800+ page tome and it deserves a careful reading and study.[16]

11. It would also be good to consult sociologist of religion Rodney Stark who has a lot to say on the question of secularization. In the following work, he emphasizes that the modern world as a whole is actually not secular but very religious. He has noteworthy points as well on the nature of secularization in Europe and the US. See Stark, *Triumph of Faith*, Introduction; chapters 2 and 10. See also Stark, *Triumph of Christianity*, chapter 21.

12. Cf. Smith, *How (Not) to Be Secular*, chapter 1.

13. Taylor, *Secular Age*,143.

14. Taylor, *Secular Age*, 19–28; 636–42.

15. Taylor, *Secular Age*, 146.

16. Taylor, *Secular Age*; to be noted particularly are: part I, chapter 2; part II, chapters 6–7; part III, chapters 8, 10, 11; and part IV, chapter 12.

"POROUS" AND "BUFFERED" WORLDVIEWS

The pre-Enlightenment Western worldview could be described as "porous"[17] because, in this view, humans and the world were, as it were, full of openings (hence "porous") through which divine and transcendent realities were thought of as being able to penetrate and influence humans in direct and significant ways. Since the Reformation and Enlightenment though, Westerners, it can be said, gradually began to acquire and adopt a "buffered"[18] view of humanity and the world—buffered because we and our world were seen to be self-contained and effectively closed to or, in short, "buffered" from the Divine and other transcendent realities. This immanent frame of reference—focused on exclusive humanism and this empirical world—has unquestionably become the dominant worldview in the West and Westerners have increasingly felt that they do not need to invoke "God" or other transcendent realities anymore to ground the meaning of life and existence. Taylor maintains that this is now our dominant "social imaginary" in the West and because of this we can indeed call our milieu a veritable secular age.

THE NOVA EFFECT AND THE AGE OF AUTHENTICITY

Now that we are squarely located and living in a secular age, we can readily observe, what Taylor calls, a "Nova Effect"[19] in our Western context. He refers to a veritable explosion (hence, "nova") of options for creating or finding significance (or "authenticity"). This began after the dominant and controlling story or scheme of significance in the West (i.e., Christianity) broke down and exploded into a plethora of possibilities for sustaining meaning at the personal and communal levels since the Renaissance. That's what the expression "nova effect" wants to convey.

Presently in the West, society by and large no longer gives institutional and social support to religion and the pursuit of spirituality. Hence, individuals must fend for themselves in order to become truly themselves or, to use a common expression nowadays, to be "authentic." This is of course reflective of our Western society's individualism. The search for authenticity in our age takes place in a context where we are offered mainly humanistic and immanent paths. At the same time, as we search for authenticity, we are

17. Taylor, *Secular Age*, 35–43.

18. Taylor, *Secular Age*, 37–42.

19. Taylor, *Secular Age*, 399.

confronted with such a mind-bogglingly massive number of possible paths (again, the nova effect), that could lead to us being authentically true to ourselves or even "spiritual" (in a sense). That ironically results in a situation in which it actually becomes difficult and confusing to choose a/one path. Despite this, it remains a crucial task to seek our own path of meaning in this supposedly "age of authenticity."[20]

The above-mentioned factors are some of the most important points that Charles Taylor makes in his landmark work *A Secular Age*. I made this digression here explaining Taylor's main points, one of the best explanations in my opinion of our secular age, because they have important repercussions on what we're trying to accomplish in this work.

To pick up once again on the metaphorical image from Asian North American literature presented in chapter 1, we in the West now are like *The Bonesetter's Daughter*'s protagonist Ruth in a few significant ways. With regard to our spiritual ancestry, our ancestors came from a metaphorical "different shore"[21] in the sense that they lived in a world that was "enchanted" or deeply embedded in religious or spiritual realities. We, on the other hand, are now in a new, very different place in the sense that we are living in and breathing the air of a secular age in which the transcendent dimension is not given much importance anymore. But there is a stark truth I want, as it were, to shout out here: If we just simply negate or forget our spiritual roots and ancestry, we would be left in the dark as to where we came from. That would result—I'd like to emphasize—in us not being fully aware of who we are and where we should be going in order to forge on toward a more holistic future in which our hearts and spirits could flourish. With that, let's now address this situation of being severed from our original spiritual roots with the help of key insights from thinkers Simone Weil and Hannah Arendt.

OUR NEED FOR ROOTS AND ITS CONNECTION TO THE BIBLE

As quoted earlier, Simone Weil upheld that "to be rooted is perhaps the most important and least recognized need of the human soul. It is one of the hardest to define." About this, Weil rightly notes that we feed these roots through "real, active and natural participation in the life of a community,

20. Taylor, *Secular Age*, 473–504.

21. This is a reference to this work's title, Takaki, *Strangers from a Different Shore*. It is meant as a double entendre.

which preserves in living shape certain particular treasures of the past and certain particular expectations for the future."[22]

I trust that by now you know that Weil's assertion of the human "need for roots" is a foundational idea for this book about the Bible and how we should relate to it as a source of our spiritual ancestry. Recall that for many of us, Christianity with its heart (the Bible) is, in effect, for better or worse, part of our heritage, a tradition in which many of our ancestors (as recent as our parents or grandparents!) were more deeply rooted. Put in a more concrete image, the Bible, I would like to suggest here, is something like *the village that raised our ancestors.*

The image of a "village" that I propose here is actually rooted in my Asian North American identity. Where I originally come from (that happens to be the Philippines and Japan, but it is also true of many other parts of Asia), family and its extended network of so many people such as uncles and aunts (Filipino, *[mga]*[23] *tito* and *tita*), cousins (*pinsan*), godfathers and godmothers (*ninong* and *ninang*, a very important relationship in Philippine society), real and extended[24] siblings (*kapatid*), and so on and so forth, virtually form a whole village that raised me and continues to support and interact with me through all the vicissitudes of life. This is exacerbated in the digital, social media age in which practically the whole village (even those I only remotely know!) wants to be friends with me on Facebook!

However, at present, many of us who are located in secularized, Western(ized) contexts often lack this "village" of support and nurture. That is also quite true in the spiritual sense. We often feel estranged and alienated from our religious-spiritual heritage, in particular our biblical roots, because we are either not familiar with the Bible and its plot, its main stories, characters, concepts, and messages or we have the impression that "all that religious-biblical stuff" is no longer relevant or perhaps even detrimental for us today.

As a result of twenty-some years of teaching biblical and religious studies to undergraduates and in various ministry settings, I strongly feel that this kind of alienation from our spiritual ancestry; in short, this kind of "rootlessness" has quite a negative effect not only on my students, but on society as a whole. Many of us don't know where we came from; for this reason, we likewise don't know where we are and where we're headed.

22. Weil, *Need for Roots*, 40–41.

23. Particle to denote "plurality."

24. The notion of "extended siblings," I would say, is way bigger and more encompassing that what is usually understood in the West.

Philosopher Hannah Arendt has made an insightful observation directly related to this in her book, *The Origins of Totalitarianism* (1951). According to her, deeply problematic phenomena such as totalitarianism are often the result of "atomized, isolated individuals," that is, people without roots and without an awareness of their cultural and spiritual ancestry. We can argue then that totalitarian movements, such as Nazism (Arendt's context) or even recent populist movements, "succeed when they offer rootless people what they most crave: an ideologically consistent world aiming at grand narratives that give meaning to their lives. By consistently repeating a few key ideas, a manipulative leader provides a sense of rootedness grounded upon a coherent fiction that is 'consistent, comprehensible, and predictable.'"[25] One can soberly conclude then that "the modern condition of rootlessness is a foundational experience of totalitarianism"[26] and, I would add, other common feelings of malaise, such as nihilism and purposelessness, that are so prevalent today. Because of this there is an urgent need to tap into our roots (a significant portion of which are religious ones) in order to know where we came from, where our traditions are based, and where/what our original "village" is. By doing this, we might have a better idea of the direction we're supposed to take in the future.

The village image is not meant only for people like me who come from an original context in which, what I would call, "village ties" among people are quite strong. The village image is meant for everyone, even in this Western context where the emphasis is generally on rugged individualism. I propose that if we dig deeply enough into our traditions and (this is ultimately speaking) our common humanity itself, we will realize that everyone yearns to have their "village of support" because, as Weil insisted, we all need roots. Hence, I would like to invite readers to get to know their roots better. When they do so, they will find out that religion-spirituality has been and still is an important part thereof, something that each one will have to accept in order to find out more deeply who they really are.

"RE-ROOTING" OURSELVES

The essential work of discovering our roots can be described as "re-rooting" ourselves in our spiritual ancestry. Concretely for people in the West, this means getting to know the people behind the biblical texts and relating with

25. See Arendt, *Origins of Totalitarianism*. This point is underlined by Roger Berkowitz in his essay reflecting on Hannah Arendt's relevance in the age of Trumpism; see Berkowitz, "Why Arendt Matters."

26. Berkowitz, "Why Arendt Matters."

these ancient biblical ancestors *as foundational members of the village suggested in this work, the nurturing community in which (even our immediate) ancestors here in the West were raised.* By that, I don't really mean to say that we have to be religious in a childish way, that is, uncritically accepting any or all of our ancestors' religious traditions. By spiritual "re-rooting," I mean instead that we first become familiar once again with the big plots and the important stories (and the ideas behind them) that comprise our religious traditions. Next, since *we ourselves are now grown-ups*, we can have a more critical sense toward the village that raised our civilization, a village which we didn't choose but were just simply born into. We ought to have both an attitude of trust and openness to rediscovering whatever is life-giving in our spiritual traditions but, at the same time, also have a healthy dose of suspicion, of wariness to spot and call out the things that are inimical to our holistic flourishing today. This may even entail rejection of parts of our religious traditions that are not beneficial to the wholesome development of our common humanity now.

THE GAP BETWEEN OUR RELIGIOUS ANCESTORS AND OUR SECULAR SELVES

When we think about the deep religiosity of our ancestors and the widespread secularization either of ourselves or those around us, it seems at first blush that there is such a deep chasm that divides our religious past from our secularized present. This is what leads many nowadays to think that there can be no further relevant link between their secularized worldview and the religious worldview of their ancestors. From another perspective though I would say that we tend to exaggerate a gap between our religious ancestors and our secular selves in a way that is quite out of proportion. Why? Because we think that we have moved too far away from them that we can no longer relate to them in any significant way. But is that true? Maybe we have to redefine the meaning of "religion" itself in order to see anew that humans have "religious" (better perhaps, "spiritual") attitudes hardwired into them no matter how apparently secularized they seem to be. Better yet, we may have to identify fresh categories that would make us realize how much we have in common with our ancestors when it comes to the areas of spiritual heritage and ancestry.

In recent years, I've increasingly felt that "religion" has acquired such a bad rap among many Westerners that maybe it is time to call for a kind of moratorium (actually, more of a "pause" than a "death" which is what "moratorium" means) on its use, much like some theologians have called for a moratorium on the use of the word "God."[27] We might be better served if we use "spirituality," "spiritual intelligence," or even fresh categories such as "meaning systems," *ikigai* (a Japanese word that means "the reason for living"), or some other alternative expression.

SPIRITUAL INTELLIGENCE: THE BOND BETWEEN OUR ANCESTORS AND OURSELVES

To restate the matter, we need to find some bond of commonality between our ancestors and ourselves regarding spiritual ancestry or else the project of re-rooting ourselves spiritually might never happen successfully. One common bond, I propose, could be found in what is being called "Spiritual Intelligence."[28] Let me describe it in a preliminary way as the deep drive hardwired in humanity that pushes us to seek for meaning, particularly by *both* journeying into our inner depths and transcending ourselves for something "bigger" (than our egos). Although "metanarratives" have been much maligned in the postmodern world, it is clear at least to me that this "meaning" humans have pursued throughout history has usually taken the form of a "total framework" (yes, a "metanarrative") that could suggest a possible explanation for why all things are the way they are and why this universe is the way it is. For example, from the dawn of time, humans were confronted with a world in which all kinds of things—living and non-living—existed. Upon observing and reflecting on that, the so-called key hardwired component in humans which I call "spiritual intelligence" began to work and some humans posited the idea that "gods" or (later on) a "God" (an unseen, *spiritual* Being who is the powerful origin of everything) created what we know as the world or the cosmos.

Why is it "spiritual" [intelligence], one may ask? The reason is simple. In humanity's efforts to propose a possible framework that would encompass the whole of reality, the explanation that was given for most of human history took the form of an order, a vast reality in which material realities were *only a part* of the total picture, located in a bigger, more fundamental, authentic, and vastly superior "spiritual" (non-visible, non-material) realm. This dominant explanation of reality is beautifully and succinctly stated in *The Little Prince* as "what is essential is invisible to the eye."[29] It is only since the European Enlightenment that purely materialistic explanations for

27. See, for example, Carl Gregg, "Do We Need a Moratorium on the Word 'God'?"

28. Bhullar, "Growth of Spiritual Intelligence," 122–31.

29. Saint Exupéry, *Little Prince*, chapter 21.

reality began to become popular and, later, dominant in wide swaths of the Western[ized] world.

WHAT IS SPIRITUAL INTELLIGENCE?

Danah Zohar and Ian Marshall in a 2000 book calls "spiritual intelligence" ("SQ") the "ultimate" form of knowledge in that it is more fundamental, and it animates the more well-known IQ (Cognitive Intelligence) and EQ (Emotional Intelligence).[30] "Spirit" of course, is basically "the animating or vital principle; that which gives life to the physical organism in contrast to its material elements; the breath of life."[31] It is important to remember that spiritual intelligence, Zohar and Marshall emphasize, *is not necessarily about being religious.* It is true that "religion" and "spirituality" have been considered one and the same for most of human history. In an increasingly secular world, however, it is good to make a distinction between religion and spirituality. Conventional religion can be described as "an externally imposed set of rules and beliefs, . . . top-down, inherited from priests and prophets and holy books, or absorbed through the family and tradition."[32] Spiritual Intelligence, on the other hand, "is an *internal,* innate ability of the human brain and psyche, drawing its deepest resources from the heart of the universe itself. It is a facility developed over millions of years that allows the brain to find and use meaning in the solution of problems. . . . [It] is the soul's intelligence. It is the intelligence with which we heal ourselves and with which we make ourselves whole."[33]

The implications of spiritual intelligence, I would say, are vitally important for us here as we review our spiritual ancestry through the New Testament. Even though we think we have gone so far from our spiritual roots because we "live, move, and have our being"[34] in a secular age while our ancestors lived their whole existence in a spiritual-religious world, we are actually linked because of the common spiritual intelligence found not only in them but also in us. We continue to seek for meaning through depth and transcendence with the same energy that our ancestors pursued the matter through more explicitly religious ways. They found that meaning in ways and forms (such as organized religion, institutional Christianity, etc.) that may not be in vogue anymore in our secular age. But being possessed

30. Zohar and Marshall, *Spiritual Intelligence*, 3–6.

31. Zohar and Marshall, *Spiritual Intelligence*, 4.

32. Zohar and Marshall, *Spiritual Intelligence*, 9.

33. Zohar and Marshall, *Spiritual Intelligence*, 9.

34. An expression originally found in the Acts of the Apostles 17:28.

by the same drive to find meaning, we can learn from their experiences and journeys in positive and negative ways. But this can only happen if we get to know our spiritual ancestry first. That, I strongly argue, is why we, especially we in the West (or in Westernized contexts), need to continue reading the Bible, particularly the New Testament, even in a secular age.

THE PRIMARY SYMBOL OF WESTERN SPIRITUAL INTELLIGENCE: "GOD"

In tackling the particular form that the spiritual intelligence of our Western ancestors took, we necessarily have to go through the big "G" word—God. This is the primary way through which our ancestors in the Bible, in Christianity and practically throughout the whole of Western history viewed life, reality, and the cosmos. Needless to say, they tried to figure out "the meaning of it all" by invoking "God." We will discuss this theme extensively in the next chapter.

3

Calling the Bible as It Really Is: The Words of Our Ancestors

The Bible, the God-Question and What Really Is "Faith in God"?

Whether we *remain* believers is, once again, nothing more or less than a choice. . . . So then, make your choice.

—Reza Aslan[1]

CALLING THE BIBLE AS IT REALLY IS

Whether they are believers or not, in many people's minds, the Bible is a book about "God." Moreover, it is often even claimed as a book *coming directly from* (even "from the very mouth" of) God. That is quite logical because for much of Western history, the Bible has been reverenced by the Christian Church as "God's word." The continuing association of the Bible with God just shows how much influence Christianity has exerted on Western civilization. With the increasing skepticism nowadays of more and more people about the "God" that Christianity has proclaimed and worshiped, interest in the Bible has understandably also waned. I'm one who can vouch for that because I witness this slow yet steady decline at our university every passing year. When I get together with colleagues in biblical and religious

1. Aslan, *God*, 170–71.

studies, one common lament we all have is that we can *no longer expect* that even the basic biblical stories, characters, and themes, which were still quite familiar to our grandparents or even parents, would still be part of so-called "common knowledge" today.

In such a secularized context, is there a better way of thinking about and understanding the Bible? What framework would be helpful to use so that people could connect with their spiritual ancestry through this collection of ancient writings? My proposal about this issue is the following: Call the Bible as it *really* is—namely, it is, first and foremost, the writings of our spiritual ancestors. Yes, that also means: Don't bring in "God" too soon into the equation!

To explain further, I have a rule for speaking about religion, God, spirituality, and other related matters which I refer to as *my* version of "Ockham's razor." Recall that a popular iteration of Ockham's razor is that "the simplest explanation is usually the best."[2] When I apply Ockham's razor to biblical or religious studies, I would say that, before anything is claimed as divine, that is, coming from or speaking about God, we have to acknowledge the simplest and most obvious fact that it is, primarily, *a human statement* that *interprets* something as having been inspired or revealed by God. In other words, the structure of any so-called "theological claim" is the following: the first, most obvious, and empirically provable thing about it is that: (1) There is a human being who makes a claim. Analyzed critically, the claim is that, (2) *according to their interpretation*, something is coming from or related to God.

Applied to the notion "the Bible is God's word," I would affirm first and foremost that it is a human statement. And then, secondly, that this statement interprets the collection of ancient literature (known as the Bible) as God's message to humanity. In a more religious age, people tended to ignore the human origins of the Bible and proceeded to acknowledge its supposedly divine origin immediately, yet—we have to say—uncritically and too facilely. They could not do otherwise; it was commonsensical in their religious culture to do so. In our secular age, many tend to acknowledge only the human origins of the Bible and dismiss the inspiration that countless generations throughout history have received from it and that made them claim it as "divine." I think that there could be a middle way between these two extremes, a way we will try to explain further as we go along.

It is crucial to keep this whole discussion in mind especially in our secular age because when we don't, that is, when we uncritically continue to call the Bible "God's word" or to rashly impute a divine seal upon it—poor

2. Kaye, "William of Ockham."

Bible!—we are actually putting undue pressure upon this collection of ancient literary works to fulfill an impossible role that it has not and never will live up to. It is my experience that a majority of the most fervent and extreme upholders of the so-called Bible's divine character, while neglecting its human origins, have actually not gone deeply enough into a historical and literary study of this classical work. Such a study will only prove swiftly that the Bible is, first and foremost, unmistakably words of our human ancestors with all their telltale foibles (as well as noble traits!).

Having clarified that matter, let's now delve into the big "G" with which the Bible has been identified in the history of Western civilization. What do we actually mean when we refer to "god"? I will use this uncapitalized form to refer to the human ideas about "divinity" seen from a neutral and non-faith-based perspective as well as the different underlying processes that are involved when the word "god" is invoked. When I revert to using the capitalized form "God," I will refer to the Being that religious believers have faith and trust in. Only when we have discussed the deep structure of human faith in "god" will we return to our main topic of how God is actually related to the ancient collection of literary works called the Bible.

"GOD" AS A "SYMBOL" OF THE HUMAN EFFORT TO WRESTLE AND DANCE WITH LIFE

One of the truest statements we can say about what it means to be a human is this: We humans wrestle with life, particularly, with its many profound mysteries, its crushing setbacks, and disorienting absurdities. After many years of studying religion, I have come to conclude that, seen from a humanistic standpoint, *god is primarily a symbol of the human effort to wrestle with life, especially its most difficult and vexing questions.* This is suggested by the Old Testament story of the patriarch Jacob who wrestles with a divine figure through the night and is given the name "Israel," which means someone who has wrestled with God and humans, in short, with life itself (Gen 32:22–32).

In other words, when humans try to make sense of life's greatest mysteries, especially great suffering (such as the one recently unleashed by the COVID-19 pandemic upon the whole world), many of us have and still continue today to invoke "god," imagining a supernatural and powerful being with the ability to stop disasters from happening or to turn things around when the situation becomes quite bad. Again, analyzed from a humanistic standpoint, trusting in a god who helps to alleviate the world's suffering can be positively evaluated as an expression of the resilience and indomitable nature of the human spirit. In this sense, faith in God is a symbol of the trust and hope that continue to live on in human hearts which in turn give us the strength and courage to face the many struggles and challenges of life. I understand and deeply respect that. At the same time, I am also mindful of its limitations which I will deal with later in this work.

On a more positive note, I must add that "god" is also a symbol of the human effort to dance with the glorious aspects of life. When we encounter beauty, love, compassion, forgiveness, and many other wonderful things, we imagine and trust that the source of such goodness and benevolence is a supreme, gracious being which many of us call "God." Thus, the idea of god seems to be, on the whole, something that human spiritual intelligence (mentioned in the last chapter) has given birth to. Its function is to propose and suggest the source of the "big picture" that helps us "make better sense of it all" as we wrestle and dance with life's many shadows and lights.

"GOD" AND SUFFERING

The litmus test of our human belief and trust in God though is in the crucible of suffering. No religious tradition I know has definite and conclusive answers to the question "Why is there suffering?" To expand on that by rephrasing it, let me say unambiguously that the "God" invoked by Christianity (to give an example very familiar to me) usually does not have answers to the big "why" question of great suffering, such as chaos-generating and deadly epidemics. It's enough to look at God's answer to the fabled Old Testament character Job when the latter requests some answers to the question of his undeserved suffering. In Job 38–39, God declares that human wisdom just cannot plumb the mysteriousness of God's ways and so it (human knowledge-wisdom) amounts to nothing before God. That is another way to say that all our human efforts to understand the wherefore and whither, the why and the "to what end?" of suffering are practically pointless in a sense because we will never get any satisfactory answers.

Even Jesus in the New Testament Gospels does not make an effort to answer these questions in a sustained way. Rather, what the Christian tradition, embodied especially in Jesus, presents is an invitation and a summons (and this is very important) first, to refrain from judging (see for example Matt 7:1 and Luke 6:37) because we really do not know everything; second, to be compassionate for the sufferings that all of us have to endure; and, third, to act resolutely and lovingly to alleviate suffering.

But the plot thickens regarding the god-question. If that is so, what use is there for "god" then? Is it any good to have faith in a God who seemingly cannot even supply us with adequate answers to our questions about the apparent random suffering that is visited upon us in life?

I think that this question is crucially important, especially for people who consider themselves religious believers. Some will simply choose to ignore it for fear of rocking the boat too much and losing their "simple childhood faith." As a scholar of religion and theology, I have wrestled with this question through the years, and I've realized that unless one faces this gnawing question squarely in the face and attempts to give some response to it, I'm afraid one will never shed a childish faith and advance to a more mature stage of faith. So let me share my two cents' worth coming from some of my efforts over a very long time to make sense of the god-question.

"GOD" AS A HYPOTHESIS ABOUT REALITY

I've already suggested considering "god" as the human effort to wrestle and dance with life. Let me ground that further by mentioning a foundational idea: "god" is just one hypothesis (among many) that our ancestors have proposed about the nature of reality, about the "meaning of it all."

One of the most useful and thorough books on the questions of God's existence and nature that I've come upon thus far has been the Catholic theologian Hans Küng's *Does God Exist? An Answer for Today.*[3] There, Küng uses a good amount of space to survey and analyze the many efforts to prove, be agnostic about, or deny the existence of God through the centuries. When he comes at last to stating his major conclusions about God's existence and nature, he starts by positing God as a human hypothesis. God as a hypothesis, Küng proposes, would be the answer to humanity's ultimate questions. Apropos that, we can say that these three following questions are probably the most important and consistent ultimate questions that human beings have asked: Who are we? Where do we come from? Where are we going?

Küng points out that if God does exist (hypothetically), there would be meaningful answers to those questions. Therefore, in answer to *Who are we?* God would be the ultimate ground of being that defines our identity: We (and all of reality) are all grounded in God; we carry in ourselves, as the Bible says, the divine image (*imago dei*—see Gen 1:26–27). Thus, God is the "primal ground" for all life and reality. In answer to *Where do we come from?* God would be the source, the creator, and the sustainer of all human and natural existence. God is then the "primal base and support"

3. Küng, *Does God Exist?*

of everything. Finally, in answer to *Where are we going?* God would be the ultimate goal in whom everyone and everything will find fulfillment.

Therefore, the ideal situation is that all human and natural life would take on a deeper meaning with this awesome "God" as the ground, support, and goal of everything that is. And that would definitely make life worth living to the full, despite the acute menace of fate and death, apparent emptiness and meaninglessness, sin, and suffering. This, I can say, is a rather sophisticated way of expressing the traditional God-believer's ultimate reasons for having faith in God.

It goes without saying that the ideal and utopian worldview described above was the one which our spiritual ancestors embraced. It is the worldview that runs firmly throughout the books of the Bible. It continues to be the worldview that many people of faith hold on to today. What has changed though in our secular age that such a worldview is now commonly contested and challenged?

REVELATION AND THE UNPROVABILITY OF GOD

Let me underline that in the reflections above, god, we can say, is a hypothesis that humans have and continue to put forward in order to make sense of life. However, there is one big problem that looms large especially in our secular age: It is commonly acknowledged in the discipline called the "philosophy of religion" that, despite the best efforts of many brilliant minds throughout history, there is actually no definitive way to prove conclusively this hypothesis that God exists. What Küng has stated above is merely that, *if* the hypothesis of God were true, then all life and existence would take on a deeper and fuller meaning—the traditional religious believer's worldview.

We also know well that many religious traditions (especially the monotheistic religions of Judaism, Christianity, and Islam) have emphasized the notion of divine revelation: that God has, it is believed, revealed to some chosen humans the very nature of the divine and also certain firm truths about God and life which are trustworthy and reliable and—important for us in this work—that revelation has been written down in books that hold great authority for the communities that revere them (the Bible, the Qur'an, etc.).

Although I don't like to enter too deeply into this line of discussion here, let me state my personal and very honest opinion on the so-called notion of revelation. I may sound like an agnostic here but bear with me: I honestly think that the concept of revelation just does not speak effectively anymore to many people in our contemporary secularized world, especially people who have not been raised to believe that there is a God. Moreover, a detailed historical study of, say, Christianity and of its different supposedly firm and solid revelations (as I have done professionally for practically my whole life as a scholar of religion and theology) will reveal instead that these grandiose claims about "revealed truths" should always be made in a modest and temperate way because all so-called "truths" (that not only Christianity but practically any religion proclaims) actually bear the telltale marks that they are all too human (more than divine!). That is, these "truths" are anthropologically, historically, and culturally conditioned in radical ways.

It is seldom acknowledged that, truth be told, these very "human" truths have been imbued with an aura of sacredness and infallibility by some authority in the tradition's history more than anything else for the purpose of forging a given community's identity through a common belief in supposedly "revealed truths," *rather* than as a witness to provable truths. For these reasons, I do not usually like to take the path of "divine revelation" when attempting to speak about "god" to present-day people (to myself first and foremost!) who are, on the whole, historically conscious and are trained to think critically through things.

Applied to the Bible, that means believing in the "truth" of the Bible is not so much believing in objective truth itself. It is *rather a matter of staying faithful to the identity of your community* that has upheld throughout history that the Bible contains these so-called truths.

Let me reiterate: For me, the more fruitful path to take when we attempt to study religion and the idea of god nowadays, especially when it is done in the context of a growing number of people (in my Western context) who consider themselves SBNR (Spiritual but not Religious), "Dones" (We're "done" with religion!), or "Nones" (We have NO religion!)—is, rather, to understand religion (and the idea that there might be a God) as first and foremost the human endeavor to search for meaning, a quality hardwired in us through what we have referred to above as spiritual intelligence. As stated, "god" functions then as a way for humans to put meaning into life or to make some sense of life—life which, many times, can be very mysterious, incomprehensible, and even absurd. That applies perfectly to our spiritual ancestors who wrote books that came to be included in the Bible.

This faith in God went unquestioned for a long time in the past when people's identities were tied to a single community that was thoroughly religious. But we live in a vastly different world now where people's identities are no longer tied to a single deeply religious community. Our individual identities rather are made up of multiple worlds (I call this "hybridity"[4]). Hence, even if some of us still belong to religious communities, the creed of the community does *not* command our full and total allegiance anymore. We usually have to make sense of it in the presence of other parts of our identity with which we identify. And that includes the parts of us that have become secularized even if we may still somehow identify as part of religious communities.

And so, we are usually faced with this question: Can there be other ways of making life meaningful besides positing the God hypothesis? Without hesitation, my answer is: Of course, there are! Believing in God is by no means the only way to "create meaning." But it is definitely the way by which most people have tried to make sense of life and reality throughout human history. Let me drive it home further by declaring in no uncertain terms that believing in God while living in the light of faith is the way by which our own spiritual ancestors created meaning for their lives. That is why it is still important even in our secular age that we study the God-question *if we are to understand what it has meant in the past to be human.* Only by learning the positive and negative lessons of the past will we create new ways to be better humans today.

AGNOSTICISM AND ATHEISM COMPARED WITH FAITH IN GOD

Toward the end of his tome on God, Hans Küng—who at this point has already surveyed and analyzed the many efforts either to prove, be agnostic about, or deny the existence of God through the centuries—draws a stark conclusion. He states bluntly that, when we stand in front of life and its utter mysteriousness, *both a denial and an affirmation of God* are rationally possible as choices that humans could make.[5] Of course, that is true in our contemporary setting in which we are presented with so many other options for "meaning-making" other than belief in God. This is also why I never judge people by their belief or unbelief in god. Doubting and denying God would have been more difficult in a past world steeped in religion where our ancestors lived. But let me underline again that *the spiritual intelligence that made our ancestors believe in a god seems to be the same spiritual sense that makes some of us doubt such a god or deny this being all together today.* What unites us all rather is a common humanity that possesses a capacity

4. Kato, *How Immigrant Christians Living in Mixed Cultures Interpret Their Religion*; Kato, "Interpretation," 63–75; Kato, *Religious Language and Asian American Hybridity.*

5. Küng, *Does God Exist?*, 568.

and a passion that try to make sense of it all while coming up with different proposals and answers.

Let's go back to the possibility of multiple choices about life's meaning. First, atheism is definitely a possible and, in many ways, perhaps even a logical option (for some) in front of life's mystery and absurdity. There is no definitive way to refute or eliminate atheism rationally. For some people, the dominant experience of reality is that it is radically uncertain and even absurd. For them, there is simply no way to "be certain" that there in fact exists a primal source and a primal support, let alone a primal goal for everything. Hence, for them, an agnosticism ("I just don't know about ultimate realities, and I prefer not to discuss them" attitude) that often tends toward atheism is the option that makes the most sense. This is very common nowadays, and it is not necessarily bad, despite what religious people usually say. In fact, agnosticism could be a sign of a healthy humility and that the agnostic person has transcended some simplistic, naïve, and childish images of god.

For some others, the dominant factors in their experience of reality are much darker: radical chaos, irreparable hurt and damage, delusion, meaningless suffering, absurdity, and nonbeing. For them, an atheism that can tend toward nihilism is the position that makes the most sense.[6] I think that this is also the reason why we should make ours the mantra made famous by Pope Francis with regard to the question of homosexuality: Who am I to judge? And, of course, Jesus said something similar long before, "Do not judge, so that you may not be judged" (Matt 7:1).

Küng asserts, however, that there is another possible choice that is *not irrational* by any means although many today think that it is so. This choice, therefore, also deserves respect and legitimacy, yes, *even in our secular age*, because it is perfectly justifiable even in a rational way. It is the position of the person of faith-trust (note that "faith-trust" might be the best description of "religious belief") who, despite the radical uncertainty and even the seemingly meaningless suffering and absurdity that characterize reality (life), still decides to have faith and trust in a primal ground, support, and goal of life and all reality—a Being commonly known as "God."

Of course, this rationally justifiable "God" should be nuanced well and explained more at length (and that is not my aim here; I will save it for another occasion). What we can say is that it is definitely not the "god" of earlier and more naïve stages of faith that arguably could not hold up against the deconstructive critiques of contemporary agnosticism and atheism (such as from the "New Atheists"). Many crude and heavily anthropomorphic ideas of god espoused by a great many religious believers are what

6. Küng, *Does God Exist?*, 569.

modern skepticism about God can attack and refute, and perhaps, rightly so. This, we can say, is the "god" that the philosopher Friedrich Nietzsche proclaimed as dead and, again, perhaps rightly so. The rationally justifiable God is a more robust and mature idea of faith-trust in a primal source, support and goal of all life and reality.

FAITH-TRUST IN GOD IS A DECISION TO TRUST REALITY AND LIFE

What I would most like to highlight here, though, is an aspect of faith-trust in God (emphasized by Küng above all other meanings in *Does God Exist?*) which has spoken deeply to me throughout my life as a scholar of religion and theology and which, I think, helps us to understand better the spiritual ancestors who we will meet in the Bible. Küng points out that both belief or unbelief in God has to do mostly with *a decision* on the part of humans (individually or collectively) to adopt either a fundamental *attitude of trust* in reality (or life) or, its opposite—a fundamental *attitude of skepticism and/or pessimism* about reality. In light of that, what used to be commonly called *"faith" (in God) is actually*—I would like to propose—*a matter of having an attitude of trust in the fundamental goodness of reality*, whether that is attached to some kind of divinity or not.

Let me further qualify that description: If analyzed deeply, what religious believers call "faith" is the decision to trust that reality (or life) is fundamentally good despite all the uncertainty, suffering, and absurdity that are part of it. Moreover, this trust in the fundamental goodness of life should necessarily translate into an active commitment to action: that is, to respect and honor and, if needed, to fight for life (taken in a holistic sense, this involves positively struggling for justice, peace, equality, freedom, etc., or, in a negative sense, struggling *against* injustice, oppression, destruction, calamities, etc.).[7]

THE PERSISTENCE OF SPIRITUAL INTELLIGENCE DESPITE THE "FALL OF GOD"

In the past, our spiritual ancestors used to think that this faith, this trust that reality is fundamentally good, could only be directed at a personal being commonly known as God. A lot of us today continue to do so. However, this

7. I have rephrased Hans Küng's expressions slightly; confer Küng, *Does God Exist?*, 572. See also Aslan, *God*, 170–71.

is no longer universally true in our secular age. Although "god" may have been a valiant attempt with a long pedigree and history to make sense of it all, since the European Enlightenment, it has lost a lot of ground to other ways of making sense of the big picture of life and reality. Science with its method of proving things by empirical methods has gained the upper hand while "god" has been relegated by many to, as it were, a dust-covered shelf as the now-irrelevant product of a bygone, pre-scientific, unenlightened age when people had to rely on "fairy tales" and mythological figures such as deities to explain how things could exist in the universe. Aside from science, there are other ways by which contemporary people try to make sense of it all. For example, British philosopher of religion Don Cupitt suggests that many people in the West today are inexorably moving toward a "religion of life" in which the main object of devotion is not some transcendent god but life itself.[8]

Important though it is, the scientific-technological way of accounting for reality is by no means a perfect way of making sense of it all. One can say that it is not even a good way to try to understand life's "bigger picture." When we start dealing with matters that conventional science with its empirical methods cannot handle, such as the mystery of pain and suffering or the question of meaning, we find that the science and technology we are so proud of, fall painfully short of meaningful responses. Moreover, we must not forget that, even in our contemporary world, the scientific and materialistic worldview that is dominant in the West is not in fact shared by a significant number of the total population of the world which is still quite religious in many ways.[9]

Let me point out here that, at first blush, although we in our secular age seem to be irreconcilably different from our religious ancestors in the past, when observed at a deeper level, one can note that we actually share a common bond with them in the form of—what I referred to earlier as—a kind of "spiritual intelligence" that seeks to find meaning in a bigger framework mainly through the quest for depth and transcendence. That restless and indomitable human spirit (rooted in our innate spiritual intelligence) continues the search for a greater meaning in every age. It is the same spirit that made humans propose the existence of God in the first place; it is the same spirit that drove them to build up religious institutions around great spiritual masters who seemed to have experientially encountered a "greater something." Connected with this is the phenomenon of religious or spiritual

8. Cupitt, *Old Creed and the New*, and Cupitt, *New Religion of Life in Everyday Speech.*

9. See, for example, the sociological data that Rodney Stark presents in *Triumph of Faith.*

experience which we shall explore further in a later chapter. Let me say at this point that, ironically, it seems to be the very same human critical sense animated by a spiritual intelligence that deconstructs frameworks or systems of meaning that do not seem to work anymore in the light of new evidence. The same spiritual intelligence continually proposes newer ways, newer "systems of meaning"[10] as we continue our evolution through history. This relentless spirit, this human drive for meaning questions the limitations of the different concepts of "god" that were proposed in the past; it replaces mythical frameworks with more rational and scientific ones. In the light of new developments, it goes on to rebel against religious institutions when it judges them to have fallen into ennui and even idolatry by just repeating the now-irrelevant and dysfunctional ideas of the past. It may bask for a while in the glittering achievements of science and technology, but the self-critical and ever-reconfiguring human critical sense animated by spiritual intelligence eventually notices the shadows of our civilization's recent achievements. Hence, it goes on to humbly concede the limitations of reason, science, and technology and searches for newer ways to give human life and existence a deeper and fuller meaning even in our present postmodern age as the contemporary interest in spirituality amply proves.

This unquenchable thirst for a fuller, more holistic meaning through depth and transcendence, this "spiritual intelligence" is what we share with all humans everywhere and in all historical periods. I would even submit that, contrary to the core monotheistic idea that "everyone is one in God" (which we cannot demonstrably prove), what can actually be demonstrably proven is that everyone is united in this human quest for greater depth and transcendence which, nevertheless, produces very different outcomes in different groups and individuals. These diverse ideas about "god" have and can divide humans against each other, unfortunately even to the extent of murderous ill-will. But there is something more basic and deeper than "god" in humans: the deep passion and drive to search for a deeper meaning of life by going deeper into oneself and transcending oneself is something we all share through our common humanity. Come to think of it, *that* indomitable questing for meaning may itself be the very thing that could lead to as authentic a "God" (with a capital "G"!) as we humans can reach this side of the grave. This unquenchable human quest for depth and transcendence is in fact what can and will, I am convinced, unite us in all our diversity.

10. An expression often used to refer to religion in the sociology of religion. See, for example, Silberman "Religion as a Meaning System," 641–63.

OUR SPIRITUAL ANCESTORS' CONCRETE FORM OF SPIRITUAL INTELLIGENCE

As mentioned, this spiritual intelligence can produce a diversity of ways and forms of finding meaning in different people today: Some may continue to hold faith in God; some may even reject the idea of a god; some may choose to pursue a personal Being as the ultimate reality; some might prefer a non-personal entity. At this point, what should concern us—we, who are digging into our spiritual ancestry in this work—is this following question: What concrete form did the spiritual intelligence of our spiritual ancestors in the Bible take?

At this early stage, let us say that our spiritual ancestors had a thoroughly deeply religious way of engaging with life. As Second Temple era[11] Jews, they understood life as being composed of an inseparable "combo" of (1) God (YHWH),[12] (2) Humans (bound in a covenant with God), and (3) Life (lived in a covenant with YHWH). We can call that the biblical Jewish view of life. We have to go further and specify that our more directly linked New Testament spiritual ancestors who came to believe that Jesus of Nazareth was the Messiah were convinced that YHWH was embodied in a definitive way in him. They thus organized their lives around this central faith principle—God as embodied in Jesus—and tried to spell out how the life and teachings of Jesus spoke to their own particular circumstances.

11. This is the historical period when Jesus and his immediate disciples lived.

12. This is the name revealed by God to Moses out of the burning bush in Exodus 3:14. Written with four Hebrew letters: *yod-he-vav-yod* and commonly interpreted to stand for *YaHWeH* although the ancient Israelites never pronounced the word out of reverence for the divine name.

4

The New Testament as a Village of Spiritual Ancestors

Dealing with the Three Worlds of the Text as a Crime Scene Investigation

The Western word that comes closest to that of *ancestor* is probably *tradition*. (I prefer the term ancestor because it is more personal.) . . . Our ancestors are those who have gone before us. . . . We stand on their shoulders; we inherit their genes, their ways, their lessons learned, their teachings, their stories, their mistakes.

—Matthew Fox[1]

A "VILLAGE" OF "SPIRITUAL ANCESTORS"

Recall that I suggested in chapter 1 that we put ourselves in the mindset of being on a quest for our spiritual ancestry much like the character of Ruth in *The Bonesetter's Daughter*, who was on a quest to rediscover her Chinese heritage and ancestry through the manuscript written by her mother. Recall too that the key metaphor that I suggested for the task we want to do in this book is that the New Testament is a (textual) "village" where a number of our important "spiritual ancestors" continue to live. Now it is time to go deeper and ask: How so?

1. Fox, *A.W.E.*, 64; 62–63. Emphases in the original.

Some of our spiritual ancestors live in the texts that were written about them: Jesus, Mary Magdalene, John the Baptist, Mary of Nazareth, to name a few. These people may never have written texts themselves, but they come alive as characters in the New Testament texts. We usually refer to the text itself as "the world within the text." Not to be forgotten however is that many of our spiritual ancestors continue to live "behind the text" because they either wrote the texts themselves (like Paul the apostle) or were part of the great metaphorical village that gave context, sustained, or received the message that eventually became the written texts of the New Testament. Some of our anonymous spiritual ancestors were given names of famous early Jesus-followers at some later point in history, such as "Matthew," "John," "Peter," "James," etc. Some of them were most probably who tradition identified them to be, such as Mark, Luke, or John ("the Seer" of the book of Revelation). We can also encounter these important spiritual ancestors behind the text when we engage in the act of reading-interpreting the texts.

And then, there are also the different readers of these texts throughout history. That includes us. These different groups comprise the world "in front of" the text. We may rightfully consider ourselves "spiritual descendants" of these New Testament ancestors in many ways: Many of us continue to have faith in Jesus, whom we believe (i.e., trust) to be "the Christ" (the Chosen One), a faith that these ancestors themselves had and handed on to the next generation. That would make the believers among us the latest links in the long chain of a faith-tradition that goes back thousands of years. However, it is also true that many of us either do not identify fully with the Christian faith anymore or do not accept it altogether. Nevertheless, because we are located in a culture and society that have been, for better or worse, heavily influenced by and even imbued with Christianity, we can say that we still are, in a profound sense, spiritual descendants of these biblical ancestors in significant ways. Therefore, I am convinced that it would be very useful for us who are now located in the West itself (or in Westernized contexts)—*whether we are religious or not, whether we are originally Western, have come to the West from non-Western lands or were born here but have family who are non-Western*—to be acquainted with these spiritual ancestors so that we could know better the origins of the Christian worldview that influenced Western civilization (our present location and context) in a crucial way.

If these spiritual ancestors continue to live through the New Testament texts, this means that we can actually encounter them if we engage in the thoughtful act of reading-interpreting which, to use theologian David Tracy's analogy, is like a conversation.[2] In short, what I want to say is: "Talk

2. Tracy, *Plurality and Ambiguity*, 1–27.

with your elders already!" But before we can do that, we should first metaphorically undertake the "journey" to the New Testament village where some of our important ancestors continue to live.

THE MOST IMPORTANT SPIRITUAL ANCESTORS

Journeying into the different worlds of the New Testament basically means taking up the text and learning to read it in an intelligent and critical manner with the aim of having a critical conversation with these texts, a conversation that could in turn influence our outlook on life. You can see how important that conversation is. Let us identify then a few key points to keep in mind as we begin our journey into this village of spiritual ancestors.

Jesus is to be regarded, of course, as the great founding ancestor of the village. After all, the movement that would eventually become Christianity[3] began because of his life, ministry, teaching, and especially the events at the end of his life that were eventually referred to as "the Paschal mystery" in the Christian tradition. That is the set of events comprising Jesus' arrest, passion, and death by crucifixion on a Roman cross. The story does not end there though. Crucial to the whole narrative are the different experiences that some early disciples had of encountering Jesus after his death on a cross. These encounters convinced them that Jesus and all he stood for had been vindicated by God. Their way of expressing that was: Jesus has been raised by God from the dead (see 1 Cor 15:4). And that in turn is simply referred to now as Jesus' "resurrection" in Christianity.

All that makes up the core of Christianity. Hence, Jesus is rightly the "great founding ancestor." Let me suggest from this point onward that we begin calling Jesus by his Jewish name: *Yeshua*. Changing how we usually call someone—a process that we can refer to as "defamiliarization"—can have the effect of making us see this person (or any other thing for that matter) in a new light. "Jesus" (or its various forms in different Western languages) has been laden with a lot of historical baggage, both positive and negative, from its common uses in history and popular culture. Moreover, when many of us hear "Jesus" here in the West today, we often cannot help but think of a blond, white guy that is found in many Western depictions of Jesus. By calling Jesus "Yeshua," the same way as his compatriots in first-century Israel-Palestine called him, hopefully we can more properly envisage

3. A long and arduous process. For more on that theme, confer this recent groundbreaking book: Vearncombe, Scott, and Taussig, *After Jesus Before Christianity*.

the first-century Palestinian, Jewish peasant-become-rabbi that Yeshua was as a historical person. Let's start that defamiliarization consistently *now*.

Next to Yeshua, though, there are other important spiritual ancestors that we should encounter in a meaningful way, beginning with the storyteller-ancestors who wrote their versions of the life and teachings of Yeshua. They are usually called "evangelists" in the Christian tradition. These gospel writers didn't attach their names to their accounts but, in time, the four earliest versions of the Gospel were attributed to the following figures: Matthew, Mark, Luke, and John. These four names, I suggest, represent the most important ancestor-storytellers in our metaphorical New Testament village. When their portrayals of the Yeshua-story (adapted to their own particular circumstances) were considered later on in time as "sacred scriptures," these gospels would play pivotal roles in shaping how Christians throughout Western history have thought about crucial themes such as God, religion, life, morality, and other great questions of existence.

Besides, note well that behind these names lie *whole communities of people*—the many men, (yes, also many) *women*,[4] and children who came to believe in Yeshua as a special embodiment of God, tried to live according to his Spirit, and went on to spread Yeshua's message and way of life to many others and to later generations of people. Eventually, this movement gathered strength and became a world religion called Christianity, the tradition that formed Western civilization in a crucial way. That tradition in turn also touches you and me (even though we may not be religious) in many significant ways up to the present day because of our location in the West.

Besides Yeshua and the four Gospel writers, I would like to add two other names that, I think, are important spiritual ancestors to be singled out in our New Testament village: First, Paul, the apostle, who played a major role in making Christianity more widely accessible to non-Jews at the beginning of the Christian movement; and, second, the author of the last book in the New Testament whom we shall refer to as "John the Seer." I add this latter one as a major figure because of the arguably important role that the text he wrote came to play, particularly in the history of Western apocalyptic thought (that is, how people imagined the world would end). I will, unfortunately, not be able to discuss John the Seer in this work for lack of space.[5]

Besides, there are other spiritual ancestors-writers I won't be able to introduce you to in this work such as Peter, James, Jude, the anonymous

4. I would like to mention in a special way McGrath's insightful work, *What Jesus Learned from Women*.

5. I direct general level readers to Gorman, *Reading Revelation Responsibly*. My own reflections on certain aspects of revelation are found in Kato, *Religious Language and Asian American Hybridity*, 133–47.

author of the letter to the Hebrews, among others. This is because I consider this work a kind of "first visit" to the New Testament village, but hopefully not the last. This time, we only have a limited time to get to know the most important village elders and thus I have singled out those, I judge to be, absolutely essential for someone to be acquainted with as they make what will hopefully be just the first of many other subsequent journeys into the New Testament village.

RELATING WITH THE SPIRITUAL ANCESTORS

For us to accomplish our aim in this work, it is absolutely crucial, I propose, to feel a certain "family affinity" for these spiritual ancestors. In saying this, I am, of course, rooted in my original Asian cultures where we often call family members and relatives with "titles of respect" to indicate how they are related to us. I propose then that we consider and call these spiritual ancestors "granduncles." It may take some time for some of you to get used to this practice but, henceforth, I will put "granduncle" (or simply "GU") before the names of these spiritual ancestor-authors. Where I come from, it makes all the difference calling your mother's brother "Uncle Pedro" or just "Pedro" (as we are wont to do here in the West more and more nowadays). We use these all-important titles to immediately establish a bond, (in most cases) a "family affinity" with the person we name. For this reason, in Japanese we attach these titles *after* the name of people (or just use the title to address them) who are related to us in a special way: *sensei* (teacher, "doctor"), *ojī-sama/obā-sama* (grandfather/grandmother), *oji-san/oba-san* (uncle/aunt), *onīsan/onēsan* (elder brother/elder sister or even someone older than one-self), to name a few. On the Filipino side of our family, we attach these titles *before* the name of the person (or again, just use the title independently) to call them: *lolo/lola* (grandfather/grandmother), *tito/tita* (uncle/aunt), *kuya/ate* (elder brother/elder sister), *ninong/ninang* (godfather/godmother), *pinsan* (cousin), etc.

This practice brings to the fore a strategy of reading the New Testament texts that I will insist on again and again in this work. This goes against the advice of many of my esteemed past professors who taught me to read the text in a supposedly detached, objective, and historical manner (although that has an important role to play as well). Instead, I propose that we read the New Testament texts *in a deeply attached and involved form* of reading with clear vested interests. Here, we are on a quest, like Ruth in *The Bonesetter's Daughter* (introduced in chapter 1), for a deeper knowledge of our spiritual ancestry and these New Testament texts are our connection with some important ancient spiritual ancestors, foremost among whom is the Great Founding Ancestor himself—Yeshua.

And so, we enter the village, walk around it, and seek out the "homes" of these different spiritual ancestors. When we encounter people, we call them "granduncle" or "grand-aunt" and tell them that we're trying to go deeper into the stories and teachings about Yeshua and his followers that continue to touch us who come from a very different world. If we show this openness, they will also open up to us and tell us about how it all began . . . but from their particular and unique perspectives. Thus, we will be put in deep contact with our spiritual ancestry, an important part of which is embedded deeply in this New Testament village.

THE NEW TESTAMENT VILLAGE: UNITY AND DIVERSITY

In this journey to the New Testament, through the acts of reading and interpretation, we will try to walk figuratively around the New Testament village and have meaningful conversations with our spiritual ancestors. Allow me here to make another digression by relating something from my life story to make this point: I was raised in a large urban area, [Metropolitan] Manila (in the Philippines), but as a child, my mother would bring me to the rural village where she grew up in the central part of the Philippines, the province of *Iloilo* located in an island called *Panay*. In that small village (we called "barrio" back then), it seemed to me that everyone knew each other and were related to each other, so much so that when a city boy like me, unfamiliar to many locals, would make an appearance, they would ask me who my mother was.

Upon mention of "Barbara" (my mother's name), a look of recognition would light up in the eyes of the village folk and they would accept me as "Barbara's kid" (*báta ni Barbara*) and thus part of the village in some way. But because I didn't grow up there, I would be regaled with accounts of how I was related to the speaker or how they knew my mom when she was growing up; I would be told village folklore and traditions, stories of past and present relatives and so on and so forth. Being an outgoing and curious boy, I really loved going around the village to talk with and do things with immediate and distant relatives. In that way, I became well-acquainted with my specific Iloilo-Filipino ancestry and that, I'm convinced, has grounded me in many deep ways.

Going into the New Testament village and familiarizing ourselves with it would be similar in some ways to my experience as a boy. Present-day readers are originally outsiders to the New Testament village but the more they "walk around" and have conversations with the spiritual ancestors who continue to live there (like GU-Paul or GU-John or GU-Mark) through the critical process of reading-interpreting, the more they will become familiar with the village, its founding ancestor, and the other village folk. They will also come to realize clearly that in this village there is both unity and diversity—unity in acknowledging the Founding Ancestor Yeshua as the Chosen One of God, but also diversity in spelling out the concrete ways by which the earliest Yeshua-followers appropriated Yeshua's life and teachings in their concrete and different circumstances.[6]

Later on when we try to get to know each particular ancestor-author, I will identify, what I will call, "*sine-qua-non*'s" (Latin), some key traits about each major ancestor-author "without which" we would not understand who they were. These traits include, to name a few, granduncle (GU) Matthew's balancing act between his beloved Jewish tradition and the newness of faith in Yeshua-as-messiah; GU-Luke's struggles as a gentile being treated as a second-class citizen of God's people and his passion for the full inclusion of fellow gentiles as part of the covenant people; GU-John's complex situation of having the heights of mystical experience while being painfully excommunicated by the Jewish synagogue for his deep insights into various spiritual mysteries.

Now it is time to elaborate on a few concrete matters that critical readers/interpreters of the New Testament have to keep in mind when they enter the New Testament village on their quest to know their spiritual ancestry better.

THE BIG "H" WORD: "HERMENEUTICS"

I was trained as a cut-and-dried biblical exegete at the Pontifical Biblical Institute in Rome in the mid-'90s. A "biblical exegete," traditionally described, is someone who prioritizes the historical-critical method to identify, first of all, what the text meant for the original author and what this author meant to convey to their original audience. I do not mean to say that I consider my training was a predominantly negative thing. In fact, I am quite happy and deeply grateful that I was trained this way. Knowing the historical-critical method is still a fundamental and important skill for me. However, at a certain point in my life as a scholar and teacher, I became more and more interested in how texts and messages are interpreted by those who receive

6. A noteworthy book on this theme is Dunn, *Unity and Diversity in the New Testament*, chapters 2, 11–14.

and engage with them. This matter falls under the academic discipline called—what I sometimes refer to as the big "H" word—"hermeneutics," the theory of interpretation. I realized that the following words of the theologian David Tracy are just so accurate. He said, "We need to reflect on what none of us can finally evade: the need to interpret in order to understand at all. . . . Every time we act, deliberate, judge, understand, or even experience, *we are interpreting*. To understand at all is to interpret."[7] However, I must confess that a serious challenge I usually encounter in my passion for hermeneutics is that the word "hermeneutics," I've come to conclude, is one of the greatest conversation-stoppers of all time. Not even some of my professor-colleagues know exactly what it is.

Since hermeneutics is in fact a not-too-easy-to-comprehend enterprise, I've been engaged for as long as I can remember as a scholar and teacher in the effort to explain hermeneutics better with the hope of persuading people (in particular, my students) about how crucially vital and also how fascinating it really is. I routinely wrestle with questions such as: What happens in hermeneutics? How is it performed? What are different types of hermeneutics in biblical or religious studies? Or, applied to my topic in this book: *What is the hermeneutical process like when you are searching for your spiritual ancestry in the New Testament?* As I've mentioned, in my experience, I've found that using metaphors or concrete images can help a lot to explain what hermeneutics is all about and even to make it quite exciting, to boot! Hence, the image of a village of spiritual ancestors in this work. And a last footnote: I usually don't use the word "hermeneutics" with students; I will use it sparingly here, but I hope you know that hermeneutics plays a key role in this work.

With that let us ask: What are some other fundamental skills to learn as we negotiate the textual village of the New Testament? I propose that we learn to distinguish better between different levels of the text by utilizing yet another metaphor for serious textual work—that of a crime scene investigation.

READING-INTERPRETING THE BIBLE AS A CRIME SCENE INVESTIGATION

For years now I've encouraged my students to embark upon biblical studies by suggesting that the study of the Bible can be made more interesting and even fun if we imagine it as a "crime scene investigation" (CSI). In this metaphor, the biblical text is tantamount to the "crime scene" (CS); the one

7. Tracy, *Plurality and Ambiguity*, 8–9.

who studies, analyzes, and interprets the text is the "crime scene investigator" (CSIr); and the events that led to the creation of the text as we know it now is the "crime." Let me walk you through the finer points of this image, helpful, I think, for textual study in general and biblical study in particular.

WHAT'S A TEXT? INTERPRETING A TEXT

First of all, when we seek to read and understand the New Testament better (or any piece of literature for that matter), it helps to remember that we are dealing with "texts." As I said above, a "text" is usually associated with something written, but that is just one of its possible meanings. We can expand the meaning of "text" to its greatest possible extent. For our purposes here let us define "text" broadly as "anything that has meaning and that can be interpreted." When we look at "text" in this way, it will be clear that a "text" can be practically anything: a written text of course, but also a piece of music, a poem, a historical event, a friend's facial expression or body language at a given moment, a movie, a work of art, a scene in nature—all of these things *can* be texts because each of them has a potential meaning and can be interpreted.

What makes texts (in the wider sense described above) so interesting is that we, who seek to read and understand them, can propose what we think they mean. That's just another way of saying: we can *interpret* them. Interpretation then is a key notion in biblical studies or any textual study for that matter. Besides, haven't you noticed that we usually make an effort to interpret the "texts" that are truly important to us? To make a sweeping yet true statement: In order for anyone to understand practically anything at all, we actually have to interpret that very thing. For instance, how many times do we have to interpret the facial expressions and body language of our parents, our teachers, our bosses, our partners, our friends, etc., in order to grasp what they are *actually* thinking and feeling? We can therefore say that the activity of interpretation (yes, the big "H" for hermeneutics) is an essential and crucially important process not only in textual study but for life itself.

It is absolutely vital then to learn how to interpret "texts" (in the widest sense possible) well so that our understanding of the things that really matter to us in life could be more precise. When it is a matter of really important things, we do not want to proceed with misunderstandings or illusions. Needless to say, good interpretation is a skill that has to be honed with the right knowledge and the right tools. And that is why I propose the following image for biblical study and interpretation.

When we've understood the importance of having good interpretation skills and have decided to grapple more seriously with some important texts in our life (hopefully, that would include the biblical text), the image of (biblical) textual study as a crime scene investigation (CSI), I've found, comes in handy for us to better understand what it is exactly we're doing when we study "texts," because it describes "the nuts and bolts" as it were of dissecting a literary text (or any "text" for that matter) in order to grasp the different nuances of meaning that this text contains.

THE DIFFERENT ELEMENTS OF A CSI APPLIED TO TEXTS

In a CSI, the only thing that is accessible to a CSIr is the crime scene. The crime itself—that is, the past event that produced the crime scene—is *no longer directly accessible* with utter finality to the CSIr or to anyone else. It has already happened; it is in the past; no one can go back to it barring time travel. When we apply this image to textual study, we see clearly that the event *behind* a given text is no longer directly accessible to us except through something that we *can* access now. That often takes the form of a written text or other mediating materials such as archaeological remains. What that past event produced is something like a crime scene that is now present to us. This CS is so crucially important for getting a glimpse of what happened in the past and understanding this past event's different dimensions, that the authorities will try to preserve the CS *as it is* to the best of their abilities (often by cordoning off and protecting the crime scene) so that the CSIrs could come in and do their job properly and well. (Additional yet optional nerdiness: that could be an apologia for the importance of the sub-field in biblical studies called textual criticism.)

Expanding the metaphor and summarizing the discussion thus far, in our case, the biblical reader-interpreter is, as it were, the CSIr who comes to the CS (which is equivalent to the biblical text) and works at the scene by carefully investigating it (an image of textual study). The purpose of this careful study is to thoroughly analyze what is *presently available* in order to determine as best as possible what might have transpired at the scene *in the past* which, as we saw, created such a CS in the first place. In other words, the CSIr seeks to get as clear a glimpse as possible of events in the past by analyzing the material remains that they can access now with all the knowledge, training, and tools at their disposal. Why such a focus on the past? It's because we hope that understanding the nature of that past event can teach us valuable lessons in the present, which will in turn help us forge a better future.

Of course, the success or failure of the CSI depends on a lot of factors but, one can say, that it relies in a major way on the competence of the CSIr. If they do their work well and thoroughly, that is, if they observe the CS very carefully, see the matter from every possible angle, do the requisite background historical research and apply a sharp wit to the analysis of all the available data, then what transpired in the past as the crime will probably successfully come to light. If the CSIr instead does a sloppy job, a less than optimal result might turn out. Of course, it is also quite possible that there are other reasons over which the CSIr has no control, such as, if the crime scene itself has been compromised or it does not of itself give sufficient evidence of the crime because of a very careful criminal. All these extenuating circumstances could prevent a CSIr from getting to the bottom of the CSI.

As hinted at earlier, in the crime scene, there is an encounter of past, present, and future. The crime belongs to the past; the crime scene, however, is in the present and acts as a window to the past for the CSIr; the results of the investigation spell out the consequences of the crime for both the present and the future as people draw lessons from "the crime" (applied to biblical study, the event or teaching).

At this point, I hope that the parallels between textual study (in this case, of the Bible) and a CSI are clearer. With such a perspective, we can take up the study of biblical literature (and all possible life-texts) with more gusto, imagining ourselves as being on a quest to understand more deeply a past event with such a significance that it changed the lives of our spiritual ancestors by "investigating" a text available to us now.

Let me add here that the "crime scene" we are investigating when we study the New Testament is in fact quite related to us because it has to do, after all, with *our* spiritual ancestry. This is why we undertake the investigation not with a detached sense but with a vested interest to discover the legacy in the past that brought us to where we are at present.

Thus, with such an image of biblical textual study, the many methodologies that students of biblical literature have to learn (such as the historical-critical method, narrative and rhetorical criticism, contextual interpretation, and many other [sometimes mind-boggling] methods)[8] will be seen in a new, more interesting light. These different methods can be more deeply appreciated as the necessary rigorous training for us to better deal with the "crime scene" that will stare us in the face every time we investigate

8. Among the many excellent aids to help students learn different methods to study biblical literature, I would like to recommend: Carvalho, *Primer on Biblical Methods*, and Green, *Hearing the New Testament*.

a biblical text. This crime scene is waiting to be unlocked in order to yield the riches of a deeper understanding and appreciation of the past and enable us in turn to reap fruits for the present and the future. But that all depends on whether we are competent and good CSIrs.

Let me also underline the following for teacher-readers: Making biblical studies interesting is a crucial factor. If or when that is accomplished, we can arguably say that at least half the work will have been done as the students themselves self-motivate to become better investigators of the biblical "crime scene."[9]

THE "THREE WORLDS" OF THE BIBLICAL TEXT: THE WORLD "WITHIN" THE TEXT

Let us go further in our efforts to learn how to properly read and interpret texts. Here, I will propose yet another important set of images for engaging in biblical study and interpretation. It is the notion, mentioned in passing earlier, that with regard to texts (such as the New Testament), we can identify three (so-called) "worlds."

When explaining the different possible meanings of biblical texts, the French philosopher Paul Ricœur thought that we are dealing with, as it were, three interrelated "worlds" with their own particular characteristics.[10] First, there is a world "within" the text. For convention's sake, let us call this "World #1" (W1). It refers to the text itself which, upon closer inspection, is actually a world in itself. Whenever a reader-interpreter is working directly with or on the text *at the level of the text itself*, we can say that they are using a method of textual analysis that is directly related to World #1. Some of you might have encountered methodologies of biblical study called narrative criticism or rhetorical criticism. They are, strictly speaking, methodologies that pertain more immediately (not exclusively though) to W1. This world within the text is tantamount to the crime scene we identified above.

The following analogy might also be helpful. We can illustrate the nature of the three worlds more clearly by referring to fantasy literature. Take the *Harry Potter* series of books as a good case in point. When we encounter for the first time a book about a young wizard called Harry Potter and his adventure with a Sorcerer's (or Philosopher's) Stone in the first volume of the series, begin reading it, and are gradually "sucked into" the story, we

9. See the following work for more elaboration on this image for biblical study: Kaltner and McKenzie, *Sleuthing the Bible*.

10. Ricœur, *Interpretation Theory*, 87–94. See also Johnson, "Literary Criticism of Luke-Acts," 159.

realize that "the world within" *Harry Potter and the Sorcerer's Stone* is a self-contained world, different from ours, where wizards and witches exist, where magic is used for good or evil, where fantastical beasts roam about. And when one is drawn into the story, one could actually "lose oneself" in this fantastical world that is distinguishable from where we are currently located but is nevertheless a marvelous world to enter and spend some time in, even only for the sake of entertainment.

THE WORLD "BEHIND" THE TEXT

The second level related to the text is the so-called world "behind" the text, which we shall heuristically term as World #2 (W2). This refers to all the historical forces "behind" the text that conspired to produce the text as we know it now. When a Bible reader has, as main purpose, the reconstruction of the history that lies behind the text, they are doing work that pertains to World #2. Put more technically, when a particular methodology employed in biblical studies is directly concerned with the uncovering of the historical backgrounds of the text, it belongs to World #2. In this regard, the method of biblical study commonly known as "the historical-critical method" concerns itself immediately with the world behind the text. This world behind the text, it should be noted, is the reconstructed history of the crime scene that we referred to above.

If one for instance wants to go beyond the text of Harry Potter to know what lies behind such a marvelous story of fantasy, one will have to deal with the figure of its famous author, J. K. Rowling. Thus, one would learn about her life story: her background, her family and relationships, her passion for writing, the different circumstances she found herself in which all worked together to make her finally imagine the persona of Harry Potter and his fascinating world; the story of how her first manuscript was rejected multiple times before it was finally accepted and published, and even what she has grown to become after she achieved fame. All of these comprise the "world behind the text" of the Harry Potter story.

Note also that by "historical backgrounds," we can refer to several different layers of history. When analyzing, for example, the gospel story of Yeshua's baptism in Mark 1:9–11, we can be concerned with whether the event as recounted in Mark really happened behind the text (that is, in history) or whether it really happened as the text portrays the event. Alternatively, we can be more interested in the circumstances that the gospel writer Mark was faced with in his community which influenced his decision to describe the story in this way with points of difference, we can note, from the parallel accounts in Matthew (3:13–17) and Luke (3:21–22). *Both* of those foci of attention pertain to W2 because they are concerned with things that happened *behind* the text of Mark that we know now.

THE WORLD "IN FRONT OF" THE TEXT

And finally, there is also a World "in front of" the text which we shall designate as World #3 (W3). It refers to the reader of the text seeking to interpret it and it is named "in front of the text" because we are usually in front of a text that we are reading. World #3 or the reader is oftentimes an individual, but it can very well refer to a group or community of people in the present (or even in the past or the future) who are trying to make sense of a text. This is particularly true of the biblical text which has been held as sacred scripture by communities of religious believers through the ages. By now, you would undoubtedly have made the connection that the world in front of the text can be identified with the crime scene investigator.

Whenever I read and study Harry Potter, for instance, I am a distinct "world," and my world encounters the world within the text (of Harry Potter) as well as the world behind the text (J. K. Rowling). When I consciously try to draw out meaning from Harry Potter for me and my students, I am engaged in creating meaning for the world "in front of" the Harry Potter text.

As with Worlds #1 and #2, World #3 is also a self-standing world: The readers of the text constitute a world in themselves. It is this reader in their world who confronts the text and tries to make sense of it. This is the one who tries to interpret what meaning and significance the text had for its original recipients in W2 but also ponders about what significance the text continues to have for themselves. Therefore, when a particular methodology (such as contextual interpretation) is directly concerned with the interpretive value of the text, it can be said to be related to World #3.

Now that we have posited that the New Testament is, as it were, the village that raised our spiritual ancestors and have armed ourselves with some useful tools for the journey, let's go visit it and immerse ourselves in it so that we could actually get to know our spiritual ancestors in a better way. *On to the village we go!*

5

Finding Our Way around the New Testament Village

The "Big Picture," the Nature of the Texts, the Old Testament Background

For somebody who thinks that the four Gospels are like four witnesses in a court trying to tell exactly how the accident happened, as it were, this [the fact that the gospels are *not* like video recordings of history] is extremely troubling. It is not at all troubling to me because they told me, quite honestly, that they were Gospels. And a Gospel is good news—"good" and "news"—updated interpretation, so I did not expect journalism.

—John Dominic Crossan[1]

The Gospels are very peculiar types of literature. They're not biographies. I mean, there are all sorts of details about Jesus that they simply are not interested in giving us. They're a kind of religious advertisement. What they do is proclaim their individual author's interpretation of the Christian message through the device of using Jesus of Nazareth as a spokesperson for the evangelist's position.

—Paula Fredriksen[2]

1. Mellows, "From Jesus to Christ."
2. Mellows, "From Jesus to Christ."

A BIG PICTURE OF THE NEW TESTAMENT VILLAGE

Now that we have affirmed that the New Testament is like a village where some of our important spiritual ancestors continue to live through texts, our task now is to actually go visit it and immerse ourselves in it so that we could get to know these spiritual ancestors better: Welcome to the village!

Let's begin by painting a big picture of our (metaphorical) village. It all started as a result of the life, teaching, and ministry of Yeshua of Nazareth set in the first century CE, mostly in the Galilee region of Palestine but with a climactic conclusion in Jerusalem. Thus, Yeshua is clearly the one we should acknowledge in this work as the "great founding ancestor" of the village. "Great" in this context would refer both to Yeshua being the *ancient* source at the beginning of the Christian tradition, as well as to *the lofty esteem* with which Yeshua's followers held him during his life and more so after his death. They came to believe that he was the promised messiah, "the Anointed One" from God to save Israel and the whole world (even!). That concept would be *ha-meshiach* in Hebrew or *ho Christos* in Greek. "Christ" then is not Yeshua's last name but an exalted title given to him by his followers.

Yeshua, a member of the peasant class, was from the village of Nazareth. At a certain point in his life, he became a public figure. He started an itinerant ministry of teaching, healing, showing solidarity particularly to the underprivileged, and sharing fellowship with all, but especially with the poor and marginalized. That is shown clearly for example in his practice of welcoming everyone to an "open table" without conditions.[3] All of those activities were geared toward proclaiming and realizing what he referred to as "the reign of God" (Greek: *basileia tou theou*).[4] His ministry attracted followers and, at the same time, incited opposition from certain powerful factions in the political-religious establishments of his time. At a certain point in his public career, he and his disciples went to Jerusalem, the political-religious center of his land. There, he was arrested and handed over to his opponents to be condemned and "terminated." Yeshua of Nazareth finally met his death, crucified as an enemy of the empire on a Roman cross around the year 30 of the common era.

Sometime after this, some of his closest followers claimed that they were witnesses of Yeshua being "raised from the dead" by the God of Israel,

3. Crossan, *Jesus*, 66–70.

4. Also commonly rendered in English as "the Kingdom of God." I will use the arguably more gender-neutral "Reign of God" in this work.

the Being Yeshua called *abba* (Father). This claim about Yeshua's resurrection gradually gained strength as the years went on and became the central proclamation of his followers. It continues to be repeated in the Christian proclamation at Easter: "He is risen!" Yeshua's followers rebooted the movement Yeshua himself started during his ministry and shifted its focus to trusting faith (Greek: *pistis*) that God had put his seal of approval on Yeshua's life, ministry, teaching, as well as ignominious death by raising him from the dead and glorifying him at God's right hand. In the light of that trusting-faith, they followed Yeshua's way within the concrete contexts where they found themselves. In fact, the earliest designation of what eventually became Christianity is recorded as "the Way" in the *Acts of the Apostles* (9:2). In the years following Yeshua's death and reported resurrection, he became acknowledged more and more by his followers in exalted ways, primarily as "Lord" (Greek: *kyrios*),[5] a term that was used of the God of Israel in the Greek translation of the Hebrew Scriptures called the Septuagint.

Trusting-faith in this great founding ancestor Yeshua, the Christ, became the defining characteristic of the movement and the communities of people who followed the way of life started by Yeshua himself. They were eventually called "Christians."[6] The movement developed into various communities scattered around the Mediterranean basin which continued to live and spread the message of the rabbi from Nazareth. In time (practically in the last third of the first century CE), certain early Yeshua-followers decided to write down accounts of what Yeshua supposedly did and taught, how Yeshua lived, how he died, and how he was proclaimed by his disciples as being raised from the dead. This kind of account written in Greek, came to be known as *evangelion*, a word that means "good news." It was later rendered into English with the word that we continue to use today—"gospel."

We know of at least twenty-two early gospels.[7] The authors did not attach their names to these accounts but in time the earliest written four gospels were attributed to Matthew, John, Mark, and Luke. Two of these names (the first two) belong to individuals who were part of Yeshua's inner core known as "the Twelve." The other two were thought to be disciples of prominent early Christ-followers.

These four names, I have suggested earlier, refer to the most important spiritual ancestors after Yeshua of our metaphorical New Testament village. We added Paul the apostle and John the Seer. Each of them stands

5. One of the best works on this topic is Hurtado, *Lord Jesus*.

6. See Scott et al., "If Not Christians, What?," 13–18. See also Vearncombe, Scott, and Taussig for the Westar Christianity Seminar, *After Jesus Before Christianity*.

7. See Miller, *Complete Gospels*.

for a community (or even groups of communities) that had trusting-faith in Yeshua and lived according to his Spirit in their own particular styles and within their own local contexts. When these early writings of the Yeshua-story (adapted to the authors' own particular circumstances) were considered in time as "sacred" and "inspired" scriptures, they would play pivotal roles in shaping how Christians throughout Western history (and wherever Christianity found itself) have thought about crucial themes such as God, religion, life, and morality.

A GUIDE FOR GETTING TO KNOW THE SPIRITUAL ANCESTORS

This is how we will proceed from here on out in our efforts to get to know the important spiritual ancestors who continue to live on in the (New Testament) village. At the beginning of every chapter, I will start with a general overview of our "crime scene" (the text). It is important to have a grasp of the general plot of the story that a particular spiritual ancestor-author recounted and other main characteristics of said ancestor-author and his work. I will limit myself to a very broad outline of each storyteller-ancestor's plot with the presupposition that if readers would like a more detailed outline of the story, they can easily consult the many excellent resources available out there (please see the bibliography for further study at the end).

What I would like to prioritize here is pointing out, what I think are, crucially important factors either about the particular ancestor himself or about the circumstances that he and his community faced because I consider them as key, even indispensable elements for understanding these spiritual ancestors and their communities. Grasping them also plays a crucial role in developing what I described earlier as a family affinity, affection for, and a critical attitude about these spiritual ancestors and their legacies. I describe these factors as *sine qua non*'s, a Latin phrase that literally means "without which." What I'll mention then in each chapter about the ancestor-authors are the pieces of information "without which" we would find it hard, in my opinion of course, to understand what "made a particular spiritual ancestor tick" (if we can put it that way).

THE TEXTS OF OUR SPIRITUAL ANCESTORS

Let us be clear though that the texts that our spiritual ancestors wrote will be our primary evidence for getting to know them. It would be good now to explain a little more about the nature of these texts. The Gospels relate a particular version of the story of Yeshua rooted at the same time in the concrete contexts in which an ancient Christian author and community-of-context were located. They are *not* historical accounts in the contemporary sense of the word in which an author tries to reconstruct on the basis of available historical material what most probably happened in the past. Instead, the Gospels are, *first and foremost, faith proclamations*. They are documents that aim to awaken trusting-faith in Yeshua as "the Christ" by recounting a version of Yeshua's story that is composed of all the following: partly remembered accounts and teachings from the tradition, as well as embellished accounts or even "constructed fiction" about historical figures and their teachings, all for the purpose of awakening faith in the targeted audience of the work. Let me reiterate that these accounts are *not* based on modern standards of historicity. So, when we listen to or read them, we are accessing the Yeshua-story through the lens of a particular ancient ancestor-author and the faith community in which they were embedded. In technical terms, we are listening to or reading the *kerygma* (faith proclamation) of some early Yeshua-followers. We *do not* have history playing itself before our eyes like a video recording of past actual events.

The letters of granduncle Paul (and other New Testament letter writers), on the other hand, deal with practical issues in different communities of early Yeshua-followers. We can observe at close quarters how GU-Paul is trying to flesh out what faith in Christ means as applied to different concrete life situations. And then, the so-called revelation to granduncle John the Seer is considered "apocalyptic literature" and is an effort to encourage Christians to hold on to the hope that Yeshua is ultimately going to be victorious over the empire that persecutes them by recounting apocalyptic visions that were supposedly revealed to the author.

These different texts seem, at first blush, to be all about Yeshua, the Christ, and what trusting-faith in him might mean for the recipients of the text. But let me emphasize an oft forgotten yet really important side of these texts: they are definitely *not only* about Yeshua. Using our metaphor of textual study as a crime scene investigation, it will become quite clear if we dig deeper into these texts that, although they (the gospels particularly) seem to speak mainly about Yeshua, these texts actually reveal a lot to us about the ancestor-authors and the circumstances that faced them and their communities. True, we are definitely interested in the great ancestor Yeshua, but no less important is what we can learn about our spiritual ancestors who wrote and received the good news about Yeshua. We would also like to learn more about the communities that occasioned the writing and the people who received those writings. From such an examination, we will try to get a better glimpse of who these ancestors were, the faith and hope that sustained them, and the concerns and challenges that a particular ancestor-author and his community faced. In this way, we will learn the necessary lessons that our spiritual ancestry can teach us. Armed with that, we can hopefully face our own present and the future with a deeper wisdom.

SOME "HEART-POSTURES" TO MAINTAIN AS WE GO AROUND THE NEW TESTAMENT VILLAGE

So here we are. We are Westerners (or Westernized people) who (metaphorically) set out from distant and very different places and have finally arrived at the New Testament village to have a more meaningful encounter and conversation with our spiritual ancestors. There are many important questions we would do well to be mindful of at this stage. Some of them could be the following: What are the presuppositions we bring with us as we enter the village? Are they accurate or misinformed? What do we need to do in order to encounter our spiritual ancestors in a real and significant way (even if it is only through texts)? What will it take to have a real conversation with these spiritual ancestors? Will we discover some significant commonalities between them and us? We ask those questions because, like Ruth in *The Bonesetter's Daughter*, we have been raised in a faraway and very different place from this village. At the same time, we have decided to go back to the village to get to know our ancestry better and, thus, become more aware where we and our ancestors came from.

At this point, allow me also to suggest some, what I'll call, "heart-postures" to have as we begin our more intimate exploration of the New Testament village. *Kokoro-gamae* is a Japanese word that literally means "heart-posture." It refers to an inner attitude that one takes toward something. So, let me reiterate the following heart-postures that, I think, will be useful for us in our quest to get to know our spiritual ancestors better.

First of all, let us once again remember that "the past is a foreign country; they do things differently there."[8] The village we are about to explore is composed of documents written in the very distant past by ancestors who lived in a bygone age, in places that are radically different from our time and present (Western[ized]) contexts. For some time now in the guild of biblical studies, we have been rightly warned of the dangers of imposing our worldviews on the biblical text because that will only make us grossly

8. Hartley, *Go-Between*. This is the first line of the prologue.

misunderstand these writings and the people behind the texts. That will in turn prevent us from having a truly meaningful encounter with writings that influenced our civilization and with our spiritual ancestors who wrote or received them.[9]

Of course, it has to be equally emphasized that, contrary to many "modern" (as opposed to "postmodern") voices urging us to be as objective as possible in our historical quests, the postmodern age has shown that *there is no completely "objective" view*. Each of us is situated in particular historical, cultural, and social contexts and, try as we might to be free of those constraints and be more objective, we will never truly be a *tabula rasa* (Latin: "blank slate") in whatever we do. Our contexts will always influence us one way or another. Hence, in order to be realistic and astute examiners of the text, we have to acknowledge our particular contexts and consider them as an essential part of the whole equation even as we try to reach out and encounter the past (be it a past text or a past person) in a meaningful way.

To add to the above, there are other heart-postures to maintain in keeping with the spirit that we have proposed in this work—that of questing to discover the spiritual ancestry of our civilization. The first would be, what I guess could be called, a "sense of family." The ancestors (they are tantamount to World #2 mentioned in chapter 4) we are trying to encounter through their writings (World #1) are, in a deep sense, part of our spiritual ancestry. In short, *they are family!* When it comes to family, we have "vested interests." We cannot be entirely "detached" and "objective."

The next heart-posture would be something I'll render as "non-judgmental listening." Yes, I know that a lot of people dislike their families because of the dysfunctions that they experienced firsthand from living with them and I do not blame in any way those for whom family experiences were so traumatic that they could no longer relate with their families in a positive way. For those who can, however, it would be worthwhile to rise above family dysfunctions and try to understand the various histories of one's ancestry by first setting aside our presuppositions and biases. A good *first* attitude to take toward our family histories (and this applies to anyone who is truly dear to us) would be *non-judgmental listening*. We try to truly listen to their stories with an open heart to discover what their experiences were; what challenges they faced; what motivated them to act and write in the ways they did; what were their backgrounds from which they became what they became; etc. Only in this way can we come closer to a clearer view of our ancestors' worlds.

9. An excellent treatment of this theme is found in Richards and O'Brien, *Misreading Scripture with Western Eyes*, 9–23.

The next heart-postures follow on the heels of the last one: sympathy and understanding. We not only refrain from being judgmental about our ancestors' stories, since they are part of our ancient family, let us also strive to be sympathetic with and understanding of whatever they will tell us. The opposite of this is a closed and hostile attitude that is, from the get-go, immediately ready to contradict and, at every chance, condemn and correct whatever we hear. This is why I urge readers to treat the New Testament books as a sort of textual voices from ancient family, in order to elicit this sympathetic attitude.

WE ARE (METAPHORICALLY) GROWN-UP CHILDREN OF AGING PARENTS

Why have I explicitly suggested the *kokoro-gamae* (heart-postures) above? It's because I am trying to create an environment in which the New Testament texts and messages are listened to, not so much in a traditionally religious way whereby we kind of revert to a childish attitude of non-questioning reverence. What I am urging here instead is something I hinted to in chapter 1: to relate with spiritual ancestors much like *mature grown-up children* would try to relate with their aging parents (and relatives). That ideal would be: to accept, esteem, respect, and possibly even love family members "warts and all," that is, with all their strengths as well as flaws. This doesn't mean that grown-up children would agree with or condone all that their parents/relatives say or do. This means rather that whatever their parents/relatives will say will be respected and reacted to in a sympathetic and understanding way, although the grown-up children might have to disagree with some points and even suggest correctives and improvements.

It all begins with the first step of an understanding and sympathetic listening. That should be followed though by a respectful yet authentic "family conversation." As mentioned in chapter 1, I have in mind a conversation between two grown-ups, members of the same ancestral and family line, characterized by mutual respect, even affection if possible, but is, nevertheless, critical and mature as illustrated by the grown-up Ruth with her mother LuLing in *The Bonesetter's Daughter*.

Thus, now that we have come to this stage, we can bring out all the tools we have at hand in order to do a proper critical reading and analysis of the texts (World #1) as well as the past events and the people that lie behind these texts (World #2). That actually comprises the sympathetic listening part mentioned above. Only after that can we make worlds 1 and 2 the springboard for the grown-up conversation that we, present day descendants (World #3), should have with the texts and the ancestors behind the texts.

GOING BACK FURTHER TO THE EARLIER BACKGROUND

For us to get to know well our New Testament village-spiritual ancestors, it is necessary that we have some acquaintance of the worldview and the different stories that were dominant narratives of the world in which they lived. In practice, that means becoming familiar with the common themes and the general plot of the Jewish Scriptures or what Christians call "the Old Testament." If you are familiar with that already, you may skip the next section and go to the next chapter. If you think you need a quick refresher, then please go over the following section.

UNDERSTANDING THE (EVEN MORE) ANCIENT JEWISH ANCESTORS

Our spiritual ancestors were all first century common era (CE) Jews (with the possible exception of granduncle Luke). As Jews who were born and lived during the time period that historians call "Second Temple Judaism" (from 515 BCE to 70 CE; let us also include the immediate aftermath of the Jerusalem temple's destruction in the years after 70 CE up to the turn of the first century), *they themselves were heirs already at that time of a long and venerable tradition* that was considered "ancient" and therefore begrudgingly respected even by their Roman conquerors. (The Romans had a deep esteem for "antiquity," that is, traditions that had a long, venerable history.)

Ancient Jews as a group had several common characteristics that we will have to keep in mind if we are to understand, what can be considered, a common Jewish worldview at the time. How do we do this? By familiarizing ourselves better with some key areas of life as expressed by the following questions:

- What were the *stories, laws, poems, and other oral and written traditions* that lay at the foundation of their worldview?
- What were the dominant *religious-cultural symbols and practices* that they valued?
- What were their most cherished *hopes* and dreams?

COMPONENTS OF THE WORLDVIEW OF THE SPIRITUAL ANCESTORS

We will be able to answer these questions by studying what Jews call "TaNaK" or "the Hebrew Bible/Jewish Scriptures" or what is widely known among Christians as "The Old Testament" (OT). What this means in practice is that, for Christians and Westerners in general, *some knowledge of the OT is necessary in order to get to know their spiritual ancestry.* That is why the OT is an essential part of the Christian Bible which, as a whole, is composed of two parts: The Old Testament (which is like a part 1); and the New Testament (which is tantamount to a part 2).

So here are some of the major points (key words will be in italics) to keep in mind regarding this Jewish background for us to understand our New Testament village ancestors who, it should be remembered, even include Yeshua (as a historical person).

First of all, ancient Jews were fiercely proud that they were part of "Israel" (taken here primarily as a people-nation) which, they believed, had been *chosen* in a special way by God to be the Creator's own special people and nation. The people of Israel were bound to God by a special "Covenant," the primary component of which was the "Law" (*Torah*) that God had given them through Moses and was, in turn, elaborated upon by the many prophets, sages, and various other teachers throughout Israel's history. In the Jewish Tradition, it is often said that there are 613 commandments of the "Law" (that number includes the Ten Commandments that are more familiar to Christians).

Ancient Jews also valued immensely the geographical "Land" (also referred to as "Israel") which, they believed, God had given to them as Abraham's descendants. The Land (of Israel) was holy but its cultic center, Jerusalem, was especially so because on it stood the Temple where God, they believed, was present in a special way.

Moreover, it is also necessary to know the general plot of an extended sacred story that, we can say, was the foundation of how our first-century Jewish spiritual ancestors understood history or the story of the world. I often refer to it as the "story-plot" or simply *"the story" that was told by parents to their children as an essential part of raising them as Jewish* and, hence, every Jewish child at the time would have learned the gist and main lessons of this storyline as they grew up. This was in turn the basis of the worldview by which ancient Jews viewed, understood, and mentally organized everything: God, the world, life itself and all the other details in their world. Having a grasp of the basic flow of this story found in the Old Testament is, therefore, essential for us to understand the common mindset of our spiritual ancestors whose voices are preserved in the New Testament village.

I divide this extended storyline into several subheadings using the following key themes: *Creation, Nation, Flight, Fight-Settlement, Kingdom(s) and Exile, Return-Rebuilding, Further Struggles with Empires*, and *Hope*. These notions, I think, can summarize well the spirit of the story that parents told their children at the time. This is the same narrative plot that the wider culture expected everyone to know well during what is called Second Temple Judaism.

This then is the main outline of the extended story that our spiritual ancestors in the New Testament village were familiar with. (Let me use the "historical present" to narrate the extended plot for vividness.)

THE EXTENDED STORY-PLOT FROM THE JEWISH SCRIPTURES/OLD TESTAMENT

Creation

God creates the world and everything in it, culminating in the fashioning of the first humans, male and female, who bear God's very "image" (Western Christians refer to this as *Imago Dei* [Latin] "God's image"). The seventh day (Saturday) is special because God rested after all the work of creation. That, it is pointed out, is the origin of the all-important Sabbath practice. The humans are entrusted with the care and stewardship of creation. They are put in an idyllic world described as a garden with the proscription, however, that they should not eat of a forbidden "fruit" (Gen 1–2).

Giving in to the prodding of a serpent in the garden, our first male and female proto-ancestors fail in this and end up partaking of the forbidden fruit. This event has often been described in Christianity as "the Fall." This act damages the once perfect relationship between God and humans and, thus, the first ancestors (commonly called "Adam" and "Eve") are driven away from the garden (Gen 3). They and all their descendants after them are burdened with suffering and eventual death as a result of this act. The dark aspect of this story often dominates the retelling of it. Let me encourage readers though not to forget that creation does not begin with an "original fall" but instead with a tremendous "original blessing" that the Creator bestows to the whole of creation.[10]

The main point of this story for ancient Jews (as well as those who continue to read this story as scripture) is arguably to explain the origin of the

10. Consult Fox, *Original Blessing*.

many unfortunate things that assail humanity and why evil and suffering are so pervasive in human life. The entry of evil-suffering into the human story is portrayed eloquently in the stories that follow in quick succession: Cain (Adam and Eve's son) murders his brother Abel (Gen 4); in time, the world becomes so evil that God decides to destroy everything and, as it were, "reboot" creation with a clean slate through a flood. God spares a limited number of the created order from the flood's destruction. Thus, Noah, his family, and a limited number of species of animals survive the destructive waters by riding out the storm in an ark (Gen 6–9); humans build a tower aiming to "reach the sky" but God confounds their plan by mixing up their languages at Babel (Gen 11).

Nation

Sometime later (always in the context of the expansion and multiplication of evil and suffering in the world), God chooses a man who is given the new name "Abraham" (meaning "father of multitudes"). Abraham is destined to be the origin and ancestral father of a nation of people who will be bound to God in a special way and a source of blessing to the whole world (Gen 12–18). Thus, the interactions between God and Abraham become key to the ancient Jewish story as a symbolic story of who the people of Israel should be. Abraham is called to trust in God (this is what "faith" is) through an invitation to leave his homeland and go to an unknown place that God will give to him (the "Land"). Abraham decides to trust in this God, accepts the invitation, and sets out for the "promised land." God makes a covenant with Abraham and all his descendants who, it is promised, will be as numerous as "the stars in the sky." The physical sign of the covenant will be the mark of *circumcision*. Abraham's descendants after him (Isaac, Jacob, and his offspring) multiply and become a clan. They eventually end up in Egypt because of a famine in the land where they were living and are initially welcomed in Egypt as guests because of Jacob's beloved son, Joseph, who had meanwhile risen from being a slave to become an important official in that land (Gen 21–49).

Flight

This phase of the story is traditionally described as "Exodus," which is also the title of the second book of the Jewish Scriptures in its Greek translation. It is a word that means "departure" of a large mass of people (hence, "flight"). After hundreds of years of living in the land of Egypt, the descendants of

Jacob are enslaved by a pharaoh who did not know Joseph. The people suffer terribly from oppression and cry out to God. God then chooses Moses as the one who will be God's agent in freeing the Israelites from slavery and leading them out of Egypt back to the land that was given to the patriarchs (Abraham, his son Isaac, and Jacob also known as "Israel" himself). In spite of the vehement efforts on the part of Pharaoh to prevent their flight from Egypt, through the power of God, the people cross the Red Sea and pass over from slavery to freedom. In the wilderness, they have different important experiences: On Mt. Sinai, they receive the Law from God through Moses; they experience the power and protection of God at every stage of the journey; and they are caught up in a cycle of rebellion and repentance with regard to their covenant with God. In the end, they have to wander the desert for forty years before finally being able to enter into the land that God had promised to their ancestors (see Exodus through Deuteronomy).

Fight (yet again!) and Settlement

After their long wandering in the desert, the Israelites are finally allowed to enter the promised land with Joshua this time as their leader. But it is not an easy task. Although "the Land" has been promised to them and was inhabited by the patriarchs before them, this time, they have to struggle and fight with other groups of people who are already there (such as the Canaanites, the Amalekites, the Midianites, etc.). (Consult the book of Joshua.) Although the promised land is divided according to the different tribes of Israel and apportioned to them in the book of Joshua, the book of Judges gives us the impression that struggles with the other inhabitants of the common area continue for a while even after the initial settlement. The Israelites are led for a while by a diverse and ad hoc group of leaders called "judges" who are raised by God when there is a need for decisive leadership during times of crisis (see the book of Judges).

Kingdom(s) and Exile

After a while, the Israelites ask for a king to rule over them. Thus, God, through the prophet Samuel, appoints Saul for this role. When Saul goes against God's directives, the shepherd boy, David, is anointed in his place to be the future ruler. David displays his mettle particularly against the Philistine "giant" Goliath whom he defeats in the battlefield. In time, after many struggles, David finally becomes king of Israel. He unites the different tribes and solidifies the kingdom with the capital in Jerusalem. His son, Solomon, follows him as king of a united kingdom. Solomon starts out as a good and wise king. He builds the first temple in Jerusalem. However, later on in life, he displays some fatal flaws such as idolatry and the imposition of oppressive measures against his people. After his death, the once united kingdom is divided into two. Ten tribes separate from Solomon's line to make up the "northern" kingdom (also) called "Israel" and two tribes dominated by the tribe of Judah make up the "southern" kingdom known as Judah. These two kingdoms are led by a succession of mostly evil kings.

These unfaithful steward-kings often lead the people of Israel (divided now into two kingdoms) astray in many ways and thus Israel (i.e., the people of God) is mostly unfaithful to the covenant in a collective way. This long and sorry history is told from a perspective that wants to teach its audience an important lesson: that unfaithfulness to the covenant and the sins of the people are what caused God's judgment that allowed many catastrophes to happen to Israel. The northern kingdom was finally devastated by the Assyrian empire in 722 BCE and its inhabitants were scattered in many different areas. The southern kingdom was defeated by the Babylonians in 587–586 with Solomon's temple destroyed (the first temple) and the leading inhabitants of Judah led into exile in Babylon. With the dispersal of the northern tribes of Israel, it was mainly the people of the southern kingdom (composed mainly of people from the tribe of "Judah," which is arguably where the term "Jews" come from) that carried on the legacy of Israel. From this point onwards, the "chosen people" of Yahweh are also commonly referred to as "Jews." The time that many Jews spent in captivity in Babylon is commonly known as the "Babylonian exile" (585–538 BCE). This story-plot is found mainly in 1–2 Samuel and 1–2 Kings.

Prophets

We must not forget the pivotal role that God's special messengers called "prophets" played particularly in this tumultuous time in ancient Israelite history. The prophets are commonly yet mistakenly thought of as people who could foretell the future. Their primary role instead in the sacred story of Israel is, above all, "to speak on behalf of God." They were called by God to be spokespersons of what God's people needed to hear at a given time, whether that be warning, correction, condemnation, consolation, guidance, or encouragement. Among the prophets are names such as Isaiah, Jeremiah, Ezekiel, and so forth (see the books of the Bible bearing the names of these different prophets).

Return and Rebuilding

Eventually, a new imperial power arises—the Persian empire under Cyrus the Great—and it conquers the Babylonian empire in 539 BCE. The Persians allow the Jews to go back to their ancestral homeland. Thus, many Jews return from the Babylonian exile and rebuild the temple in Jerusalem. This new temple is known as the "Second Temple," and this is why the historical period in which there is a second temple standing in Jerusalem is called "Second Temple Judaism" (until its destruction by the Romans in 70 CE). The resettlement of "Palestine" (this is an alternative term to refer to the area that we've been calling "Israel" so far) after the Babylonian exile is *particularly important for us because it is toward the end of this second temple Judaism era that the people who were going to start the Christian tradition—Yeshua and his earliest followers—lived.* The last seventy years of this epoch as well as its immediate aftermath are especially noteworthy for us who are trying to better understand the environment in which our spiritual ancestors lived.

(Note well: The final years of the divided kingdoms are described in 2 Kings and Second Chronicles. Different events and teachings related to the Persian or Babylonian exilic periods are scattered in various books of the Old Testament such as the prophetic books, Esther, Psalms, etc.)

Further Struggles with Empires

The resettled Jews in Palestine enjoy relative peace and stability during the Persian period (539–330 BCE). We can say that there is something like a religious and cultural revival during this time brought about by the rebuilding of the Jerusalem temple and the city's walls (see the books of Ezra and Nehemiah). One can say that the dominant lesson emphasized so far was that fidelity to the covenant between God and Israel is reemphasized as of utmost importance for the land and people of Israel: Obviously, faithfulness guarantees Israel's flourishing and its opposite, unfaithfulness, brings about disaster (many scholars often point out that this is the main message of the school of ancient scripture editors called the "Deuteronomistic" school).[11]

But then again, a new imperial power flexes its muscles with the appearance of Alexander the Great of Macedonia (356–323 BCE), whose lightning conquests during his relatively short life extends his Hellenistic empire to an area that comprised one of the largest empires the world had ever seen up to that point. ("Hellenistic" refers to the Greek language and

11. See Knight and Levine, *Meaning of the Bible*, 70–71, 396–98, 403–15.

culture.) His death at the age of thirty-two though cuts short that conquering march and his generals divvy up his Hellenistic empire amongst themselves. Two of these, the Seleucid Empire based in Antioch-on-the-Orontes River in ancient Syria (in modern-day Turkey), and the Ptolemaic Empire based in Egypt, fought for a while amongst themselves for control of certain areas including Palestine. In this way, Palestine at this time was controlled alternatively by one or the other of these two Hellenistic empires. When the Seleucid ruler, Antiochus IV Epiphanes, forced the Jews to adopt Hellenistic practices that violated the tenets of their faith, they revolted against their Seleucid overlords in what is called "the Maccabean Revolt" (because it was initially led by the family of a certain Judas "Maccabeus" [meaning "God's hammer"]). They were successful in a limited way with their revolt. That allowed the Jews to be independent for a while (142–63 BCE). (Consult the books of the Maccabees.) However, that all came crashing down when the Roman general Pompey conquered Palestine in 63 BCE as part of the expansion of the new imperial power—Rome. Thus, the Roman occupation of Palestine begins and goes on until the early seventh century CE when it passes over to the invading Muslim armies.

Hope for the Coming of God's New Order or "Reign"

Sometime after the Babylonian exile (around the third century BCE), a type of literature commonly described as "apocalyptic" begins to appear. These apocalyptic writings are filled with mysterious and cryptic language and symbols that express a strong hope that God would directly intervene in history to defeat evil. Evil is, of course, identified with the empires that conquered and oppressed God's land and people. Future apocalyptic events are imaged as cosmic and catastrophic events. Throughout their history, the people of God always looked back to the past, particularly, to the foundational event when God freed their ancestors from slavery in Egypt, in order to draw hope that God would deliver them again when they need God's help. One can say that with their continuing experience of being conquered and oppressed by one empire after another, the Jews had to add an extra way to cope with suffering by envisioning a glorious future when God would act once again in power to defeat Israel's enemies and restore the chosen people and nation to a glorious state. Many Jews held the belief that God would send a chosen one, a "messiah"-like figure who would be akin to Moses and David of old and be the agent of God's deliverance and healing (consult Daniel and some books that are classified as "intertestamental" or "pseudepigraphal" literature such as the book of Enoch).

And Here We Are: The Times of Yeshua and His Followers

With this we are caught up. It is here where we come at last to the particular context in which our New Testament spiritual ancestors lived: Yeshua, his immediate followers, and later generations of people (who would eventually come to believe in Yeshua as the Messiah sent from God and write about him) are located in this late Second Temple Jewish context (and its immediate aftermath). The more we understand it, the more we also come to better grasp their hopes and dreams, the causes that moved them to live as they did, the reasons why they came to trust and have faith that the rabbi-healer from Nazareth named "Yeshua" was the long-awaited Messiah of God, sent to deliver them and usher in the reign of Israel's God.

And with this, we can continue our visit to the New Testament village and get to know each of the important spiritual ancestors in part II.

PART II

Our New Testament Spiritual Ancestors

What They Faced, What They Believed, and What They Handed Down to Us

6

Mark and the Tragic Messiah

Tragedy as the Wellspring of Compassion

Some later Christian poets and theologians clearly believed that they could use Greek tragedy to make Christian meaning. That is the stunning creative achievement that I am suggesting Mark first imagined.

—Louis A. Ruprecht Jr.[1]

GRANDUNCLE MARK AND HIS WORK: FIRST IMPRESSIONS

It's time to get to know in a more up close and personal way, our first spiritual ancestor-storyteller, granduncle ("GU") Mark and his work, to be called here simply as "Mark." My first dominant impressions of GU-Mark and his work are the following: His Gospel is short compared to others, often fast-paced, offering something like a "no-frills" account of Yeshua's life and teaching. But here and there peppered throughout the Gospel, we notice some very curious things such as: Yeshua is frequently misunderstood, even by his own family (e.g., Mark 3:21); When his identity is correctly understood, he strangely doesn't want this truth to be proclaimed openly (1:34); From the beginning, the opposition to Yeshua (in the form even of murderous intent!) is already marked (3:6). What's the deal here? Who is

1. Ruprecht, *This Tragic Gospel*, 80.

this ancestor-storyteller, GU-Mark? What led him to construct this kind of story? What lessons is he trying to teach us? Here is my attempt to answer those questions.

HOW MARK'S PROTAGONIST BECAME MY PREFERRED IMAGE OF YESHUA

Books are like different people we encounter in our daily lives. Many of them are quite ordinary; some of them are especially good; a few are unpleasant. Once in a while, however, we cross paths with a book that is life-changing and, for a biblical scholar like me, that usually means a book that occasions a tremendous "aha" moment within me about the biblical literature that I'm already familiar with to begin with. Several years ago, I encountered one such book called *This Tragic Gospel: How John Corrupted the Heart of Christianity* by classical and religious studies scholar Louis Ruprecht Jr. As suggested by the title, the book is mainly about the Gospel according to GU-John. I thought though that, in a way, it was very much also about the Gospel of GU-Mark because it makes its case by contrasting John with Mark and how each Gospel portrays Yeshua quite differently. It shows that Mark, the earliest gospel to be written, presents Yeshua as a man of sorrows, a tragic figure full of pathos. On the other hand, John's Yeshua is the diametrical opposite of Mark's: Yeshua (in John) is definitely "untragic"; his Gospel is, in Ruprecht's words, "antitragedy"[2] for the Yeshua described there is self-confident, always in control of things, more divine than human; in short, John's Yeshua is a gloriously triumphant figure, even as he dies on the cross!

I've always had the impression that this gloriously divine Yeshua of John has been the more preferred and beloved image in much of Christian history.[3] What struck me keenly though was this book's insistence that Mark's haunting portrait of Yeshua is the earlier and arguably original image of Yeshua among our earliest Christian ancestors. It is also the source of what is supposed to be Christianity's defining trait—compassion, more popularly known as "love" (or "charity" or "mercy"). What John did was to replace Mark's more original Yeshua-image characterized by tragedy with a diametrically opposed glorious and triumphant figure. In so doing, however, he subverted Mark's compassion-inspiring Yeshua with a more grandiose, dominating and, instead of compassion, awe-and-fear-inspiring figure that would eventually have a lot to do, Ruprecht claims, with Christianity

2. Ruprecht, *This Tragic Gospel*, 7.

3. New Testament scholar Candida Moss calls John "Everyone's Favorite Gospel" in Moss, "Everyone's Favorite Gospel Is a Forgery."

developing ominously into a "line-drawing, border-defining, heresy-hunting religiosity that became even more violent when it attained imperial power in Rome."[4]

As I was struck with how I was warmly and powerfully drawn to Mark's portrayal of Yeshua as a tragic figure, rich in poignancy and pathos but, at the same time, why I was left cold and sometimes even annoyed at John's too lofty and glorious portrayal of Yeshua, I had an epiphany. I realized with clarity that this was because, for a good part of my life, I've been an immigrant, a person who stayed for extended periods of time in places far from my familiar and cozy, original homeland. Moreover, I've shared a lot of common experiences with fellow immigrants and even worked for them in various ways in church-ministerial contexts, especially when they faced tough and painful situations. What I've learned in all these years of migrant life and ministry is that *pathos* is one of the main features that characterize the vast number of immigrants. Why? Because anxiety, alienation, fear, and other painful experiences are what many of them face in a new and hostile place and these in turn sear their souls deeply to such an extent that those sufferings produce in them a particular way of being-in-the-world, as well as a characteristic way-of-viewing-the-world.

So, what exactly is "pathos"? The *American Heritage Dictionary* defines this word as "a quality, as of an experience or a work of art, that arouses feelings of pity, sympathy, tenderness, or sorrow."[5] I've noticed that immigrants, who have lived through many difficult experiences yet have processed these experiences in a holistic way in themselves, usually respond with compassion when faced with the pathos of the world. That is precisely what the Gospel of Mark wanted its readers to experience and that was why the sorrowful and suffering Yeshua of Mark, not the confident, glorious Yeshua of John, captivated me.

OUR NEW TESTAMENT ANCESTORS AND THEIR TEXTS

Recall that, here, we are trying to become more familiar, even enter into a kind of relationship of kinship/ancestry with our spiritual ancestors in the New Testament by going deeper into the works they left us for the purpose of finding some key points that would make us grasp, what I can only describe as, their essence, their core, what "made them tick." Negatively put, I would like to identify these New Testament ancestors' *sine qua non*'s—that

4. Ruprecht, *This Tragic Gospel*, 5.

5. "Pathos," *American Heritage Dictionary*.

is, just two or three things about each one *without which* we would not "get" them. In the limited space we have then, I will underline just a few points which I think are absolutely necessary to understand the spiritual ancestor in question. Let me also add that this is a fruit on my part of many years of reading, studying, and teaching the New Testament. I honestly admit though that, in the final analysis, it is my *limited* perspective that has to be complemented by the learned opinions of other scholars as well as the personal critical reading of the readers themselves.

GRANDUNCLE MARK, HIS TEXT, AND ITS CIRCUMSTANCES

Let's backtrack a bit and go over more basic things about the Gospel called "Mark." Granduncle Mark is acknowledged by the majority of biblical scholars as, chronologically speaking, the first of our New Testament ancestor-storytellers to write a work that we now know as a "gospel." The date of composition is usually put around 70 CE. This is the reason why we will be introduced to him first of all although his work does not appear first in the New Testament; it's GU-Matthew's Gospel that does.

"Gospel" (in Greek, *evangelion*) literally means "good news." This word appears at the beginning of Mark (1:1; 1:14) because GU-Mark wanted his community to understand that his account of the life, teachings, and works of Yeshua was (in GU-Mark's mind) good news for them. This also explains in part why Christians began to use the word "gospel" to refer to accounts of the life and teachings of Yeshua: they came to believe that God accomplished the work of making people whole through the life, work, teaching, death, and resurrection of Yeshua. And *that*—in the Christian worldview—is indeed good news for all.

Mark is the shortest of the four Gospels: It has sixteen chapters (compared to Matthew's twenty-eight; Luke's twenty-four; John's twenty-one). Mark can be described as a fast-paced, no-frills account of Yeshua's activity, especially in the first half. In fact, many of the sentences in this gospel begin with "and" in various English translations. Frequently, we find the expressions "and immediately" and "and again." Does this reflect oral preaching, as has been suggested by some scholars? It's plausible.

Unlike in Matthew and Luke, there are no stories about how Yeshua was born. In the very first chapter, we are already confronted with a grown-up Yeshua who is baptized by John in the Jordan river, receives a revelation that He is God's beloved son, survives his temptation in the wilderness, and begins his public ministry. The story goes on to show us that Yeshua teaches with authority, performs works of power (for example, heals the sick and drives out evil spirits), calls disciples to follow him, all the while proclaiming through this flurry of activity that his teaching and works have something crucial to do with the coming of God's reign in the here and now.

MAIN CONTOURS OF THIS GOSPEL'S STRUCTURE

One can divide Mark into three parts: (1) Yeshua's Ministry in his "home province" (territory) of Galilee (1:16–6:6); (2) The Journey to Jerusalem (8:22–10:52) during which Yeshua continues to teach and heal; (3) Jerusalem where Yeshua's Passion and Death occur (11:1–15:47). These three parts are sandwiched in-between an introduction (1:1–15) and a conclusion (16:1–8). In Mark's case, the introduction presents John the Baptist announcing the messiah's coming and Yeshua's baptism in the Jordan river by John; while the conclusion deals with the empty tomb and, in its original ending, the mysterious and cryptic last story of the women who came to anoint Yeshua but end up fleeing the tomb with fear (16:8).

This tripartite structure (with introductory and concluding portions serving as bookends) is worth noting and remembering well because two other ancestor-authors, GU-Matthew and GU-Luke, are practically going to replicate the very same structure in their own works some ten to fifteen years after the writing of Mark. They would even heavily borrow from GU-Mark's story and edit it (technically called a "redaction") according to their own needs and plans. For this reason, Mark, Matthew, and Luke are called "Synoptic" Gospels. That word suggests that we can read these three similar gospels together, comparing and contrasting them to see what things are similar or different among them, all the time hoping to get a deeper insight into the nature of each of these writings and the people behind them.

THE STORY THAT GRANDUNCLE MARK TOLD

To summarize, GU-Mark tells the following general story about Yeshua: He begins his public ministry in Galilee. At a certain point, he embarks toward Jerusalem with his disciples while continuing to teach and minister to people along the way. He finally reaches Jerusalem in what is to be his last week. Yeshua continues to teach and perform signs there, but there is decidedly an atmosphere of impending tragedy: This part begins with a deeply apocalyptic chapter (chapter 13); there are increasingly hostile exchanges between Yeshua and those who oppose him (e.g., 11:28); finally, Yeshua's enemies look for a way to arrest and kill him (14:1); in a gesture that foreshadows a coming tragic event, Yeshua allows himself to be anointed by a woman in Bethany for his coming burial (14:8); and then, Judas, one of the twelve, agrees to betray Yeshua (14:10). With that, the Passion narrative (in the strict sense) begins, and it concludes with Yeshua's tragic death and burial (at the end of chapter 15). The last chapter, chapter 16, in its original form is a mere eight verses short. We do not even have a resurrection appearance of Yeshua, just a clear message that he has been raised and awaits his disciples in Galilee (vv. 6–7). It ends, though, in an intriguing and mysterious way with the women, who has just witnessed the white-robed young man's announcement of Yeshua's resurrection, fleeing the tomb. The explanation given is: "for they were afraid" (v. 8).

POSSIBLE CIRCUMSTANCES BEHIND THIS GOSPEL

An ancient tradition suggests that Mark (the Gospel) might have been written in Rome by the John Mark mentioned in Acts 12:12, who was supposedly acting as a kind of secretary and interpreter to Peter, yes, "the" Peter—Yeshua's prominent disciple. Moreover, the Gospel is also frequently associated in tradition with the persecution of Christians in Rome by the emperor Nero of "Nero fiddles while Rome burns" fame. Christians were scapegoated as the ones who caused the tragic event and were persecuted as a result. More recently, some scholars have proposed a context for Mark rooted in the Jewish Revolt against Rome (66–74 CE) in Palestine. This scenario suggests that Christians did not support the cause that motivated many Jews to go against Rome, probably because their faith in Yeshua as the Christ made them transcend what they viewed as narrow Jewish nationalism. This led to their being marginalized and treated in a hostile way by the Jewish leadership.[6] Based on those possible historical scenarios, it is probable that GU-Mark wrote this Gospel while living within, and bearing with, *a situation characterized by intense suffering*. This painful context—which was most probably brought about by marginalization and persecution—crucially influenced the work.

In the case of Mark, the above-mentioned suggestion from tradition (particularly of a connection with persecution) seems to make a lot of sense compared to some strands of the tradition about the other Gospel authors, such as GU-Luke being a physician, GU-Matthew being a tax collector, or

6. For example, Marcus, "Jewish War," 441–62.

even GU-John—the presumptive author of a good Greek literary text—being the apostle who was originally a fisherman from Galilee, described in the Acts of the Apostles as being "uneducated" (Acts 4:13). Therefore, I consider that the idea of GU-Mark writing out of a context of intense suffering is not only quite plausible but is in fact the first and major key (or *sine qua non*) for understanding this spiritual ancestor. The reason being that this piece of information jibes well with, what I think, is a major characteristic of Mark's story about Yeshua, namely, that it is the story of a Messiah (Yeshua, of course) who, as it were, lives out a very tragic story. Let me unpack that statement.

YESHUA AS A SUFFERING MESSIAH

Upon close analysis, it is clear that GU-Mark's portrait of Yeshua is predominantly as a misunderstood, opposed, and suffering Messiah.[7] This is obvious throughout his ministry in Galilee, his journey to Jerusalem, and the final week in the holy city itself. Everywhere and always, Yeshua is up against great odds, whether they be opposition from his enemies (e.g., 3:22) or even his family (3:21), misunderstanding on the part of the disciples (e.g., 10:37–38), and, finally, the agony of his passion and death. Nowhere, however, is the suffering Messiah motif in GU-Mark's Gospel clearer than in the account of the agony of Yeshua in Gethsemane before his death (14:32–42).

GU-Mark describes Yeshua there as "distressed and agitated" (v. 33), praying that the cup of suffering pass him by but courageously resigning himself ultimately to do the Father's will and not his own (v. 36). GU-Mark's Yeshua in Gethsemane, gripped by sheer terror in the face of death, is the figure par excellence that inspires compassionate pity (pathos) in the readers.

Unfortunately, this is only the beginning of greater tribulations because Mark's tragic Passion account continues with Yeshua being arrested, condemned, denied by Peter (his closest disciple), flogged, made to wear a crown of thorns, mocked by soldiers, and finally handed over to be crucified. On his way to Golgotha after having been flogged, Yeshua becomes too weak to carry the cross, so much so that the soldiers even have to constrain a passer-by, Simon from Cyrene, to relieve Yeshua for part of the way (15:21). Historically speaking, we can say that the soldiers do this *not* out of mercy but so that the poor, condemned man could last long enough to be "properly" crucified on the cross! Finally, Yeshua is nailed to the cross. After a while, darkness comes upon the whole land and Yeshua plaintively cries out using

7. As we see, for example, in the title of this chapter on Mark found in this introduction to the New Testament: Van Voorst, "Gospel of Mark," 148.

words from Ps 22:1, "My God, my God, why have you forsaken me?" (Mark 15:34, even quoted in Yeshua's native Aramaic for greater effect! *"Eloi, eloi lema sabachtani"*). In this way GU-Mark shows us that at the very climax of the story—the protagonist's death—Yeshua feels completely abandoned by everyone, *even by the very God* whose reign he steadfastly and courageously proclaimed. Thus, Yeshua in Mark ends in an utterly tragic way an utterly tragic life. Louis Ruprecht's verdict is stark, "Mark's gospel emphasizes the totality of the failure."[8]

THE MESSIANIC SECRET

There is a well-known recurring theme in Mark that scholars frequently refer to as "the Messianic Secret." This is the curious phenomenon in Mark in which Yeshua's identity as Messiah is supposed to be some kind of secret. That is, Yeshua admonishes people who correctly discern that he is the Messiah not to tell others his identity. We can see this concretely in several passages: For example, Yeshua commands the demons who know who he is to keep silent (1:21–27); he orders a man healed of leprosy not to tell anything to anyone (1:44); when he asks his disciples the core question of who he is and they, through Peter, correctly discern that he is the Messiah, he sternly orders them not to tell anyone about him (8:30); when Yeshua is transfigured in front of Peter, James, and John (thus making it plain that he is indeed the Messiah), he nevertheless orders them not to tell anyone what they have seen (9:9).

Why the secrecy about Yeshua's true identity? One can make a good case that the reason behind this phenomenon is that GU-Mark wanted Yeshua's role as Messiah to be understood correctly. How? The answer for me is plain: In the *crucible of suffering*. So, where in the story of GU-Mark does Yeshua reveal his true identity? Only in 14:60–65 in front of the high priest when he knows that revealing his identity as Messiah will only trigger his fatal condemnation by the powers-that-be. In other words, only when his passion and death are sure does Yeshua feel free to "broadcast" openly and unambiguously his identity as the Messiah. Did this really happen in history or was it a creation of GU-Mark, the author? One really cannot say for sure although one can make a strong case that it is primarily GU-Mark's literary strategy to emphasize a message dear to his heart—that Yeshua's role as the Messiah could only be understood correctly when viewed from the point of view of suffering and death.

8. For more details, see Ruprecht, *This Tragic Gospel*, 65. Cf. also the whole of chapter 3.

This is also connected intimately with the curious anecdote in 15:33–39 in which a centurion, when he witnesses Yeshua's utterly tragic death on the cross abandoned by everyone (even by God!), suddenly "gets it" and confesses, "Truly this man was God's Son." Now this can be utterly baffling for someone who does not read this gospel carefully. How could the centurion intuit that Yeshua is the Son of God from such a tragic death? It becomes even more intriguing when we realize that what the centurion understood is the most important message that GU-Mark wanted his listeners and readers to understand. We can say this from the way he introduces his work in 1:1 when he says, "The beginning of the good news of Jesus Christ, *the Son of God*." That's the very faith that the centurion has acquired upon seeing the tragic Messiah give up his life after having undergone much suffering on the cross. It is only when one experiences the tragic story of Yeshua that one can see who he is correctly—that he is the suffering Son of God!

CASE IN POINT: YESHUA IN THE GARDEN BEFORE HIS ARREST

Let's go back and reflect more extensively on the account in chapter 14 of Yeshua's agony in Gethsemane as a case in point for claiming that GU-Mark's Yeshua is the suffering Messiah par excellence. In the above-mentioned work *This Tragic Gospel*, author Ruprecht instructively imagines a small town in which our early Christian ancestors gather around a fire to listen to storytellers tell of Yeshua's life and death, particularly, about what happened to Yeshua on the night of his arrest. One of the storytellers is GU-Mark and, as we have seen above, his retelling of the tale of Yeshua's agony in the garden as well as his entire story of Yeshua's life and ministry is utterly tragic. On this count, GU-Mark can therefore be considered a "tragedian, a Christian poet building on the classical Greek models," using the genre of tragedy to make Christian meaning.[9] Writing ten-to-fifteen years after GU-Mark, GU-Matthew defers to GU-Mark's version of the story and practically copies it into his gospel. GU-Luke also follows the general outline but shortens it and makes Yeshua's suffering less intense so much so that a later scribe felt he had to add a story about Yeshua sweating blood because of sheer agony (Luke 22:43–44). Was this later scribe trying to reproduce a bit of the "tragedy" of GU-Mark's original story?

Back to our imagined campfire with GU-Mark. Among the campers around the fire that night, Ruprecht imaginatively suggests that there was a young man (whom we will come to know in time as GU-John) who is

9. Ruprecht, *Tragic Gospel*, 80.

not happy at all with the "tragic" way in which GU-Mark tells the story of Yeshua in the garden as well as his utterly tragic version of Yeshua's life in general. The young GU-John thinks rather that his hero Yeshua had to be more composed, more in-control of the situation, and more majestic than GU-Mark's story suggests. Later on, this Christian will go on to write his own version of the story in which Yeshua is no longer a tragic Messiah (as GU-Mark portrayed) but a glorious one, always in-control of events, even during his passion and death. Although GU-John's Gospel was to be written a good twenty to thirty years after Mark, it would be enlightening here to contrast GU-Mark's story with the revised version that this "unhappy camper" was going to write in time because it brings out more clearly the message that, I feel strongly, GU-Mark had most at heart when writing his Gospel.

GU-Mark, the tragedian, painted a picture of a Yeshua before his arrest in chapter 14 of his Gospel as "distressed and agitated" (v. 33). He makes it clear to his closest friends, Peter, James, and John, that he is so "deeply grieved, even to death" (v. 34) that he asks them to keep vigil with him. As Yeshua withdraws to pray, he is described as so terrified at the prospect of death that he asks his *Abba* (Father) to take away the cup of suffering (v. 36) but touchingly and faithfully maintains at the same time, "yet not what I want, but what you want" (14:36). When he sees that his closest disciples have allowed themselves to be overcome by sleep, he does not hesitate to express his hurt and disappointment saying, "Could you not keep awake . . . ?" (v. 37).

GU-John's Yeshua, on the other hand, is nothing at all like this character in Mark who is in deep agony. Yeshua (in John) is calm, composed and even "know[s] all that was to happen to him" (John 18:4). He self-declares who he is by uttering—what could be GU-John's way of identifying Yeshua with Yahweh—"*I am* he" (v. 5). While GU-Mark's Yeshua offers no resistance to those who arrest him, GU-John's Yeshua, when confronted by the cohort of soldiers and temple police, identifies himself with God's very name and his word is so powerful that his mere reply makes those sent to arrest him fall to the ground (v. 6). And then very curiously, when Simon Peter cuts off the ear of the high priest's servant, Yeshua reprimands him and declares (in words that are a dead giveaway of what GU-John was trying to do in his version of the story), "Put your sword back into its sheath. *Am I not to drink the cup that the Father has given me*?" (v. 11). That is practically the complete reversal of Yeshua's anguished prayer (in Mark) requesting his *Abba* to take away the cup of suffering if that was at all possible. The unhappy camper-turned-Gospel-writer has transformed Yeshua in this garden scene from a tragic and anguished Messiah (GU-Mark's portrayal) to a triumphant, glorious savior, who has no fear in the face of a death that he has nonchalantly and confidently accepted as the will of his Father. This glorious Yeshua of GU-John just further showcases the tragic hero of GU-Mark's Gospel. Not to be forgotten however is the stark truth that the first and original written record of the Yeshua story known to us is as a person crushed with sorrow, a figure that was supposed to inspire a profound pathos in the original audience.

But lest we stray away from the story and intention of GU-Mark's version of the Yeshua story, let's reflect on the *effect* of GU-Mark's tragic story on listeners-readers of the Gospel in the past and in the present.

GRANDUNCLE MARK'S TRAGIC PROTAGONIST AND CHRISTIAN COMPASSION

I mentioned at the beginning that I am strongly drawn to GU-Mark's portrait of a suffering messiah with all the pathos oozing, as it were, from that tragic figure. It must be because I've become more aware of the world's pathos through some experiences I've had in my life-journey so far. On the other hand, GU-John's composed, confident, and glorious Yeshua strangely leaves me unmoved. This is curious even for myself because I recall that in a more youthful and perhaps more naïve time before I left my homeland where I was born and raised in a well-to-do and privileged family, I used to find John's version of a gloriously triumphant Son of God profoundly moving and comforting. What has changed? How was I changed? I can think of no other answer to this other than that I've become more aware of the world's pathos through a number of experiences I've had, especially through my encounters and work with immigrants and other underprivileged people. I recall that in most cases I felt utterly helpless and could do nothing more than lend a sympathetic ear and accompany them with compassion (literally in the Latin sense, *cum* + *patire*, "suffering with"). In those painful encounters with human suffering, I have had the humbling experience of encountering the suffering messiah—GU-Mark's, not so much GU-John's.

It is actually in the tragic and suffering Yeshua that we can most surely find the essence of what GU-Mark was most probably trying to convey through his gospel—compassion. He, like the Greek tragedians before him, presents suffering as the great reality in life and being able to look at suffering straight in the eye, especially in the case of Yeshua, constitutes the great skill that he wanted his community to acquire. The gospel seems to say that the reality of suffering is what will teach those who follow the suffering Messiah the most profound truths about life and about faith, above all, about compassion and the utmost importance of having this in their hearts.[10] GU-Mark is the one who starts a genre we know as "gospel" which, as we already

10. Ruprecht, *Tragic Gospel*, 89.

heard, means "good news." This might seem counterintuitive to us now but the basic message of this good news is, in the words of Hegel, "salvation is through suffering, not from it."[11] Let me state my second *sine qua non* about GU-Mark then as a rather "temperate" case (not widely acknowledged by many biblical scholars): He also seems to be a "tragedian," similar in some respects to those Greek authors who wrote great tragedies in order to communicate life's greatest lessons.

The pathos of GU-Mark's suffering messiah can be something that acts like a "heart tenderizer" as it were, especially for those who have gone through and are mindful of the suffering in the world. In my case, this tragic messiah resonates particularly with the difficult, painful, and sad experiences I know personally or vicariously as an immigrant. These have definitely worked to "tenderize" my heart in such a way that I have emerged from them resolving firmly to view and relate to the world with a more tender and compassionate heart, especially for those who likewise encounter difficult, painful, and other negative experiences in life.

I imagine that there were similar dynamics that lie behind why GU-Mark highlighted a Messiah of sorrow for his community, which was probably undergoing the great suffering of persecution and the disruption and destruction that accompany it. Yeshua, the Messiah of many sorrows, would have been a very familiar and profoundly comforting presence because GU-Mark and his fellow community members encountered him over and over again in the trials and sorrows that they themselves faced.

As mentioned, GU-John, it can be said, profoundly changed at some later point the form and message of what was arguably GU-Mark's original, tragic "gospel" genre because his Yeshua is not the tragic protagonist of Mark but a triumphantly glorious, divine figure. It is ironical, perhaps even sad that GU-John's messiah became in many respects the most influential image of Yeshua that would dominate Christianity for much of its history.

THE PASSION OF GRANDUNCLE MARK'S COMMUNITY

We have almost no concrete knowledge of what GU-Mark and his community might have undergone, an experience which gave birth to the Gospel of Mark and its tragic story. But let us use our creative imaginations, now better informed by biblical studies, to appreciate and have compassion for the suffering that many of our early spiritual ancestors went through. The catastrophic events that befall "other" people, especially those far removed

11. Quoted in Ruprecht, *Tragic Gospel*, 87.

from us because of geographical distance or historical distance, can be quite difficult for us to appreciate, especially in this age in which we are desensitized by so much virtual violence we see on our screens. This does not change the fact that, long ago, some of our ancient spiritual ancestors, in their efforts to make sense of it all, tried their best to follow Yeshua, the Christ, who was for them the suffering Messiah par excellence. That tragic and pathos-inviting figure ironically gave them the strength to continue in Yeshua's path, hoping that they themselves might also have some share in the hopeful proclamation we find at the end of GU-Mark's text, "He is not here [in the tomb]. . . . He has been raised" (16:6).[12]

Thus, we have learned that granduncle Mark and his clan were probably located in a context of great suffering, a circumstance often identified as persecution by biblical scholars. From that painful context was born his dominant portrayal of Yeshua as a suffering Messiah: the chosen one of God who was nonetheless misunderstood, opposed, plotted against, betrayed, abandoned, sorrowful and even in despair at the very end of his life on the cross. In this way, GU-Mark, it seems, wanted to impart the lesson to his community that to "follow Yeshua on the way" of life and discipleship (see Mark 10:52) boils down to facing life's inevitable suffering with courage while not losing hope and compassion, as the way still leads to a tomb that is empty and a promise of encountering the risen one (Mark 16:6–7). Indeed, the dominant image of Yeshua in GU-Mark's Gospel as a suffering Messiah invites the Yeshua-follower to contemplate him with pathos and compassion. Hopefully, that same compassion would be the dominant way to view all human suffering, even the whole of life and reality.

12. The order of statements has been changed from the original order in Mark for emphasis.

7

Matthew: Balancing the Old and the New

Grafting Faith in Yeshua onto Jewish Tradition

The gospel of the kingdom announced by Jesus, believed in by the disciples . . . is by its very nature a blend of continuity and discontinuity with the old (i.e., the [Old Testament] as ordinarily understood). At its heart the gospel consists of "new things." But for Matthew these "new things" presuppose and are fundamentally loyal to the "old things" (cf. 5:17–19). The Christian Torah scholar or "scribe" is one trained in the mysteries of the kingdom who is able to maintain a balance between the continuity and discontinuity existing between the era inaugurated by Jesus and that of the past.
—Daniel Hagner[1]

GRANDUNCLE MATTHEW AND HIS WORK: FIRST IMPRESSIONS

It's time to get to know a second spiritual ancestor-storyteller, GU-Matthew and his work, which we shall refer to simply as "Matthew." If we would go through a quick browse of the Gospel, our first dominant impression of

1. Hagner, *Matthew 1–13*, 402.

GU-Matthew is that he seems to be very Jewish in that he knows and values deeply the Jewish roots of Yeshua's way. This is obvious by observing how he quotes extensively from the Jewish scriptures (e.g., 2:6; 5:43; 8:17; 12:40, and many other places),[2] how he painstakingly tries to present Yeshua in very Jewish terms, namely, as the new and greater Moses (as expressed for example in aspects of his account of Yeshua's birth) and the long awaited "Son" of the great King David of long ago (e.g., 12:23). So, we ask once again: Who was this spiritual ancestor-storyteller? What was his background? What was he trying to hand over to his community (and us) as precious tradition? Here are my efforts to get to know GU-Matthew better.

NAVIGATING BETWEEN PAST TRADITION AND PRESENT CHANGE

At the beginning of the 1971 movie *Fiddler on the Roof* (I'm more familiar with the movie than the original play), we are shown a fiddler playing his instrument while precariously perched on the roof of a house. With that in the background, the protagonist, Tevye, explains that the fiddler on the roof is a symbol of him and his people in their early twentieth-century Ukrainian-Jewish village of Anatevka, "trying to scratch a simple tune without breaking his neck." From this, he draws the lesson that the secret of balance is "tradition." As we go on with the story, we gradually understand that the fundamental issue that Tevye and his co-villagers confront is how to navigate between tradition (revered principles and practices handed on to them from their Jewish past) and the disruptive winds of change that blow through their lives in their setting in early twentieth-century Ukraine where anti-Jewish sentiment is growing stronger.

I often use this vignette from *Fiddler on the Roof* to introduce the Gospel of Matthew to my students because it captures one important feature of the "first" Gospel (named so because of its position in the New Testament): Like the villagers of Anatevka in early twentieth-century czarist Russia, GU-Matthew appears to be deep within a process of serious negotiation between his Jewish tradition (the compendium of revered notions and practices from the past) and his newfound faith (in his "present") that Yeshua of Nazareth is the long-awaited Messiah of Israel and the "fulfillment of the Law and the Prophets" (Matt 5:17). And that, if we may use Tevye's musings once again, "isn't easy" at all. Like Tevye and his family, GU-Matthew seemed to be trying to navigate the turbulent waters where past and present meet with the intention of preserving what was best in the tradition and applying it to the

2. Just, "Quotations from the Old Testament."

new order that he believed God had wrought through Yeshua, the Christ, God's Son ("Son of God" is used multiple times in this Gospel to refer to Yeshua, e.g., 4:3; 14:33; 26:63). This is a new order that, GU-Matthew is convinced, does not abolish but instead "fulfills the law and the prophets" (5:17).

With that in mind, let me apply to GU-Matthew the title "Rabbi" from the get-go. You may already know that this means "teacher" in Hebrew. Even Yeshua is called "rabbi" in the Gospels (e.g., Matt 26:25). It seems that in the ancient Jewish communities as well as the earliest Jewish-Christian communities (after all, the earliest Christians were almost all Jews!), the rabbi played many important roles. But what strikes me as particularly noteworthy and applicable to GU-Matthew's case is that, in effect, the rabbi in the ancient Jewish community was some sort of bridge or intermediary between past and present; specifically, between past tradition and present circumstances. The term "rabbi" itself seemed to have been widely employed only in the latter part of the first century CE, namely, around the time GU-Matthew wrote his Gospel.[3] But in the long history of the people of Israel, prominent figures who were considered in a broad sense as "rabbis" (that is, in some teaching-leadership role even if they were known by other titles such as "priests," "prophets," "sages," "kings," etc.) had some salient common traits: On the one hand, they were profoundly adept in the knowledge and wisdom that were part of the long history of Israel and, on the other hand, they had the skill to apply that wisdom *from* the past *to* the present context where they and their people were located.

As we know from various Old Testament stories, the people of Israel had a long turbulent history. Each new age brought new circumstances and problems. In these crucial moments, it was these rabbi-like figures who stepped in, plunged deeply into Israel's tradition, brought out of its rich store some necessary wisdom and guidance, and applied these to each new age's peculiar needs. In Matt 13:52, there is a mysterious verse that is unique to this Gospel:

> Therefore every scribe who has been trained for the kingdom of heaven is like the master of a household who brings out of his treasure what is new and what is old.

Who is the "scribe" being referred to here? It might very well refer to Yeshua who, in the newness of his teaching and ministry sought to recast the older traditions and bring them to fulfillment (as inferred in 5:17). However, it is often suggested that GU-Matthew makes a sort of cameo appearance here because this was precisely the project he was engaged in when composing

3. See, for example, Lapin, "Rabbi." Cf. also Zacharias, "Rabbi as a Title."

this Gospel. He was bringing out of his treasury the "new" proclamation that Yeshua of Nazareth is in fact the Messiah sent by God but, at the same time, he backed that up with many precious strands from the venerable "old" tradition to show that Yeshua was in fact the fulfillment of the "Law and the Prophets." Again, here we more clearly see the "scribe-rabbi" acting as a bridge or intermediary between past and present.

In the turbulent era in which GU-Matthew and his community lived, there must have truly been an urgent need to bridge past and present. Let us therefore continue our quest in earnest to better get to know GU-Matthew's identity and the circumstances that faced his community.

PEERING BEHIND THE TEXT OF MATTHEW

Matthew is positioned as the first book in the New Testament canon. This placement is probably because of GU-Matthew's emphatic message peppered throughout the Gospel that Yeshua is the fulfillment of numerous prophecies contained in Israel's tradition. That tradition is largely found in what Christians now know as the Old Testament, the first part of the Christian Bible. Early Christians understandably felt that putting Matthew first in the New Testament would serve as the perfect segue to the Old Testament and the logical opening to the rest of the New Testament as it clearly shows how Yeshua continually fulfills the Jewish scripture in various ways. Most New Testament scholars today agree though that, chronologically speaking, Matthew was not the first Gospel to be written. This runs contrary to how some important early Christians thought, most prominent among them, the influential church father, Augustine of Hippo. We already learned that Mark was probably the first Gospel to have been penned (around 70 CE). Matthew came out probably ten to fifteen years after that.

Like Mark, Matthew was written in the aftermath of the temple's destruction in Jerusalem by Rome in 70 CE. We cannot underestimate the cataclysmic nature of this event for all Jews at the time and its huge impact on all aspects of Jewish life thereafter. After all, together with "the Law and the Prophets" (the Torah and the rest of the Jewish scriptures), the temple was a central feature of Jewish identity and religious life in Second Temple Judaism (515 BCE–70 CE). Jews firmly believed that God dwelt there in a special way and that the worship and sacrifice that were rendered at the temple had a special character that no other place on earth could have.

When it was mercilessly destroyed by the Romans, Jews were suddenly confronted with a "temple-less" Judaism. How does a whole people survive such a traumatic event? Even more importantly, how could Israel continue without the temple? In response to this, there may have been various points of view but what eventually emerged as the most authoritative was the creative position that influential rabbis put forward. We can say this because the dominant form of Judaism that eventually emerged out of that catastrophe, a form that remains to our day, is in fact commonly known as "Rabbinic Judaism." Rabbinic Judaism is a remarkably creative reinvention of the tradition that takes, as central element, the Torah and its various interpretations and commentaries by influential teachers in the tradition and no longer relies on the Temple.

But this was not the only Jewish response in the aftermath of the Temple's destruction. We can situate GU-Matthew's community in this context as one "minority report" which advocated to other Jews the message that Yeshua of Nazareth, *is* in fact the Messiah sent from God and that in him the covenant has been brought to a glorious fulfillment. According to GU-Matthew's Jewish-Christian community, although Yeshua was crucified by the Romans as an enemy of the state in the 30s CE, through the resurrection, God put the seal of approval on Yeshua and made clear that he has a pivotal role in God's plan.

The inevitable consequence of that position, however, is that, since the covenant has already in fact found its apex in Yeshua (the Messiah, the Christ), nothing else in the tradition equals Yeshua in importance: not the destroyed temple and (scandalously!) not even "the Law and the Prophets" so zealously advocated by prominent Jewish rabbis at the time as the new *central* factor in the tradition. GU-Matthew even seemed to have thought that Yeshua is comparable to the great Moses and King David as shown for example by the clear references in Yeshua's birth stories (chapters 1 and 2) to the familiar stories of Moses and David. In fact, we can make a good case that GU-Matthew believed that Yeshua surpassed even Moses and David in importance from key passages in his text (e.g., 19:7–9; 22:41–45). If Moses and David are the two greatest figures in the Tradition, who then is this Yeshua who surpasses even these two great pillars of the Jewish tradition? This is the question that would have intrigued GU-Matthew's Jewish compatriots. We can think of his Gospel as being an extended answer to that question and, more importantly, a desperate effort to win over his fellow Jews to faith in this Yeshua—whom he believed was—the anointed one of God. Since this could have been one of the original intentions of GU-Matthew, it makes a lot of sense that he employed the above-mentioned strategies in his Gospel to pitch this message to his audience. In retrospect, now we know that, unfortunately, GU-Matthew's efforts were in vain because most Jews eventually rejected his central message. But at the time of writing, GU-Matthew might have thought that he was making a good case for Yeshua with some possibility of success.

We learned above that in GU-Matthew's time there was an urgent need for a teaching presence that could serve as an intermediary between past tradition and present circumstance. It is clear that, in the aftermath of the temple's demise, the Jews needed rabbis who could immerse themselves deeply into the tradition and draw out precious "treasures" (13:52) from it to help people cope with some very harsh circumstances. The rabbis of the Pharisee party did that in creatively refashioning Judaism from the ashes of the temple's destruction. Rabbi Matthew was also clearly trying to do that in his gospel: He draws from the Jewish tradition's treasures and brings out old and new teachings by connecting and contextualizing Yeshua squarely in the ancient prophecies and figures of the Jewish tradition and applying them to the One he believed was the pivotal figure in God's fulfillment of the covenant made long ago with Israel. The big disappointment of this effort though is, in effect, GU-Matthew's message was eventually rejected by most of his compatriots.

THE MAIN CONTOURS OF GRANDUNCLE MATTHEW'S STORY

Matthew is one of the so-called "Synoptic Gospels" together with Mark and Luke. Scholars have lumped these three together because they could be read as it were "with one eye" (a possible understanding of the word "synoptic") because they are quite similar to each other in many striking respects.

We can therefore say that, apart from the first two chapters in Matthew where we find stories related to the birth of Yeshua ("the infancy narratives"), it basically follows Mark in structure in the sense that Yeshua begins his public ministry in his home territory of Galilee (4:12) and continues to do so until chapter 16 of the narrative where there is a clear reference that "he must go to Jerusalem" (16:21). From this point onward, Jerusalem plays some prominence in the story line leading all the way to Yeshua's arrest and death there in chapter 27. Chapter 28, the last one in Matthew, differs from Mark (in Mark's original version that ended abruptly in 16:8 without an appearance of the risen Yeshua) in the sense that GU-Matthew explicitly relates that the remaining disciples go back to Galilee where Yeshua appears to them as the risen one, commissions them to go and "make disciples of all nations," promising to be with them always "to the end of the age" (28:19–20).

But let us go further and also examine where Matthew's originality and special characteristics do appear. Here we can point out that there is a peculiar and special structure that GU-Matthew, it seems, intentionally shaped and arranged his text into—a structure that, when considered carefully, shouts out as it were a message that GU-Matthew wanted to convey in keeping with his general intentions and circumstances.[4]

Let's consider Matthew's infancy narrative (chapters 1–2) as one bookend, so to speak; and the Passion, Death, and Resurrection narratives (in chapters 26–28) as the other bookend. In-between those two points, we can find *five* easily distinguishable—let's call them "booklets"— each in turn divided into a narrative section that could be treated as a "part 1" and a discourse section that acts like a "part 2." Structurally then Matthew appears in this way:

Introduction: Infancy Narrative: Chapters 1–2
[1a] Narrative: 3–4
[1b] First Discourse: "Sermon on the Mount": 5–7
[2a] Narrative: 8–9
[2b] Second Discourse: "Missionary Instructions": 10
[3a] Narrative: 11–12
[3b] Third Discourse: "Collection of Parables": 13
[4a] Narrative: 14–17
[4b] Fourth Discourse: "Community Instructions": 18
[5a] Narrative: 19–22
[5b] Fifth Discourse: "Sermon on Eschatology": 23–25
Conclusion: Passion and Resurrection Narrative: 26–28

Upon closer inspection, one can notice that many of the materials (particularly, things Yeshua was supposed to have said) unique to Matthew itself (they're not copied from GU-Matthew's presumed source—Mark) are contained in the above-mentioned five discourses. Does this five-part structure exist only in the minds of scholars? It does not seem to be so because at the end of the sections, there is usually a clear indication that GU-Matthew intends to conclude a sub-division of his story with words such as "when Jesus finished saying these things . . ." (7:28) or words to that effect (see also 11:1, 13:53, 19:1, and 26:1).

Many scholars consider this five-part structure as quite significant. Why? Obviously, the number five has a very important meaning for Jews as it evokes of course the all-important "Law" with its five books of Genesis, Exodus, Leviticus, Numbers, and Deuteronomy, traditionally thought of as being written by the great Moses himself. That's why this part of the Hebrew Bible is also known as "the Pentateuch" (*penta* meaning "five" in Greek). I sometimes jokingly refer to this structure as a "Torah Sandwich" because a

4. Just, "Five Major Discourses of Jesus."

"Torah-like structure" is contained within an introduction and conclusion that can be thought of as the upper and lower bread slices of a sandwich.

It was, of course, not just coincidence that GU-Matthew divided Yeshua's teachings in his version of the gospel into five parts. It was probably a deliberate attempt to proclaim that, in Yeshua's teachings, we have a kind of "New Torah," a fresh guide to living the covenant that God has brought to fulfillment in Yeshua, the Christ. Moreover, by means of this structure, we can say that GU-Matthew was actually proclaiming Yeshua as the new Moses for his age and contemporaries and for all subsequent ones (see 28:20).

YESHUA AS THE FULFILLMENT OF ISRAEL'S HOPES

Put yourselves in GU-Matthew's shoes and try to think for a moment what would be a convincing and weighty way to make a case to your fellow Jews that Yeshua of Nazareth is indeed the longed-for Messiah sent from God? I'm sure that high on the priority list of your strategies would be likening Yeshua to familiar key figures in the Jewish tradition. And that is precisely what GU-Matthew is trying to do. In his Gospel, he often presents Yeshua as some kind of new Moses or new David for his milieu. This is the reason why there are numerous references in Matthew that point either to Moses, the greatest prophet in the tradition, or to David, the greatest king in the tradition, both of whom were chosen and beloved by God and sent to carry out crucial roles for Israel.

Therefore, having a familiarity with the Jewish Scriptures (what Christians know as the Old Testament) is important for grasping what GU-Matthew is trying to do in his Gospel. We can even call GU-Matthew's way of writing a kind of *midrash* in the wide sense.

WHAT IS MIDRASH?

Midrash partly comes from a word (*darash* in Hebrew) that means "to search for." In the broad sense, it's a quest (a search) to make the ancient tradition, particularly its scriptures, meaningful enough to speak with insight and authority to one's present circumstances. One possible way to do this is take verses from several sources in the Tradition, string them together and interpret them in a way that gives meaning to a more contemporary situation. Religious historian Karen Armstrong explains *midrash* as applied to a tradition's scriptures thus: ". . . weaving scriptural verses together to create a story that injected meaning and hope into the perplexing present."[5] Another possible broad description of how GU-Matthew is doing *midrash* is that he presents a contemporary event or figure (Yeshua of course) as being related with or even similar to past events and figures (Moses, David, Joseph, Jonah, etc.), again for the purpose of deriving meaning for his present circumstances. We can illustrate that through the various ways by which GU-Matthew links Yeshua with the figures of Moses and David.

HOW IS YESHUA LIKE MOSES?

We already mentioned Matthew's five-part structure that echoes the five books of the Law and inevitably likens Yeshua to Moses who was thought of as the one who wrote the books of the Law and bequeathed them to Israel. GU-Matthew goes further in his efforts to present Yeshua as Moses-like. In the birth narratives, Yeshua is presented as being at the center of a plot by the jealous King Herod to be exterminated because he is destined to be the new king. Since Herod did not know the exact location where he could find Yeshua, he "blanket-kills" all male babies under two years old in the Bethlehem area in the hope of putting an end to this new threat to his power (2:16–18). When GU-Matthew's contemporaries heard this midrash-like story, they would have of course associated this terrible act of infanticide with the similar carnage that happened in Egypt when the great Moses was born (Exod 1).

When Yeshua's legal father and guardian Joseph is informed of this potentially fatal plot, he takes his bride and the child, and departs for Egypt to shelter there from Herod's threat. In like manner, "Egypt" conjures up once again the figure of Moses who grew up there. "Joseph," Yeshua's father, was another connection to the tradition because it was Joseph, Jacob's son, who went to Egypt as a slave but rose to become a figure of authority there and providentially served as the one who saved Jacob's whole clan from starvation in Canaan. Besides, (the Old Testament character) Joseph is linked with Moses who was born in Egypt generations later as a result of Joseph's bringing the whole clan there.

Yeshua is also like Moses, Israel's teacher par excellence, in Matthew. He goes up the mountain in chapter 5, takes up the traditional posture for teaching (seated) and begins what is famously known as "the Sermon on the Mount" (5:1–2). Curiously, what is delivered on a mountain in Matthew is delivered on a plain in Luke (Luke 6:17–19). Why does GU-Matthew make Yeshua deliver his teaching on a mountain? Of course, because no

5. Armstrong, *Lost Art of Scripture*, 196.

one would have missed the clear connection between Yeshua teaching on a mountain and Israel's great teacher Moses receiving the law on Mount Sinai (Exod 19:3).

HOW IS YESHUA LIKE DAVID?

For GU-Matthew Yeshua is also the new David. He begins his Gospel with a genealogy of Yeshua which is divided into three parts, each of which contains "fourteen generations" (Matt 1:17). Why fourteen? Because fourteen was a sort of numerical code for David's name and was immediately recognizable by GU-Matthew's original target-audience. Each letter in the Hebrew alphabet has a numerical value. "David" in Hebrew has three consonants: "Daleth" ("D," having a numerical value of 4) "Vav," ("V" = 6), and another "Daleth" (D = 6). If one adds the numerical value, it comes up to fourteen and that is how this number becomes the numerical equivalent of "DaViD." It is clear then that the aim of this genealogy is to show that Yeshua is, firstly, David's descendant, but not only that. With the triple confluence of fourteen generations from Adam until Yeshua, GU-Matthew's Jewish audience is prompted to see the mysterious providence of God working through generations to produce someone who was destined to be a new David. It is also plain that Yeshua being born in David's city, Bethlehem, is another clear strategy to link him with Israel's greatest king.

This aim of GU-Matthew is made even more obvious by the frequent use of the title "Son of David" (used in Matthew ten times), six of which are applied explicitly to Yeshua.[6] One can make a good case that when Yeshua is explicitly linked to David in Matthew, Yeshua's identity as "a new David" is given prominence.

Of course, David was revered as Israel's greatest king as well as the ruler "after God's heart" (1 Sam 13:14). By presenting Yeshua as the new David, GU-Matthew had an urgent message for his contemporaries as they navigated the troubled times in which they lived: Yeshua, the new David, sent by God for this urgent time, is the most trustworthy One. He is beloved by God like David (as proclaimed in his baptism, 3:17) and it is he who will eventually lead Israel to the Kingdom of Heaven (that is how GU-Matthew expresses the "Kingdom of God" in his gospel).

6. Mullins, "Jesus, the 'Son of David,'" 117–26.

YESHUA FULFILLING NOT CANCELLING THE LAW AND THE PROPHETS

In Matthew, we find a proclamation that is not found in the other Gospels: "Do not think that I have come to abolish the law or the prophets; I have come not to abolish but to fulfil" (5:17). This verse holds a crucial role for understanding the gospel's nature and message. By that we know that GU-Matthew believed deeply that Yeshua was the "fulfiller" and fulfillment of everything Israel held dear (expressed by the expression "the Law and the Prophets") and that even Israel's greatest religious and historical figures—Moses and David—are not equal to Yeshua in importance. One can say that these deep convictions of GU-Matthew are expressed in a title he often ascribes to Yeshua in his Gospel: "Son of God." This is the title that the awestruck disciples ascribe to Yeshua after he displayed amazing power that could even make him walk on the sea and calm the tumultuous stormy seas (14:33). It is also the same title that Peter gives to Yeshua after Peter answers correctly the question of who Yeshua really is in God's scheme of things (16:16).

BRIDGING PAST AND PRESENT

We can say that the earliest Yeshua movement was an offshoot and a constituent part of Second Temple Judaism. Not only were Yeshua and all his earliest disciples Jews, but everything they did was understood to be an effort to contribute to the renewal of Israel and to—what they deeply believed was—the fulfillment of the covenant promises of God to their nation and people.

We have seen how GU-Matthew and his community lived in a tumultuous age in which the Jews lost so many precious symbols of the Tradition (like the temple and the priesthood) and in which the immediate future direction of Israel as a people and as a nation was as yet a big unknown. Within the ranks of people who believed that Yeshua was the Messiah and the mediator between God and humans, there seemed to have been those who thought that it would be better to sever ties with the past, in particular, the attachment to "Israel." We can say this based on negative anti-Jewish parts that we find in some strands of the New Testament such as those found in the Gospel of John.

What about GU-Matthew? What did he think about this matter? It is probably fair to maintain that he moved in the opposite direction. For him, cherishing the most precious elements of the Tradition, such as Law,

Prophets, Wisdom, etc., was a must if Jews were to navigate the very turbulent waters of their present. Concretely, GU-Matthew tried his best to make a case for affirming the Tradition on the one hand, while proclaiming that the promises of the Tradition have now been fulfilled in the One whom God had sent—Yeshua, the Son of God. Of course, he sought to tie the future destiny of Israel to this messiah sent from God.

I would say that GU-Matthew could be considered a sort of careful "conservative" (in a positive sense). I don't use that term in the sense of "reactionary" which is more properly used of an attitude that resists any new change to how things were in the past. No, (careful yet balanced) conservatives are indeed loath to dispense rashly and summarily with the past and rush headlong into the latest fashions because their concern is to preserve the best of the tradition and make it speak to the contemporary age. That balanced attitude guides their steps as they seek to press forward in an uncertain present and future. All communities and groups actually need these careful conservatives if they are to avoid potential disasters that forgetfulness of the tradition might cause. I am making the case that GU-Matthew was one such rabbi for his community and we can see that careful attitude in the Gospel he penned.

RECONCILING JEWISH TRADITION WITH FAITH IN YESHUA

Summing up, we can say that the following factors are the essential points, the *sine qua non*'s to understand GU-Matthew and his community. The gospel text in our possession is arguably already a result of a more mature state of reflection on the part of GU-Matthew. The text gives the impression that he has already reconciled his original Jewish heritage with his faith in Yeshua, rejected by many of his Jewish contemporaries. GU-Matthew proclaims this reconciliation of his faith in Yeshua-as-Messiah with his Jewish heritage through some strategies such as peppering his Gospel with presentations of Yeshua fulfilling ancient prophecies from the Jewish scriptures, stating unambiguously that Yeshua has come "not to abolish [the law and the prophets] but to fulfill [them]" (5:17) and structuring his gospel around five clear sections, thus presenting Yeshua's teaching and ministry as the new Torah (the first five books of the Hebrew Bible sacred to Jews).

In all this, GU-Matthew was struggling to find a balance between, on the one hand, his attachment and devotion to the sacred tradition inherited by his people Israel, and, on the other, his conviction that Yeshua was indeed the promised Messiah sent to Israel to fulfill God's covenant with them. In fact, Yeshua is so important for GU-Matthew that he dares to identify him as the embodiment of God, applying to him the epitaph mentioned in Isaiah 7:14, "Emmanuel" ("God-with-us"; see Matt 1:23). This balancing act, like the fiddler on the roof, was a difficult one to pull off. Indeed, we can say that GU-Matthew's strategy and claim did not go well with most of his Jewish compatriots because Yeshua was not acknowledged in large part as the Messiah by Israel.

Nevertheless, GU-Matthew bequeathed forever to the circle of people (who would continue a movement that would eventually become Christianity) the foundational principle that Yeshua's nation and people, collectively known as *"Israel," was always going to be a fundamentally important part and parcel of the tradition*. This is clearly shown in how the Christian church embraced the Jewish scriptures (often referred to as "the Old Testament") with its stories and teachings, as an integral part of its own sacred Scriptures.

Moreover, GU-Matthew's message is particularly important and insightful for us who struggle to figure out how, on the one hand, we can continue to valorize our spiritual traditions from the past while, on the other hand, find ways to make them relevant in the very different and difficult contemporary contexts in which we find ourselves.

8

God Plays No Favorites

The Compassionate and Radical Inclusiveness of God in Luke-Acts

[Peter said,] "If then God gave the same gift to them [the gentiles] as he gave to us [Jews] when we believed in the Lord Jesus Christ, who was I that I could withstand God?" When they heard this they were silenced. And they glorified God, saying, "Then to the [g]entiles also God has granted repentance unto life."

—Acts 11:17–18

GRANDUNCLE LUKE AND HIS GOSPEL: FIRST IMPRESSIONS

A book today always carries the name of its author. It wasn't so in the ancient world. In fact, a good number of ancient literary works were written anonymously. That is true—unfortunately for many of us who love history—of the New Testament Gospels. "Mark," "Matthew," "Luke," "John" were all attributed to these works after a good deal of time had passed since the gospels were written down and circulated.

In this chapter, one major thing to affirm first of all is that the third Gospel ("Luke") and the work called "The Acts of the Apostles" are two parts of a single long saga.[1] In short, contemporary New Testament scholarship considers the two works as one long story with a coherent plot and thematic development that is divided into two parts in the Christian canon. The author most probably wrote this work in the late first century (80–90 CE).[2] Although Luke-Acts primarily reflects the theological concerns of the author and his recipient community in the late first century CE,[3] there are some elements in the work that can give us glimpses of historical matters both in the life of the historical Yeshua and the earliest Christian communities.[4]

The third Gospel was ascribed by tradition to a certain Luke who is mentioned in the Pauline letter to the Colossians (4:14) as "the beloved physician" and also a companion of Paul himself (see also Phlm 24 and 2 Tim 4:11). Historically speaking, that attribution is possible but there are other alternative theories about the authorship of Luke and, just like all the other Gospels, we cannot be a hundred percent sure that the attribution of the work to the physician Luke is historically accurate. Nevertheless, let us accept convention and call the third Gospel's author in our usual way here as "Granduncle Luke." I will also take for granted the widely accepted idea that GU-Luke was originally a gentile who had become either a proselyte or a God-fearer, that is, was converted or strongly attracted to the faith of Israel sometime before he became a follower of Yeshua's way.[5] That is a crucial presupposition of this study, as will be shown later on.

It may be purely coincidental but the ascribing of this Gospel in tradition to "a physician" perhaps by happenstance is still, I consider, a happy event because it is fair to say that if there is anything that should be an outstanding characteristic in a physician, it would certainly be compassion—the ability to "suffer with" (which is what the root meaning of "compassion" is in Latin—*cum* + *patire*) or to "feel with" those who are in distress and to have a heart full of tender mercy for the various ills and miseries of humanity. The intriguing thing is that the third Gospel's arguably most prominent feature (definitely a *sine qua non*) is precisely the prominence it gives to Yeshua's compassionate attitude to various classes of underprivileged people. It is as if this Gospel was written from a compassionate physician's point of view! So, whether or not GU-Luke was indeed a physician is beside the point; we can say with a certain degree of certainty though that he wrote with a tender heart for all humanity, especially the most underprivileged ones.

1. See, for example, Brown, *Introduction to the New Testament*, 75.
2. Johnson, "Luke-Acts, Book of," 4:403–20.
3. Maddox, *Purpose of Luke-Acts*, 16.
4. For more on this matter, see Marguerat, *First Christian Historian*.
5. See, for example, Brown, *Introduction to the New Testament*, 268.

SOME BACKGROUND CIRCUMSTANCES OF THE GOSPEL

The immediate motive for GU-Luke's writing this work in two parts can be deduced from the dedication found both at the beginning of the gospel and reiterated at the beginning of the Acts of the Apostles which, as we said, is like the second part of GU-Luke's extended story:

> I too decided, after investigating everything carefully from the very first, to write an orderly account for you, most excellent Theophilus, so that you may know the truth concerning the things about which you have been instructed.[6]

Let's see what we can gather about GU-Luke, the person, from these words. He seemed to have the ability to conduct (what we would now call) "research" in the broad sense and write orderly accounts. That means: he was a person with a good education and some literary ability. The latter part of the dedication shows a zeal for "the truth" regarding his topic which, if we can express it succinctly, was what the good news (the "gospel") about Yeshua, the Christ, was and how that Gospel came to be spread far and wide, even to "the ends of the earth" (see Acts 1:8).

The primary recipient of the text is a personage called Theophilus (literally, "someone who loves God" or someone "beloved by God"). We learn that the purpose of his account is so that this Theophilus would know the truth of what he has been instructed in. Let me point out that, through this short introduction of GU-Luke, we can catch a glimpse of the zeal for the gospel and for educating people in the faith that our early spiritual ancestors had.

Moving on with the narrative, what stands out to me most of all is that compassion seems to be a very important theme for GU-Luke. In fact, in what has come to be called the "Canticle of Zechariah" in Luke 1, GU-Luke lets these words be proclaimed by John the Baptist's father, Zechariah:

> 76 And you, child, will be called the prophet of the Most High;
> for you will go before the Lord to prepare his ways,
> 77 to give knowledge of salvation to his people
> by the forgiveness of their sins.
> 78 By *the tender mercy* of our God,
> the dawn from on high will break upon us,
> 79 to give light to those who sit in darkness and in the shadow of death,
> to guide our feet into the way of peace.

6. Luke 1:3–4 NRSV.

If we analyze these verses closely, we can see that "the salvation of [God's] people" (v. 77) will be wrought "by the tender mercy of our God" (v. 78). And since these verses are addressed to "the child" who, at this point in the story, is still in the womb of his mother Mary, we are given a clue that this child will play a crucial role in the plan to save everyone precisely through "(God's) tender mercy(!)." As we follow GU-Luke's story, we slowly but surely realize that Yeshua is indeed the "tender mercy of God" personified!

In this chapter, I suggest that we get to know some key characteristics (the so-called *sine qua non*'s) of the spiritual ancestor-storyteller behind Luke-Acts by picking up sections of his two-volume work *that are unique* to this body of writing and not found in the other gospels. This is a valid strategy because by identifying these unique passages that GU-Luke took pains to add to a plot that he basically got from GU-Mark, we can see his "special concerns" and, hence, we can also glimpse what "made him tick," what moved him deeply as he wrote the story that we can see developed in Luke-Acts.

BIRTH NARRATIVES

Matthew, Mark, and Luke, as we know, are usually grouped together in a category called "Synoptic Gospels" because they have quite a few similarities between them. "Synoptic" could be understood to mean "[can be] seen together." If we turn this common similarity on its head though, a close comparison of the Synoptics will reveal where one work is different from the other sometimes in obvious ways; other times, in subtler ways. These differences, I submit, insightfully reveal the peculiar characteristics and personality of the authors and their communities of location. We have to have an eye for detail then and try to see what lies behind even the subtlest differences. If we take for example the commonality between Luke and Matthew—that is, of both works having a part that tells us the circumstances that surround the birth of the Messiah (something that is not present in Mark and John)—we can ask: How did each particular ancestor-storyteller shape their own birth narrative? By answering this question, we can get a glimpse of each author's unique personality.

Going to particulars, although both GU-Matthew and GU-Luke wrote "Christmas stories," we can immediately perceive a major difference: Are you aware, for example, that it is *only* in Luke that Joseph and Mary have to move from Nazareth to Bethlehem because of a census ordered by the emperor in faraway Rome? In Matthew, there is no mention of a census and no such journey and, if you were a Yeshua-follower of GU-Matthew's community and heard the Christmas Story for the first time, you'd just simply assume that Joseph and Mary were already living in Bethlehem when Yeshua was born.

In short, GU-Luke's Christmas story is, in some ways, more dramatic. Aside from the arduous journey from Nazareth to Bethlehem that Joseph and the pregnant Mary have to undertake, when they finally reach King David's hometown (also Joseph's ancestral town), there is no room at the inn! Hence, Mary has to give birth to her baby presumably in a place meant for animals because she wraps Yeshua in swaddling clothes and lays him in a "manger," a feeding trough or box-like structure for domestic animals (2:7). Following that, the people who visit the new-born savior and Messiah (2:11) are not important figures (such as Matthew's sages from the East, Matt 2:1) but lowly and poor shepherds who happen to be keeping watch over their sheep in the fields (2:8). Commentators have pointed out that shepherds were some of the most underprivileged people in this society at the time.[7]

Try to notice how GU-Luke's story is intentionally making you feel as you read his story. Of course, you, the reader, already know that Yeshua is an exalted personage. He is called by such lofty titles as "Son of the Most High" early on in the story (1:32). Why does it happen that there is no room in the inn for the parents of the "Lord" (1:43)? How can this chosen one of God be born in a shelter for animals and laid in a manger?

These details betray GU-Luke's message and—if we may state it in no uncertain terms—his "agenda." He is showing Yeshua, the Messiah and savior, as being born in the lowliest possible place and being visited by some of the most marginalized in his society. We can only conclude that the salvation that this Yeshua will bring is directed in a privileged way to the poor, the lowly, the suffering, and the oppressed.

THE "PROGRAMMATIC PASSAGE"

According to the story narrated by GU-Luke, when Yeshua is about to begin his public ministry, he goes into the synagogue of his hometown Nazareth and proclaims these words from the scroll of the prophet Isaiah:

> 18 "The Spirit of the Lord is upon me,
> because he has anointed me
> to bring good news to the poor.
> He has sent me to proclaim release to the captives
> and recovery of sight to the blind,

7. See, for example, Keener and Walton, *NIV Cultural Backgrounds Study Bible*, 1744 (note on Luke 2:8).

to let the oppressed go free,
19 to proclaim the year of the Lord's favor."[8]

The narrative continues by saying that when Yeshua had read these words, he astonishes the assembly by claiming, "Today this scripture has been fulfilled in your hearing" (v. 21), thus effectively claiming that he himself is "the anointed one" who is supposed to enact the liberative works of which the prophet Isaiah spoke. We know the people become hostile to Yeshua with this revelation because they end up driving him out of town with the murderous intent of hurling him down the cliff on which Nazareth is built (v. 29. This can be readily understood even now if one visits the modern city of Nazareth).

Although the story of Yeshua returning to his hometown and being received in a hostile way is common with Matthew (chapter 13) and Mark (chapter 6), the insertion of the passage from Isaiah is unique to Luke and that should make our ears perk up in attention for unique and "peculiarly Lukan" qualities. The quote from Isaiah is of course intentional. It reveals how Yeshua in GU-Luke's story is going to realize God's liberating compassion in a special way: He is going to bring liberating salvation to the most underprivileged: the poor, the captives, the blind, the oppressed. All these people, as we shall see in GU-Luke's unfolding of Yeshua's story, are going to be the privileged recipients of Yeshua's compassionate ministry of salvation.

PARABLES UNIQUE TO LUKE

Two of the most beloved parables in the entire New Testament are The Parable of the Good Samaritan (Luke 10) and the Parable of the Prodigal Son (Luke 15). Both of them, let us remember, are found *only* in Luke and for that reason they are prime candidates for us to peer behind the text and see the peculiar characteristics of GU-Luke. It is no surprise that both of them emphasize the compassionate salvation of God toward the disadvantaged. One may even wonder whether these tales of God's compassion really come from GU-Luke and put into Yeshua's mouth! Even if that were so, there is no doubt that they correctly and faithfully mirror the compassion that was the prime driving force behind Yeshua's own ministry and teaching.

For instance, the good Samaritan wonderfully exemplifies in the most concrete way GU-Luke's image of Yeshua who wants his listeners to extend compassion even to one's enemies (6:27) and thus let this compassionate service overcome the mutual hatred that Jews and Samaritans had for each

8. Luke 4 (from Isa 61:1–2; Lev 25:10).

other at the time. If we turn to the so-called parable of the prodigal son and analyze it carefully, we can make a case that the main protagonist is not really the son but the father who is "decadently" prodigal in his compassionate love for his son who does not deserve it. This is made clear if we put the story into its proper historical and social context. The son asks his father for his share of the inheritance while the father is still alive. This, it may be understood, is an utterly disrespectful act and is tantamount to spitting in his father's face by acting as if he could not wait for his father to die. The father gives him whatever he asked for. That action on the part of the father could be considered somewhat pathetic because the father does not uphold the dignity and honor expected of him in this patriarchal society. After having exhausted the resources from his father, the son returns home. The father does not only refuse to mete out any punishment; rather, he lovingly accepts the wayward son unconditionally and even slaughters the prized calf in a feast prepared in his son's honor. Here again we see an astonishingly prodigal kind of compassion toward someone despised by others who think of themselves as respectable (such as the elder brother). GU-Luke's point is that the most important thing to strive to attain is having such prodigal kind of love because it arguably best reflects the character of God.[9]

BE COMPASSIONATE AS YOUR HEAVENLY FATHER

Luke 6:27–36 is part of Luke's Sermon on the Plain. There Yeshua lays down a radical demand to his followers: That they are to love even their enemies! This went over and beyond what—Yeshua's audience would have commonly thought—was stipulated even by the Law (e.g., Lev 24:20 "an eye for an eye"). There is a parallel passage in Matt 5:43–48 within the so-called "Sermon on the Mount." Both passages give instructions to "love your enemies" as modern Bible editions point out with their sub-titles. However, one can notice that there is a crucial difference in the concluding statement of Yeshua's talk when Luke's version is compared to Matthew's. As the reason for the command to love even one's enemies, Matthew offers, "Be *perfect*, therefore, as your heavenly Father is perfect" (Matt 5:48). Curiously, Luke has this concluding statement: "Be *merciful*, just as your Father is merciful" (Luke 6:36 in the NRSV). The difference in one word "perfect" as opposed to "merciful" (I prefer "compassionate") gives us a glimpse into GU-Luke's clear intention: He prefers to cite God's mercy and compassion as the ultimate justification for the commandment whereas GU-Matthew uses the

9. See, for example, Hamm, "Luke," 1076–77.

concept of "perfection." If there was a quality of God that could be cited for emulation, it is, for GU-Luke, compassion-mercy. That is, without doubt, GU-Luke all over! It is consistent with all his other emphases on the value of compassion. One may wonder what the original word-concept was in Matthew and Luke's common source (called the "Q" source by scholars). Was it "Be perfect" or "Be compassionate"? We may never know the answer to that but, whatever it may have been, we know GU-Matthew and GU-Luke's intentions as they picked the key words as their ultimate reason for emulating God.

We can say that in his Gospel, GU-Luke generally portrays Yeshua as the living embodiment of compassion. All this comes to a climax in the final scene of Yeshua's earthly life in Luke (Luke 23). He is hanging on the cross. To his right and left are two criminals likewise crucified. When one of them derides Yeshua and mockingly asks him to save them, the other rebukes him and instead humbly asks Yeshua to "remember him when he comes into his kingdom." At this, the dying Lukan Yeshua shows mercy to the criminal and promises that he would be with him in paradise (Luke 23:39–43). Compassion toward, what Christian tradition has called, "the good thief" is Yeshua's final crowning achievement in GU-Luke's Gospel.

VOLUME TWO: THE ACTS OF THE APOSTLES

In GU-Luke's second volume, the Acts of the Apostles, we see Yeshua raised up to heaven at the beginning of the book while charging his disciples to continue the work of spreading the good news by being his witnesses "in Jerusalem, in all Judea and Samaria and to the ends of the earth" (1:8). One can argue that one of GU-Luke's main aims in this second volume was to show us how the gospel message spread westward from Jerusalem throughout all the earth, in the way mentioned in this previous verse (1:8), with Rome being "the ends of the earth."[10] Indeed, by the end of the story, we find Paul, Christ's intrepid missionary, reaching Rome and "proclaiming the kingdom of God and teaching about the Lord Jesus Christ with all boldness and without hindrance" (Acts 28:31).

In between those two bookends, we find many elements in Acts that can speak to the theme of spreading the good news beyond Israel's borders. We see missionaries like Peter (e.g., 9:32–43), Philip (e.g., 8:4–8) and, of course, Paul (e.g., 13:1–52) being led by the Spirit to take up an itinerant lifestyle in order to spread the good news and actualize the presence of the kingdom of God (similar to what Yeshua does in the Gospel). We see

10. See, for example, Harris, *Exploring the Bible*, 351.

persecution displacing Yeshua's followers from their original location but resulting in the spread of the gospel, particularly in Judea and Samaria (Acts 8:1).

Allow me now to focus on a particular facet of Luke-Acts that I think is key to understanding GU-Luke and his original audience. It is clear in Acts that the author is heavily invested in the "gentile question," that is, how to deal with gentiles who wanted to be part of the Jesus movement. Many scholars accept that GU-Luke was probably himself a gentile, most probably the only gentile author in the New Testament corpus. If we consider this vested interest of GU-Luke in the gentile question more closely, one can hypothesize at this point that the main message that he wanted to convey through his two-volume saga was that the gentiles are now included and empowered in God's plan of salvation, a plan that has its roots in God's covenant with the people of Israel.[11]

GRANDUNCLE LUKE'S MAIN AGENDA

To expand on this for emphasis, I propose that everything in the whole saga of Luke-Acts is actually geared toward demonstrating that the gentiles are now fully included and empowered in the salvific plan of God for the world, a plan which began with Israel (the Jews), but which was still opposed by many Jews and even by Jewish followers of Yeshua at Luke's time of writing. This is GU-Luke's main point. We can even say that this is his main "agenda," which colors the whole of his retelling of the story of Yeshua and his earliest followers. I would even say that his emphasis in the first part of his saga (the Gospel), of Yeshua having a predilection for the underprivileged, the poor, the marginalized, and the oppressed, is merely an illustrative tool, a foil even that GU-Luke utilizes to focus, in the second half of the saga, on his real concern. And what was that? It was for the quintessential underprivileged ones on the cosmic stage of history, the group commonly known in Greek as *ta éthnē* (literally, "the nations"), a group we commonly know as "the gentiles."

WHO WERE THE "GOD-FEARERS"?

Before we proceed, an important clarification is needed on the so-called "God-fearers" (Gk. *theosebeis*).[12] We can say that these were the particular

11. See, for example, Bock, *Theology of Luke and Acts*, 300–301. Note also this book's subtitle, which practically states the dominant theme of Luke-Acts (*God's Promised Program, Realized for All Nations*).

12. Crossan and Reed, *In Search of Paul*, 23–24.

class of Gentiles that we are interested in as we consider GU-Luke and the communities related to him. In the New Testament, the following Greek expressions: *phoboumenoi ton theon* ("the ones fearing God," e.g., Acts 13:16, 26) and *sebomenoi ton theon* (in various forms, "the ones worshiping God," e.g., Acts 17:4, 17) are the ones that indicate these "God-fearers."

To contextualize the matter better, let's begin by saying that the cosmic worldview of ancient people was broader than the typical secular worldview of time and space in vogue in the West today. If we use the ancient Hebrew worldview as an illustration, the ancient cosmic worldview consisted of a vast cosmic-spiritual realm of which the material world and humans along with it were just one small part. Peculiar to the ancient Hebrew worldview was the following unambiguous claim: The people of Israel, by virtue of God's election and covenant, were the privileged people in this cosmic order, and the land of Israel, even geographically speaking, was the holiest and most significant place on earth.[13]

In this context, when gentiles became interested in the faith of Israel, and followed some of its aspects (this could be a general description of the so-called "God-fearers"),[14] their worldview underwent a kind of paradigm shift to becoming identified with the ancient Hebrew cosmic imagination of God's realm and Israel's privileged place in this order. We can even claim that these gentiles became, psychologically speaking, spiritual migrants, as it were. They migrated in their minds *from* whatever cosmic order they formerly espoused *to* the operative one in which most Jews lived at the time, a worldview in which God and God's chosen people-nation-physical realm had supreme importance. Let us call these gentiles here using the terminology used in Luke-Acts for them, namely, "God-fearers."[15]

The so-called God-fearers were "Gentiles who were attached to Judaism's sophisticated monotheism, high moral standards and system for maintaining one's righteousness through observance of the Law."[16] However, when they moved toward considering Israel's faith seriously and the worldview that came with it, ironically, they experienced marginalization. In the cosmic order, in the "kingdom of God" as imagined in the conventional Jewish worldview at the time, the gentiles were basically marginalized

13. For more on this, see Oden, "Cosmogony, Cosmology," 1:1162–71, particularly, 1162–64; 1167–71. Also, Patrick, "Election-Old Testament," 2:434–41.

14. Recall that we accept the suggestion that Luke *was* such a person.

15. For more on this, see, for example, McKnight, "Proselytism and Godfearers," 835–47, particularly, 846–47; Feldman, *Jew and Gentile in the Ancient World*, 342–832; Crossan and Reed, *In Search of Paul*, 23–41. A messianic Jewish perspective on God-fearers can be found in Janicki, *God-fearers*, 39–48.

16. Soards, "Historical and Cultural Setting of Luke-Acts," 33–47.

and outside the covenant. Non-Jews were not even on the radar screen of the conventional purity charts.[17] They were simply out of the picture. God's covenant was, first and foremost, for Jews. For one to have fuller access to the covenant, one had to be part of the people of Israel.

In practice, this mentality translated into less-than-friendly attitudes and actions on the part of some Jews toward gentiles. For the sake of fairness, it must be mentioned that there is also evidence that many Jews were favorably disposed toward gentiles, particularly gentile proselytes and God-fearers. However, it is difficult to deny that more often than not, because of many particular circumstances, there were, at the same time, negative general attitudes on the part of Jews toward gentiles (including even gentile proselytes to Judaism and, of course, God-fearers as well).[18] Jewish studies scholars Adi Ophir and Ishay Rosen-Zvi claim that this is heavily supported in the rabbinic literature particularly from the second century onward:

> [We] should also mention the "God-fearers," the partial Judaizers, discussed extensively by scholars. The fact that the rabbis use this category is cited in scholarly literature as proof that they were positively inclined toward missionizing. But *the proof is in fact in the opposite direction*. Epigraphic evidence shows that "God-fearers" were closely associated with Jewish communities in the diaspora. Not so for the rabbis. Under their binary scheme, *they considered the "God-fearers" as Gentiles* tout court. . . . The rabbis deprived these categories of their ambiguous, hybrid position. *Gerim*, apostates, "Canaanite" slaves and Samaritans are grouped with Israel. *God-fearers remain Gentiles* and "Noahides" is but another name for Gentiles. . . . [We] assert that . . . *the general rabbinic trend was to erase the possibility of a hybrid existence on the borders of the Jewish community and to create the Gentile as a perfect asymmetrical counter-concept.*[19]

Admittedly, the above quote is based on rabbinic literature from the second century (GU-Luke lived in the first century) onward and describes an attitude originally found in Palestinian Judaism rather than Diaspora Judaism (GU-Luke seems to be dealing more with the latter). But such a general attitude on the part of the rabbis did not spring up overnight, it is safe to conjecture. Negative attitudes on the part of many Jews, especially the rabbis, were most probably a feature of Judaism, both Palestinian and

17. On the topic of the consequences of such a worldview as shown in the thinking about purity and the place of Gentiles in this scheme, see Malina, "Clean and Unclean," particularly, 159–62. See also Wright, "Unclean and Clean (OT)," 6:738–741.

18. See McKnight, "Proselytism and Godfearers," 840–41.

19. Ophir and Rosen-Zvi, *Goy*, 196–97. The emphases are mine.

(to a lesser extent but, nevertheless, still present) also in Diaspora Judaism where we should locate GU-Luke.

Given that, it is no surprise that when the Jesus movement was rebooted because of Yeshua's resurrection, a general negative and exclusionary attitude toward gentiles continued to hold sway even among the earliest followers of Yeshua. Is it any wonder that the first great crisis faced by the early Jesus movement/Christian community was deciding what place the gentiles would have in God's kingdom on earth, in the community of Yeshua-followers?

GRANDUNCLE LUKE AS A "SPIRITUAL MIGRANT"

My first major suggestion here is that GU-Luke (whom we consider here as a God-fearer? or proselyte?)[20] *can somehow be considered a migrant, particularly, in a spiritual or psychological sense*, because he went through a kind of cognitive and spiritual migration from an original Greco-Roman religious worldview to a Second Temple Jewish religious worldview when he began to believe that in this worldview lay, as it were, the "promised land." In connection with this, we can say that migrants are basically people in search of a "promised land." In GU-Luke's case, "the promised land" could be understood as the realization that in Israel's faith and covenant with God lie the truth, the truth of a better or deeper spiritual-religious state. However, when GU-Luke underwent this kind of spiritual migration, he probably found himself, an earnest gentile seeker, treated and marginalized in many different ways as a second-class citizen in the new cosmic-religious order which he espoused because he was not fully a Jew, ethnically and in practice. New Testament scholar Marion Soards comments thus about this matter:

> The status of the God-fearers in relation to Jews was ambiguous. At times . . . they are highly regarded, but because they were uncircumcised, God-fearers were still considered to be unclean;

20. The question marks here mean that I do not commit myself to establishing whether Luke was still a God-fearer or already a proselyte. Moreover, there are suggestions that it is still possible that Luke was a Jew. For example, Robin Griffith-Jones offers the possibility that Luke could have been a Jewish slave who was a highly educated secretary of a gentile master and who adopted his master's name. See Griffith-Jones, *Four Witnesses*, 190. I follow John Dominic Crossan's suggestions, convincingly argued for me, that Luke was a pagan sympathizer of the Jewish religion or "God-fearer." See Crossan and Reed, *In Search of Paul*, 40–41.

> and so, they were subject to discrimination within the context of the Jewish culture and the life of the synagogue.[21]

That situation brought GU-Luke, and many others like him in the first century, pain and various forms of suffering. These experiences are very much comparable to the many challenges faced by migrants in search of a better state and place, but who end up being treated and marginalized as second-class citizens precisely in the place they thought they would find a better life.

GRANDUNCLE LUKE'S "AHA" EXPERIENCE

Faced with such challenges, we can justly conjecture that GU-Luke resolved to do a deep reading, accompanied by an equally deep discernment of salvation history in the light of what transpired in Yeshua, the Christ, and the experiences of his earliest disciples. Upon doing so, he had the epiphany that it was indeed God's passionate will that the covenant be truly inclusive now of *his* kind of people, the gentiles, and that they no longer should be second-class citizens but full-fledged, proud members of God's reign, God's community and God's *ekklēsia* or church (for example used in Acts 9:31; 11:26) on earth. He then decided to set down this unique experience of enlightenment in a narrative form by which he would demonstrate and argue that the salvific action of God—whose culmination is the liberation, full inclusion, and valorization of the gentiles in the universal plan of salvation—could be traced to the radical spirit of religious-social boundary-crossing, the inclusion of the marginalized and despised, and the extraordinary openness of Yeshua the Christ, the chosen one of God. This, I think, is the key to understanding this spiritual ancestor-storyteller, a factor without which (*sine qua non*) we would not get what it is GU-Luke is trying to do in his two-part saga.

A GOOD LENS FOR READING LUKE-ACTS: IDENTIFYING ITS MAIN "AGENDA"

Reading Luke-Acts in this light brings many unique insights and allows us to understand the different levels in the worlds "within the text" and "behind the text." Hence, I propose that GU-Luke's real agenda in his two-part saga is to proclaim that, through everything that transpired in Yeshua, God has finally made clear that all the nations (literally, *ta éthnē*, usually translated as "gentiles") are now full members of the covenant. This can be considered the "hidden agenda" (if I may call it that) of why GU-Luke portrays Yeshua in

21. Soards, "Historical and Cultural Setting of Luke-Acts," 40.

the Gospel as dominantly privileging the underprivileged, such as sinners, women, the poor, the sick, the lowly, and so forth. This is why he makes Yeshua's last act the forgiving of a criminal hanging beside him on the cross and admitting him into paradise (Luke 23:43). This is finally also why GU-Luke ends his Gospel by declaring clearly that:

> Thus it is written, that the Messiah is to suffer and to rise from the dead on the third day, and that repentance and forgiveness of sins is to be proclaimed in his name *to all nations*, beginning from Jerusalem. (Luke 24:46–47; emphasis mine)

Here, we see again that for GU-Luke, the covenant is rooted in God's relationship with Israel (symbolized by Jerusalem), but now it is extended to "all the nations." The disciples are witnesses of this (Luke 24:48). The promised Holy Spirit, which Yeshua will send from on high, will enable and empower them to carry out the mission of realizing this (Luke 24:49).

It is clear that in GU-Luke's Gospel, the radical spirit of inclusiveness and openness displayed by Yeshua of Nazareth to those who were marginalized and excluded was directed to people in Yeshua's own limited Palestinian historical context. In the Acts of the Apostles though, this same radical spirit of inclusivity and openness is primarily directed to the group that Jews considered excluded from God's covenant with Israel—the gentiles. Needless to say, in the Acts of the Apostles, Yeshua is no longer physically present to realize God's radical inclusivity. Rather, it is the Holy Spirit, which Acts 16:7 explicitly calls "the Spirit of Jesus," who, through the disciples of Yeshua, continues the radical program of inclusivity and openness and enables the disciples to apply this spirit to new places and situations, especially through God's chosen emissary, Paul.

To reiterate, the theme of including and empowering gentiles lies at the very heart of the second part of GU-Luke's saga. This is the reason why he painstakingly describes the wonderful event on the day of Pentecost in which the gospel is understood and accepted by multitudes of people from all over the world (Acts 2:1–47). This is the reason why he shares with us the incident of the widows of the Hellenists being neglected in the food distribution, a problem which results in the appointing of the seven "servers" (or "deacons" in traditional language) in Acts 6. This is the reason why GU-Luke frequently mentions and makes heroes of either diaspora Jews or gentiles: Barnabas is from Cyprus (4:36); one of the seven servers (all of them most probably diaspora Jews or Hellenists themselves) is Nicolaus, "a proselyte from Antioch" (6:5); an Ethiopian eunuch is baptized by Philip, the Hellenist deacon (8:38); and, of course, Saul is from Tarsus (8:11).

Acts chapter 10 deserves special mention. Peter has a vision which, if analyzed closely, is very troubling because God commands him to eat animals that the same God was supposed to have explicitly forbade Israel to eat according to the covenant (see Lev 11; Deut 14:3–21). During the Maccabean era, many Jews gave up their lives for these laws (1 Macc 1:62–63). The vision is meant to convince Peter to perform an action on behalf of a Gentile. Hence, he baptizes a centurion from the Italian Regiment named Cornelius (Acts 10:1, 34–48) who is, significantly, "God-fearing" (Acts 10:2). At the baptism, Cornelius and his family receive the Holy Spirit shown by the gift of tongues and the text of Acts says (NRSV), "the Holy Spirit had been poured out *even* on the Gentiles (*kai épi ta éthnē*)" (10:45).

CONCLUDING REFLECTIONS

At this point, it is good to remind ourselves that we share a common faculty with our spiritual ancestors, one that we have earlier called "spiritual intelligence." This is a deep desire that urges us to seek to better understand "the meaning of it all," one that leads us to construct a big coherent framework that could encompass all things—material and spiritual—in the universe. What is GU-Luke's particular contribution to this endeavor as expressed in his two-volume work? We have thus far surveyed his work and what we can certainly claim at this point is that GU-Luke understood that the same God who made a special covenant with Israel in the past was now in the process of making it clear, first, through the life and ministry of Yeshua and, second, through the ministry of Yeshua's disciples (found in the Acts of the Apostles), that God's "tender mercy" is for all people, Jew and gentile alike. In other words, God (or as some in our secular context prefer, "the universe") is inclusive and seeks to embrace everyone and everything, particularly those who have been up to this point marginalized and oppressed. We cited that this view of the divine was most probably rooted in GU-Luke's experience as a God-fearer who was treated somehow as a second-class member of the covenant people.

As a follower of "the Way," GU-Luke was convinced that the essence of Yeshua's way was inclusive compassion. We can therefore claim that GU-Luke's work is something like a mirror that reflected Yeshua's unconditional heart of mercy for all, especially for those who were oppressed, marginalized, and underprivileged in his world. In the Acts of the Apostles, GU-Luke develops this into a particular theme that, I have argued, was his real agenda. GU-Luke wanted to say that gentiles are now fully included in God's plan of salvation.

In summary, GU-Luke went out of his way to write not only an account of Yeshua's life but also a second work that dealt with what happened to Yeshua's followers and their communities in the aftermath of Yeshua having gone back to the One who had sent him. In this, GU-Luke was trying to tell us that the covenant that God made with Israel was now, through God's anointed One, Yeshua, being offered beyond Israel to the wide-world of the gentiles, the ones who were hitherto considered in various senses as marginal and second-class citizens. We can feel the passion of GU-Luke for the full inclusion of the gentiles as full-fledged members of God's people. GU-Luke's lasting legacy to us then is his message of (God and Yeshua's) *inclusivity*. He brings this to the fore in the Gospel where he spotlights the predilection of Yeshua for those who were outside the mainstream, for the marginalized, for the oppressed and downtrodden. He brings his narrative to its high point in the Acts of the Apostles where he focuses on how the message of Yeshua is, in stages, brought to, realized, and accepted joyfully by the gentiles, mainly through the work of Yeshua's intrepid apostle Paul and his collaborators.

9

The Fourth Gospel's Mystical and Divine View of Yeshua

The Excommunicated Mystic and His Community

With that background [of Jewish mysticism in the first century], quite suddenly John's gospel began to unfold before me as a work of Jewish mysticism and the Jesus of John's gospel suddenly became not a visitor from another realm, but a person in whom a new God consciousness had emerged.

—John Shelby Spong[1]

JOHN'S INFLUENTIAL PLACE IN CHRISTIANITY

Although commonly acknowledged as the last to have been written among the four canonical Gospels, the Gospel according to John (also called "the Fourth Gospel" or simply "John") is the one that has arguably exerted the greatest influence on how Christians throughout history have thought about the central figure that lies at the heart of the Christian tradition—Jesus Christ, worshiped by Christianity as the divine Son of God and clearly portrayed as so in John. Moreover, although it is hard to prove empirically, John seems to be the favorite Gospel of a great many (most?)

1. Spong, *Fourth Gospel*, 8.

Christians.[2] It is even more urgent then to catch a glimpse of the spiritual ancestor-storyteller behind this influential text. Let's start our quest by describing a class of people that our author, granduncle John, has often been associated with. I refer to those known as "mystics" because, as we shall see, GU-John seems to have been one himself.[3]

MYSTICS AND SIGNS

What is a "mystic" anyway? We "ordinary" people often think of mystics negatively as a "weird" bunch because we reckon that there is a vast, perhaps even unbridgeable difference between them, the spiritual elite, and us, ordinary folk. To start off, they're people who search for and, to a certain extent, have experienced the most transcendent or sublime dimensions of reality. Hence, mystics claim that they know the Sacred *through experience*. Since many of us are not engaged in such a quest or have not had experiences that could be considered "mystical," we feel that mystics live at a radically different sphere from the one we inhabit and therefore perceive them as part of an unreachable, super-elite class of humans.

Mystics usually put a great value on "signs" and "symbols" because their profound spiritual experiences are hard to express in ordinary language and even harder to grasp using ordinary human concepts. This is why they frequently have recourse to these signs and symbols to express at least a part of the profound depth and glorious transcendence of their spiritual experiences. From this, we should also say that "glory" is another common theme of mysticism.

What does all this have to do with GU-John anyway? A thoughtful reading of the gospel he left us will reveal that he seemed to have been a mystic himself.[4]

Before we continue, let me insert an important caveat here about the authorship of the Fourth Gospel. Many scholars consider the final product (the Gospel as we know it now) to be the result of a long and complicated process of text composition, editing, and transmission. That means, multiple people were involved in the history of the version of the text that has come down to us. Hence, when we refer to a "Granduncle John" here, it is

2. See also Fortna, "Gospel of John and the Historical Jesus," 223.

3. See, for example, Spong, *Fourth Gospel*, 8–10; Griffith-Jones, *Four Witnesses*, 281–83.

4. Again, see Griffith-Jones, *Four Witnesses*, 7 and Spong, *Fourth Gospel*, 51–54.

more appropriate to think of a corporate author or even perhaps a group of key people behind the text, rather than a single individual.[5]

To return to GU-John as a mystic, there are strong indications that the original spiritual ancestor behind the text was trying to put into words, what we could very well describe as, a profound mystical experience of Yeshua, the Christ, identified as the "Word" of God (see for example John 1:1). In order to convey these sublime insights, he included in his gospel certain acts of Yeshua that he called "signs" (e.g., John 2:11; 20:30) which, he hoped, would reveal better to his community (and his readers) the glory of Yeshua, sent from the Father (YHWH) as the only-begotten Son of God (cf. John 1:14).

JOHN AND THE EAGLE

The Gospel of John is frequently associated in Christian art with an eagle. There are many possible reasons for that but let me point out just one here.[6] The eagle is known to be "the king" of the mighty birds of prey. It flies high in the sky, unparalleled in its majestic form, power and strength, and its far-reaching vision. Among the Gospels, the Gospel of John can very well be compared to an eagle in terms of the power and transcendence of its theological vision. It shows this from the very beginning when the Gospel hits the road running on a lofty theological note, expounding on the mystery of the "Word" of God who "was with God and was God" and who "became flesh and lived among us" (John 1:1, 14). From that soaring start, John maintains a high-octane theological level throughout his Gospel, emphasizing Yeshua as the eternal and glorious Word of God-in-action so that his readers could come to faith that this Yeshua is indeed "the Messiah, the Son of God, and that through believing [they] may have life in his name" (John 20:31).

SOME GENERAL FEATURES OF JOHN

John is commonly acknowledged to be the last of the canonical Gospels to be written, possibly around a date in the 90s or the end (or even turn) of the century. By the time of GU-John's writing, many early Christian communities would have been already familiar with the Synoptic portraits of Yeshua presented in Mark, Matthew, and Luke, particularly in their oral forms. We

5. Brown, *Introduction to the New Testament*, 117, 131–32.

6. For more information on the four symbols of the canonical Gospels, confer Felix Just SJ, "Symbols of the Four Evangelists."

can speculate that GU-John probably thought: It is time to have a new style of portraying Yeshua. All the Gospels have, as common goal, the awakening of faith in their listeners/readers that Yeshua is the Messiah sent by God. John further qualifies that this faith would result in "life in [Yeshua's] name" (John 20:31). It is useful then to ask at this point: What distinguishes John from the others and what gives it its specific character? Why did GU-John write quite a different version of the gospel from the earlier Synoptic Gospels? I propose that GU-John was, first of all, an early Christian mystic and as such he meant to lead his audience on a spiritual-mystical journey "through signs to glory."

In GU-John's story of Yeshua, the tale begins not with matters of Yeshua's birth in Bethlehem (as in Matthew and Luke) but in the eternal realm of God where the "Word" (Greek, *logos*) is with God (John 1:1). GU-John quickly identifies this Word with "life" and "light" (1:4–5) so that when the name "Jesus Christ" finally appears in the narrative (1:17), the reader makes the necessary connection that this Yeshua is the revealing embodiment of God the Father, as well as the life and light that come from this gracious Being. From there, GU-John develops his story by gradually showing who Yeshua really is, first through "signs" (Greek, *semeia* [plural]—a prominent concept in the first half of John). And then in the second half of the gospel, GU-John puts the spotlight on the theme of "glory" (Greek, *doxa*[7]), frequently referring to God and/or to Yeshua. This is the reason why it is a common practice among scholars to divide the structure of John's gospel into two main parts: The book of "signs" (John 2–11) and the book of "glory" (John 12–20).[8]

THE BOOK OF SIGNS

In John 2, we find the famous story of the Wedding at Cana where Yeshua turns the water into wine at the behest of his mother. At the end of the story, GU-John comments thus, "Jesus did this, the first of his signs, in Cana of Galilee, and revealed his glory; and his disciples believed in him" (2:11). Note that the miracle of Yeshua turning the water into wine of the best quality (v. 10) is called a "sign." The Gospel writer connects this first of Yeshua's signs with a revelation of his "glory" which in turn enables his disciples to believe in him (faith).

7. *Doxa* can be described as glory, splendor, brilliance, revealed presence of God, God himself. See Aland, *Greek New Testament*, 48.

8. Just, "Various Outlines of the Fourth Gospel."

After this first sign, GU-John goes on to relate other signs performed by Yeshua which take the form of, to use the traditional word, "miracles." He heals an official's son (4:46–54); he cures a man who was ill for thirty-eight years (5:1–18); he feeds the five thousand by multiplying loaves and fishes (6:1–15); he walks on the lake to help his disciples when they are caught up in rough waters (6:16–21); he heals a blind man (9:1–41). To cap it all up with a "biggie," Yeshua brings his dead friend Lazarus back to life (11:1–44). Note well though that this last sign has an important role to play in the transition from the "book of signs" to the "book of glory." It is the occasion for many to "believe in Jesus" (11:45). At the same time, it is also the catalyst that leads Yeshua's enemies to begin plotting to put him to death (11:53). And Yeshua's death in John, as we shall see, was actually his moment of glory.

Aside from those signs, there are other parts in this so-called book of signs in John that give the listener-reader a hint of the identity of Yeshua. Among them we can include: Yeshua's conversation with Nicodemus (3:1–21); the witness of John the Baptist (3:22–36); Yeshua's own elaborations on his identity (8:12–59 and 10:7–18; 22–39). In this way, when the audience work their way through the book of signs, they, according to GU-John's plan, are drawn more and more into the quest of discovering in a deeper way the real identity of the protagonist Yeshua. If that happens, GU-John hopes that the listeners-readers catch a glimpse of the glory that will be more clearly revealed in the second half of the book, appropriately referred to as "the book of glory."

THE BOOK OF GLORY

From chapter 12 onward, the theme of "signs" seems to take a back seat while references to "glory" become more prominent. What we should not miss is that "glory" is intimately connected with the theme of "death." It is as if GU-John is clearly asserting that one cannot be separated from the other. This is exemplified in the following passage:

> Jesus answered them, "The hour has come for the Son of Man to be *glorified*. Very truly, I tell you, unless a grain of wheat falls into the earth and dies, it remains just a single grain; but if it *dies*, it bears much fruit."[9]

It is evident that GU-John, unlike GU-Mark, treats Yeshua's death not so much as a tragedy but rather as his moment of glory. It is a different take,

9. John 12:23–24.

although the Christian tradition has rightly come to consider the two different portrayals as complementary. If we quote two other passages from this "Book of Glory" in John, the message becomes crystal clear.

In John 13:21–30, Yeshua drops a bombshell during the Last Supper. He distressingly reveals that one of his closest friends is going to betray him (v. 21). When the betrayer, Judas, is identified through a symbolic gesture on the part of Yeshua (the other disciples curiously miss the hint though!) and leaves to set in motion events that will lead to Yeshua's arrest and death, Yeshua solemnly declares:

> The Son of Man has been *glorified*, and God has been *glorified* in him. If God has been glorified in him, God will also glorify him in himself and will glorify him at once.[10]

And then, in the solemn prayer of Yeshua at the conclusion of his long Last Supper discourse, he also prays, "Father, the hour has come; *glorify* your Son so that the Son may *glorify* you" (John 17:1).

There is no doubt that GU-John wanted his community to consider Yeshua's death as the very moment when he attains the glory he had "before the universe was created" (17:5). His death—expressed in a thinly veiled way as being "lifted up" (on the cross)—is the very means by which Yeshua will draw all people to himself (12:32). This is how the Father is going to be glorified (12:28).

IN JOHN, GLORY IS LINKED WITH LOVE

I would like to add here that this theme of glory is most certainly connected with the theme of love. I say this because of the many references to love in this so-called book of glory. Some of the most prominent are the following:

> I give you a new commandment, that you love one another. Just as I have loved you, you also should love one another. By this everyone will know that you are my disciples, if you have love for one another.[11]

> They who have my commandments and keep them are those who love me; and those who love me will be loved by my Father, and I will love them and reveal myself to them.[12]

10. John 13:31–32.
11. John 13:32–35.
12. John 14:21.

> As the Father has loved me, so I have loved you; abide in my love. If you keep my commandments, you will abide in my love, just as I have kept my Father's commandments and abide in his love.[13]

> This is my commandment, that you love one another as I have loved you. No one has greater love than this, to lay down one's life for one's friends.[14]

Moreover, after Yeshua is raised from the dead, he gives the gift of peace to his fearful disciples (20:19); he also forgives Peter for his threefold denial by entrusting him with a shepherd's duty over the flock (21:1–19). In all of these intense moments, God's glory (which is Yeshua's glory as well) is made manifest in a concrete way as acts of love to his closest friends (cf. also John 15:15). At the end of the day, I think GU-John wanted to say that it all boils down to the glory of love.

JOHN'S MESSIAH OF GLORY

When I discussed GU-Mark's Gospel, I mentioned classics scholar Louis Ruprecht's work *This Tragic Gospel: How John Corrupted the Heart of Christianity*. There he imagines some of our early Christian ancestors gathering around a fire to listen to storytellers tell of Yeshua's life and death, in particular, what happened to him on the night of his arrest and condemnation. One of the storytellers, it is imaginatively suggested, was none other than GU-Mark who depicts Yeshua's agony in the garden, as we have already seen, in such a tragic way, comparable to the well-known tragedies in the Greek literature of the time. As we saw earlier, this was meant to produce pathos and, more importantly, compassion which, GU-Mark seemed to think, should be considered the foremost Christian virtue.[15]

In the audience, we can imagine, was a young man who was to become GU-John, the evangelist. He was disturbed at the "tragic" way in which GU-Mark told the story of Yeshua's life. He thought that his hero Yeshua had to be more—for want of a better expression—"divine-like" and not, he must have thought, the pathetic and tragic messiah that GU-Mark presented. Such a divine figure would be shown better in a portrayal of a Yeshua that would be more composed, more in-control of the situation (even of his death!), and more majestic than the evangelist GU-Mark's pitiable Jesus.

13. John 15:9–10.
14. John 15:12–13.
15. Ruprecht, *This Tragic Gospel*, 37–40, 55–66.

This is why this young Yeshua-follower would later go on to write his own version of the story in which Yeshua is no longer a tragic Messiah but rather a glorious one, always in control of matters (never controlled)—even during his passion and death. GU-John's Gospel was to be written a good twenty to thirty years after Mark. His version of Yeshua's person and life certainly reflected the feelings he had as an "unhappy camper" when listening to GU-Mark's tale of a tragic Messiah, especially in the garden scene (Mark 14:32–42) where Yeshua is in extreme agony in the face of death.

As we have hinted to above, John's Yeshua in the garden (see John 18:1–11) is nothing at all like the distressed Messiah in Mark who elicits pathos from all who behold him. This Yeshua in John is nothing short of majestic when he faces his impending death: He displays calm, composure, willing acceptance, and even "know[s] all that was to happen to him" (John 18:4). He self-declares who he is by uttering—GU-John's way of identifying Yeshua as closely as possible with Yahweh—"*I am* He" (18:5) when confronted by the cohort of temple police asking for a certain "Jesus of Nazareth." Note well that this response of Yeshua that identifies himself with God's very name ("I am") contains such power that it makes those sent to arrest him fall to the ground (18:6)!

And then, very curiously, when the disciple, Simon Peter cuts off the ear of the high priest's servant, Yeshua reprimands him and declares (in words that are a dead giveaway of what GU-John was trying to do in *his* version of this story which, arguably, is his corrective of the earlier Gospel of Mark), "Put your sword back into its sheath. *Am I not to drink the cup that the Father has given me*?" (18:11). That is practically the complete reversal of Yeshua's anguished prayer in Mark requesting his *Abba* to take away the cup of suffering if that was at all possible (Mark 14:36). The unhappy camper-turned-gospel writer has completely transformed Yeshua in this garden scene from the earlier gospels' tragic and anguished Messiah to a triumphant, glorious savior, who has no fear in the face of death, a death he has nonchalantly and confidently accepted as the will of his Father. This indeed is the glorious Yeshua that GU-John had in mind and sought to portray in contrast to GU-Mark's tragic Messiah.

Thus, we can say that GU-John significantly changed the form and message of what is arguably the original "gospel" genre from GU-Mark. His image of Yeshua is not the tragic protagonist we find in the earlier, arguably original form of the gospel but rather a triumphantly glorious and divine figure. Although the Fourth Gospel's Yeshua also suffers and dies, his being lifted up on the cross is, as we have seen, understood rather as a glorification (John 12:23) and, unlike Mark's tragic Messiah, John's Yeshua does not show indecision, worry, or fear. This glorious Yeshua is always sure of himself; he knows everyone and everything; his death does not come because of circumstances beyond his control; it is the very outcome of giving up his life willingly for his sheep (John 10:18). GU-John's Yeshua is, without doubt, a majestically triumphant Messiah.

GU-Mark's tragedy was certainly designed to create an emotional response of pathos in his audience, a response in which "pity and fear and compassion are essential"[16] when one beholds the suffering and tragedy-laden Yeshua who in turn symbolizes the tragic aspects of human life. On the other hand, GU-John's very different retelling of Yeshua's story as glorious, seemingly unaffected by the horror of the cross, makes us wonder why GU-John wanted to change GU-Mark's tragic Messiah?

PEERING BEHIND THE TEXT: THE EXCOMMUNICATED MYSTIC

Ruprecht seems a bit harsh in his evaluation of GU-John's portrayal of Yeshua. He reflects that in changing Yeshua's portrayal from tragic to glorious, GU-John subverted GU-Mark's compassion-inspiring Messiah with a more grandiose, dominating and awe-and-fear-inspiring figure that would eventually have a lot to do with Christianity developing into a "line-drawing, border-defining, heresy-hunting religiosity that became even more violent when it attained imperial power in Rome."[17]

I have to say though that I do sympathize with Ruprecht's comment: I find GU-Mark's tragic Messiah a beautiful depiction of Yeshua. More importantly, I agree with Ruprecht that a tragic Messiah, rather than GU-John's glorious, divine one, might be more helpful to foster compassion and respond more properly to the pain of the world. At the same time, I feel I cannot leave the Gospel of John without trying harder to look at it again through the eyes of compassion that I learned from GU-Mark and do my utmost best to probe for GU-John's human face and the possible experience behind the text. When I do so (and I hope it is the same for you, readers), scales fall, as it were, from my eyes and I actually see the pathos of GU-John and his community coming to the fore.

The world behind John's text actually suggests a community that might have been living in fear and facing great odds. GU-John's community seemed to have been driven out of the synagogue ("excommunicated"!) apparently because their so-called "high Christological beliefs" were seen

16. Ruprecht, *This Tragic Gospel*, 7–8.

17. Ruprecht, *This Tragic Gospel*, 5.

to compromise conventional Jewish monotheism.[18] By "high Christology," scholars usually mean a view of Yeshua that tends toward portraying him more as divine than human. In a Roman empire that was not too accepting of "new" faiths, being deprived of some measure of inclusion in Judaism (respected even by the Romans because of its antiquity) exposed the Johannine community to the peril of marginalization and persecution. To cope with this apparent danger, it needed to develop a strong inner coherence. This historical situation can account for John's preoccupation with Yeshua's identity and his apparent anti-Jewish attitudes that are depicted in the Gospel. This also changes my reaction from dislike to compassion for the struggles of the Johannine community which dealt with this suffering by laying claim to a Yeshua who could not show any weakness and is firm in his repudiation of his enemies, often troublingly just called "the Jews." This apparently strong, even gruff (to his adversaries) kind of Yeshua is arguably GU-John's community's effort to encourage itself in the face of adversity. Thus, I realize that pathos is actually present in the whole human condition. Sometimes, it just takes more effort to see it.

THE FOURTH GOSPEL'S HOSTILITY TOWARD ADVERSARIES

The Fourth Gospel has been frequently cited as quite harsh to the group it calls in Greek *ioudaioi*. This is a plural form in the Greek (the singular is: masculine *ioudaios*, feminine *ioudaia*) and it is still commonly translated into English as "the Jews."[19] There is a movement to stop translating this term as "Jews" and to use instead the term "Judeans" which refers to the people of the southern part of Palestine in Yeshua's day. Thus, one can avoid a general anti-Jewish sentiment. But since "the Jews" has had such a long history in English usage as the translation used for *ioudaioi*, let me continue using it here to make my point without prejudice to the valid arguments of those who favor "Judeans" as the better way to translate the term.

The term "the Jews" is used sixteen times in Mark but a whopping seventy-one times in John, many of them with a negative, hostile meaning. In fact, "the Jews" in John are so identified with unbelieving hostility

18. The term *aposunagōgos* (Gk. Literally "excluded from the sacred assembly/synagogue" or, more commonly, "excommunicated") is found in John 9:22; 12:42; 16:2. For more information, see also Brown, *Community of the Beloved Disciple*, 66–69; Lincoln, *Gospel according to St. John*, 82–89; Casey, *Is John's Gospel True?*, 111–39.

19. For a more detailed explanation of the different nuances of *ioudaioi* and the various issues related with translating it, confer Garroway, "Ioudaios."

toward Yeshua and his message that early Christianity scholar Elaine Pagels can claim that John tells Yeshua's story as a cosmic conflict between light and darkness, between Yeshua's followers and the sinful opposition of the offspring of Satan, the latter being identified with "the Jews" (see John 8:44). In short, the Jews in John, according to the same Pagels, are a symbol of "all evil."[20]

New Testament scholar Maurice Casey actually makes John's anti-Jewish character a major reason for rejecting it as a distortion of the nature of Yeshua's person and message.[21] Theologian Rosemary Radford Ruether states that in the Gospel of John, "the philosophical incorporation of anti-Judaic midrash reaches its highest development in the New Testament." According to her, *the proclamation of Yeshua as divine demanded, as foil, a group that would reject the claim.* That group is what the Gospel of John calls "the Jews." Rejection of Yeshua's messianic claims and his divinity by this group becomes, as it were, "the left hand of Christology."[22] From these disturbing remarks from scholars, one can readily understand then the reason why James Carroll, in his popular history of the relation of the church with the Jews, has this sobering conclusion: "Christology itself is a source of Christian contempt for the Jews."[23]

It behooves us then to put the Fourth Gospel's relationship to the Jews in a better perspective. The first factor to note is that John's pejorative reference to the enemies of Yeshua as "the Jews" *must be firmly set against the background of*—what we showed above as—*the Johannine community's adversarial relationship with the synagogue.* To elaborate further, the community seemed to have been in some way estranged or excommunicated from the synagogue[24] sometime before the Gospel was written, apparently for its placing Yeshua, identified as the "Logos" (the "Word"), in as close an association as possible with YHWH ("the Father" in John). This had, in the final analysis, put the community outside of the acceptable parameters

20. Pagels, *Origin of Satan*, 105. This statement has to be tempered by the acknowledgment that not all uses of the term "the Jews" are unilaterally negative in the fourth gospel. Indeed, in some cases, there is evidence of a more divided response to Jesus, not excluding an "initially positive response" (see, for example, 8:31; 10:19–21; 11:45; 12:9) as observed by Lincoln in *Gospel according to St. John*, 71. See also Anderson, *Riddles of the Fourth Gospel*, 38–39, to see the whole range of uses (positive, neutral and negative) of the term "the Jews."

21. Casey, *Is John's Gospel True?*, 2, 223–29.

22. Ruether, *Faith and Fratricide*, 111.

23. Carroll, *Constantine's Sword*, 102.

24. The term *aposunagōgos* (Gk. Literally "excluded from the sacred assembly/synagogue" or, more commonly, "excommunicated") is found in John 9:22; 12:42; 16:2.

of Jewish monotheistic faith.[25] In that light, one can see that the term "the Jews" has both a historical and symbolic meaning. Historically, it refers to the hostile religious leaders of Palestinian Judaism (many of whom were located in the territory called Judaea) who had a direct hand in the persecution and death of Yeshua, hence the suggestion to translate *ioudaioi* as "the Judaeans."

We should keep in mind though that *symbolically* "the Jews" in John *does not primarily refer to Jewishness as such but rather to unbelieving hostility* on the part of persons or groups who refuse to believe in what GU-John's community proclaimed about Yeshua. In Christian history though the term has unfortunately invited anti-Jewish sentiments and has been the cause of countless terrible acts committed against Jews. When the original context of its use is firmly kept in mind, it becomes clear that the term *does not refer to all Jewish people*. One can even argue that GU-John extends it to include Christian dissidents as when mention is made for example in John 8:31 of Jews "who had believed" in Yeshua.[26]

Let me talk briefly here as a Christian theologian. When one attempts to situate this theme of "John and the Jews" in the context of Christian discipleship—that is, knowing and following Christ and how such a discipleship should help people to continue a process of lifelong and continuous conversion by learning to love others in a more universal way, *one realizes keenly that GU-John's text does seem to have problems in its attitude toward its adversaries*. This is a serious charge that has to be answered in a more satisfactory way.

There are indications that somewhere along the way in GU-John's community, true faith in Yeshua came to mean that one had also to accept certain "doctrines" about Yeshua (for example, his being the "Logos," his being one with the Father, etc.) deemed to be correct teaching in the community. Theologian Donald Gelpi even suggests that in GU-John's community, heterodoxy (incorrect belief) forced the community to realize that "doctrinal beliefs give definite shape to religious practices," that "the deed of faith . . . encompasses not just Christian moral striving but doctrinal assent as well" and that "Christian orthopraxis expands to include Christian orthodoxy."[27] However, even if we grant the above, the crucial question is: Does that make hostility toward adversaries, who do not believe what the Johannine community believed, right and justifiable? If we answer "yes," then the next

25. Again, see Brown, *Community of the Beloved Disciple*, 66–69, and Lincoln, *Gospel according to St. John*, 82–89.

26. NRSV translation. See also Brown, *Community of the Beloved Disciple*, 78–81.

27. Gelpi, *Firstborn of Many*, 50–51.

burning question is: Is this attitude not the root of the pernicious principle, "Error has no rights"?

INSIGHTS FROM THE SOCIAL SCIENCES

These questions could very well be posing interrogatives in an anachronistic way and, therefore, unfairly. Biblical scholars who use the social sciences in their research have pointed out that, in the Mediterranean world of the early Christians, vigorous debating between individuals or groups with opposing views was a fairly common cultural practice rooted in the concepts of honor and shame. To contemporary Western sensitivities though, these debates can seem to be an extremely offensive process of insulting one another. Those debates/arguments between individuals or groups involved a challenge from one and a corresponding response by the challenged party. Those dynamics were necessary in order to preserve or enhance the honor of one's clan or to avoid shame for one's group of affiliation. The hostility that we find in the Fourth Gospel toward its adversaries might have been a part of such dynamics which seem so offensive to us now but were more acceptable in that world as part of the encounters of daily social life.[28]

Besides, the world of first-century Judaism was immensely complex and diversified. There were many groups within Judaism and practically all of them were, as it were, jostling with each other as to which was the best way to live out the covenant with the one God of Israel.[29] The conflicts of the early Christian communities (among which can be traced the genesis of GU-John's community) with its opponents must be seen against this background. The conflicts between those who believed in Yeshua and the larger Jewish community which rejected this claim, were, at the earliest stage, intra-Jewish affairs. Seen in the context of the wider Roman Empire, Judaism was a "licit" religion. Being a part of a recognized religion (although perhaps also marginalized in some ways like the earliest Christian communities) gave one's group some measure of legitimacy in the empire's overall social structure. GU-John's community should be situated in this context so that its polemic against its adversaries may be understood better.

28. Consult, for example, Plevnik, "Honor/Shame," 106–15. See also the sections on Challenge and Riposte in Malina and Rohrbaugh, *Social-Science Commentary on the Gospel of John*, 146–51.

29. For further reading on this matter, I suggest Chilton and Neusner, *Judaism in the New Testament*, particularly, chapter 1. Also Shanks, *Christianity and Rabbinic Judaism*, particularly, chapters 1, 4, and 9. A succinct survey can also be found in Harris, "Diverse World of First-Century Judaism."

The harshness with which GU-John's text addresses its adversaries somehow betrays the deep anxiety and fierce anger of his community at being expelled from a recognized and licit religion.[30] We can see then that the small Johannine community was fighting for its survival against the bigger and long recognized institution of the synagogue. In such a fight, harsh polemics on the part of the "weakling" (originally, the Johannine community) would not have done huge damage to the stronger party (the synagogue).

But that is not all there is to this matter. GU-John and his community could never have foreseen what happened later on in Christian history. Fast forward to the late-300s of the common era and all that changed when, under the Emperor Theodosius, Christianity became the official religion of the Roman Empire after his predecessor Emperor Constantine turned it almost overnight from a persecuted sect to Rome's favored religion. When that shift happened, words that were once uttered by a small insignificant community (i.e., GU-John's Yeshua-followers) against a larger, more established one (Judaism—the synagogue) were now "canonized" as part of the sacred scriptures of a powerful imperial church. This development had deadly consequences for the named adversaries—the Jews. That started what would become in time Christianity's long history of a deep anti-Jewish attitude which would occasionally rear its ugly head in the form of horrible atrocities against individual Jews and their communities down through the ages, culminating in Hitler's "final solution," which can arguably be considered the apex of anti-Jewish sentiments in history.

CONCLUSION

GU-John, writing toward the end the first century, is the spiritual ancestor who suggests more strongly than others that Yeshua was a unique embodiment of the One God and thus was to be identified as closely as possible with the divine being Israel knew as YHWH. How did he reach this conclusion? I suggest that he did through his own deep spirituality which I have referred to here as "mysticism." GU-John's mysticism and its conclusion did not sit well though with the Jewish community and led to him and his community being excommunicated, that is, thrown out of the synagogue.

Of course, Yeshua, the Christ, being an embodiment of Israel's God is a strand of thought found elsewhere in the New Testament. We have mentioned GU-Matthew calling Yeshua "Emmanuel" ("God-with-us"). GU-Paul also describes Yeshua as the "image of God" in several places in letters he wrote or in those attributed to him. However, we can say that it

30. Gelpi, *Firstborn of Many*, 107.

was GU-John who identified Yeshua most closely with Yahweh to the point that he could be acknowledged in this gospel by lofty statements such as: "the Word was God" (John 1:1), "one with the Father" (10:30), and even "My Lord and my God!" (20:28). Thus, in his story, GU-John sought to present the Yeshua walking the dusty roads of Palestine and living on this earth as something like an exalted divine being-come to "dwell among us" (1:14) although he was also human at the same time; an exalted messiah who knew everything that was going to happen to him (18:4) and as one who freely lay down his life (10:17) to "draw all things" to himself (12:32).

Furthermore, what makes GU-John's story so crucially important for the Christian tradition is that it is precisely this narrative that can act as the most direct springboard for us to see how Christianity as a whole and its institutional embodiment called "the Church" later on came to formally define their christological belief: Yeshua or (to revert to his more familiar Western name) Jesus *is* God-incarnate (the teaching is officially known as the "incarnation"). This teaching became the very centerpiece Christianity's institutional creed. That development in turn accounts for the fact that Jesus becomes the hero-archetype, the savior-archetype par excellence in Western culture and even in contemporary pop culture as can be seen in Harry Potter, Frodo Baggins, even Superman (among many others) who arguably are all Christ-figures.

10

Saul-Paul: From Persecutor to Apostle

Everyone Is "One in Christ"

There is no longer Jew or Greek, there is no longer slave or free, there is no longer male and female; for all of you are one in Christ Jesus.

—Paul of Tarsus[1]

Paul was not simply a mystic . . . he was a *Jewish Christ mystic*. . . because [he] was a Jew and in his own mind never ceased being one; . . . because the content of his mystical experiences was Jesus as risen Christ and Lord. Afterward, Paul's identity became an identity "in Christ." And as a Christ mystic, he saw his Judaism anew in the light of Jesus.[2]

YOUNG SAUL AND HIS GREAT AWAKENING

This chapter is about a spiritual ancestor-author who did not write a gospel in the strict sense like the others we've already met so far. However, he has a very large presence in the New Testament village because of the

1. Gal 3:28.
2. Borg and Crossan, *First Paul*, 26.

many letters that bear his name and also because he is arguably the one mainly responsible for making the movement that began with Yeshua more open to non-Jews, that is, more, shall we say, "gentile-friendly." That, in turn, resulted in Christianity eventually developing into a world religion, no small feat for a movement that began humbly in an obscure part of the Roman empire among peasant Jews. We are referring of course to another vitally important spiritual ancestor, granduncle Paul, the apostle. "Saul" was his Jewish name and GU-Luke's use of two names in the Acts of the Apostles to refer to this ancestor gives us the impression that he was known as "Saul" before his conversion and "Paul" after that, but this usage is probably a stylistic distinction on the part of GU-Luke to accentuate the great change that happened to this fascinating New Testament character. It is more accurate to say that the apostle, who was raised outside Palestine in the Jewish diaspora, had two names from the very beginning, a reflection of his diaspora Jewish identity.[3]

To further add to his prominence and fame, granduncle Paul's life is particularly intriguing because he began as a furious persecutor of the early Yeshua movement. If we go by the famous accounts in the Acts of the Apostles, at a certain point in GU-Paul's life, he did as it were a 180-degree change of direction after a dramatic event "on the road to Damascus" in which he encountered the Risen One who commissioned him to bring the good news about Yeshua himself to "the nations" (that is, the gentiles).

I'm convinced that understanding the nature of this experience is the absolute key to grasping GU-Paul and all he said and did. It is the *sine qua non* writ large. Hence, I will begin by suggesting a possible interpretation of the famous so-called conversion experience of GU-Paul. GU-Paul's encounter with the risen Christ (see Gal 2:15–16; Acts 9:1–19) was an experience that is, firstly, similar and comparable to various religious-spiritual experiences across cultures and throughout history. Through it, he touched—what various spiritual practitioners say is—the authentic, deeper, non-dual (or unitive) nature of reality. Hence, this pivotal event was a profound epiphany, enlightenment or awakening experience by which GU-Paul was shown that everyone and everything are interconnected and can even be considered as "one" that is, enveloped and encompassed by a gracious transcendent reality commonly known as God. In GU-Paul's case, however, he understood that God, as well as the oneness of everyone and everything in this divine being, happens "in Christ" (another very typical Pauline expression. See, for example, Gal 3:28). That is, the cosmic unity of everyone and everything in God happens through the mediation of the chosen one—Yeshua, the Christ.

3. Brown, *Introduction to the New Testament*, 423.

THE PRE-DAMASCUS PAUL: REACTING TO A PERCEIVED TRANSGRESSION?

GU-Paul is introduced to readers in the New Testament as "Saul," a persecutor of fellow Jews in Jerusalem who were following "the Way" of Yeshua (Acts 19:23) because they considered him the Christ, the chosen One of God (Acts 8:3). This is corroborated by GU-Paul's own testimony in Philippians 3:6. Here, he calls his action of persecuting the church "zeal." Zeal for what, we might ask? We can surmise that GU-Paul perceived that the new way that believers in Yeshua were propounding and living was a kind of transgression of GU-Paul's understanding and interpretation of his beloved Jewish tradition. They were introducing an element into the tradition that, for him, was a falsehood, perhaps even an aberration.

We can assume that the earliest groups of Yeshua-followers were proclaiming that "God [had] made [Jesus, who was crucified] both Lord and Messiah" (Acts 2:36). Of course, GU-Paul, at this early stage, vehemently disagreed with that for many reasons. One could have been the commonsensical Jewish idea that someone seemingly accursed by God (because he was "hung on a tree"; cf. Deut 21:23) could not be the chosen one of God. Besides, there is a strong indication that Yeshua's ministry (in word and deed), although fundamentally a movement to renew Israel for the coming of God's reign, went against a number of prominent, authoritative, and mainline first-century Jewish interpretations on how to live Israel's covenant with God. We know from his own reference that the pre-conversion Saul belonged to the Pharisee party (cf. Phil 3:5; also Acts 23:6) and, since there is quite a significant number of gospel stories that clearly show the differences and arguments between Yeshua and the Pharisees, we can again reasonably conclude that the young Saul objected to what Yeshua and his followers taught, did, and stood for, on a number of important issues.

THE CONTEXT OF THESE INTRA-JEWISH DIFFERENCES

The first-century Jewish world in which Yeshua and his immediate followers (among whom was GU-Paul) lived, was characterized by great diversity: Different Jewish groups coexisted with one another in all their different ways of understanding and interpreting how best to live as a covenant people of the God of Israel. One major strand of thinking attributed Israel's painful historical experiences of and domination by various empires to the belief that God had allowed these historical disasters to befall the chosen people because of its sins and infidelity to the covenant.[4] In response to that, some prominent and influential groups, such as the Pharisees (GU-Paul's original group of affiliation according to Phil 3:5), insisted on a more conscientious observance of all the stipulations of an expanded version of the Law ("written" and "oral" Law) in daily life for the purpose of remaining truly faithful to God and to better safeguard Jewish identity. One unfortunate result of this was probably some stratification of the society according to levels of observance because of the insistence of groups such as the Pharisees of the importance of fulfilling "expanded" conditions of the Law, ultimately in order to be more properly considered "holy as God is holy" (Lev 19:2).[5] Biblical scholar James Charlesworth even comments, "as the requirements for purity were increased, the ability of the average religious Jew to remain pure decreased."[6]

In Yeshua's thoroughly religion-imbued social world, one dominant and authoritative way of understanding what it meant to be a covenant people of YHWH was an effort to have "additional regulations . . . to observe the Torah and apply it to the whole of life."[7] This stricter understanding and lifestyle were espoused by Pharisees and Essenes among others. We should also add though that a significant majority of the people at the time understandably could not observe all the additional stipulations proposed by these more rigorously observant groups.[8]

It is fair to say that Yeshua and the movement around him probably tried to shift the emphasis from this influential and even authoritative interpretation of what it meant to be a covenant people (focused on fulfilling conscientiously the stipulations of the expanded version of the Law to be holy like God), to a different paradigm, one that put the accent instead on God's compassion embracing everyone (particularly, those considered sinners, outcasts, the unworthy, etc.) with the consequent view that imitating God's radically compassionate inclusivity was, for Yeshua and his followers, *the better way* to be holy as God is holy.[9] In the Gospels, there are

4. Also known as "the Deuteronomistic history."

5. Borg, *Meeting Jesus Again for the First Time*, 46–61.

6. Charlesworth, *Historical Jesus*, 109.

7. Casey, *Jesus*, 319.

8. Casey, *From Jewish Prophet to Gentile God*, 17–20.

9. Of course, "holy" and "compassionate" were not mutually exclusive concepts even in first-century Judaism. What I refer to here though is the particular stress, either on "observance" or "a more welcoming and compassionate inclusion." See, for example, Matt 5:43–48; also, Luke 6:36: "Be merciful, just as your Father is merciful." See also Borg, *Meeting Jesus*, 50–58. For greater detail, see Borg, *Conflict, Holiness and Politics in the Teachings of Jesus*, particularly chapters 4 and 5. I am well aware that there are

many deeds and teachings of Yeshua that underline the principle, "I desire mercy not sacrifice" (e.g., Matt 9:13, echoing Hos 6:6). This emphasis was apparently continued by the earliest followers of Yeshua in the wake of their experience of the resurrection. That could have been a major factor why Yeshua and the movement around him rubbed GU-Saul, the Pharisee,[10] in the wrong way and prompted him to be committed to eliminating this troubling new group.

THE "CONVERSION" EVENT

Thus, we encounter a young man in the Acts of the Apostles who was trying to stamp out the movement centered on Yeshua of Nazareth as the risen Messiah. There, the young Saul is portrayed as "breathing out murderous threats against the Lord's disciples" (Acts 9:1). This gives us the impression that he was probably obsessed with clamping down on the new movement (as the incident involving the death of the Yeshua-follower Stephen shows). It is at the height of Saul's effort to purge his Jewish world of followers of Yeshua's Way when he has a life-changing religious experience.

The Acts of the Apostles describes the event in very dramatic ways. That has made Luke's story the established and most beloved account of GU-Paul's so-called conversion. According to this retelling in Acts 9, Saul, in his zeal to seek out Yeshua's followers, asks the high priest for permission to arrest such people in Damascus. As he was on the road to Damascus, a light flashes around him and he is dramatically addressed by a mysterious voice: "Saul, Saul, why do you persecute me?" (Acts 9:4). Thus, he encounters the risen Yeshua who identifies with the people Saul is persecuting. Saul is then directed to go to Damascus where he is healed of his temporary blindness and baptized by a disciple named Ananias. It is to this Ananias that Yeshua reveals his plan to make Saul "the instrument to bring [his] name before the Gentiles" (Acts 9:15). That is the most well-known version of Saul's conversion. This is not the place to discuss its historical merits,

important objections to Borg's portrayal of Jesus's social context in this regard. For example, Paula Fredriksen, "Compassion-Is-to-Purity-as-Fish-Is-to-Bicycle," 55–67; also Thiessen, *Jesus and the Forces of Death*, 9. These objections have to be kept in mind. I still think though that what I have stated, at least in the main text above, is still an important factor to understand the social worlds of Jesus and Paul. See also Sanders, *Jesus and Judaism*, particularly chapters 9 and 10.

10. An important recent resource on the topic of Paul as Pharisee is Fredriksen, "Paul, the Perfectly Righteous Pharisee," 112–35.

but we have good reason to think that GU-Luke probably embellished the account in significant ways.[11]

In contrast to that famous story, the more mature GU-Paul himself, later on in his authentic letters, is unfortunately and disappointingly more reticent and abstract in his references to this so-called conversion event. Galatians 1:15–16 says:

> But when God, who had set me apart before I was born and called me through his grace, was pleased to reveal his Son to me, so that I might proclaim him among the Gentiles.

Notice that there are no flashing lights or spiritual voices. Analyzed soberly, these are descriptions of, what we can say are, how GU-Paul understood or interpreted the experience (whatever its real nature was) that he had years after the event. Hence, I think that there is quite a lot of wiggle room for how we could interpret the world behind the text of GU-Paul's references to his conversion (as paradigm shift), as well as the world behind the text of GU-Luke's more famous, probably embellished story in Acts 9 (and elsewhere).[12]

A SPECIAL CALL ACCOMPANIED BY A PARADIGM SHIFT

What GU-Paul experienced "on the road to Damascus"[13] is usually referred to by Christians as a "conversion" experience. I strongly feel that "conversion" may not be the best way to describe what GU-Paul went through because this term has been frequently understood wrongly as the young Saul converting from Judaism to Christianity. This traditional view mirrors more the convictions of reformation-era Christians rather than first-century history.

The historical reality was that GU-Paul *never* abandoned his Jewish faith. Rather, he had a seismic shift in perspective, but *always as a Jew.* He underwent a transformation from viewing Yeshua and his Way as perhaps some kind of cancer to be excised from the community of Israel, to realizing that *Yeshua was in fact the One designated by the Divine as the climax of the covenant* between God and Israel. What did that imply? For GU-Paul, God

11. On this question, see, for example, Pervo, *Mystery of Acts*, 151–56.

12. A good collection of essays on Paul's conversion is Longenecker, *Road from Damascus*.

13. I will continue to use "on the road to Damascus" here only for sentimental reasons. Some scholars doubt whether it even happened "on the road" to Damascus. The expression, however, has a classical status.

now graciously willed to extend the covenant *fully* to everyone else through Yeshua, the Christ, thus fulfilling the promise made to Abraham long ago when God had declared that Abraham's descendants (Israel) were to be in time a blessing to the whole world (see Gen 12:3).[14] In more concrete terms, that meant that, now, even the Gentiles could, through Christ, be members of God's people. Thus, everyone is "one in Christ."

In this way, GU-Paul's experience might be better described as a "calling" combined with a "paradigm shift" (among other possible terms). Just like the prophets of old were called to a new phase of life in order to perform a special mission, GU-Paul felt himself called to be the herald of God's radical opening of the covenant to those who hitherto had not fully partaken of its blessings—the gentiles.[15]

GU-Paul's so-called "conversion" or "calling" is also frequently described as a religious experience. In fact, one can properly call it GU-Paul's own religious experience of the risen Christ (see 1 Cor 15:8–10), better yet, the "cosmic" Christ. New Testament scholars Marcus Borg and John Dominic Crossan refer to GU-Paul as a "Jewish Christ mystic"[16] in order to heighten the aspect of religious experience with regard to what he went through "on the road to Damascus" (again, whatever the nature of that experience was).

WHAT IS RELIGIOUS EXPERIENCE?

For the purpose of analyzing GU-Paul's experience properly, we should start with the most basic category by asking: What exactly is the nature of religious experience? Applied to GU-Paul, I want to ask further: Can we take GU-Luke's famous story in the Acts of the Apostles of an apparent apparition of the risen, cosmic Christ to GU-Paul literally, as most Christians have done throughout history? Or is that already an embellished *interpretation* of the event? There is definitely a need to re-contextualize GU-Paul's conversion story in a wider field, a contextualization that takes more serious consideration of sociological, anthropological, cultural, and even psychological studies. In line with that, even a cursory study of more contemporary accounts of religious experience that attempt to be more impartial, more objectively faithful to what has been experienced, and less embellished by concrete religious symbolism and images from a specific tradition (such as

14. Wright and Bird, *New Testament in Its World*, 379–81.

15. See this succinct explanation of the new perspective on Paul: Lopez, "New Perspective on Paul."

16. Borg and Crossan, *First Paul*, 19.

Christianity), seems to suggest one common denominator running through different so-called religious or mystical experiences across different historical epochs and traditions: the overcoming of the duality between self and others (i.e., *nonduality*) and a more heightened *unitive* awareness of the universe.[17]

Take the following account of a spiritual experience from New Testament scholar Marcus Borg as a case in point:

> They (my religious experiences) were moments (sometimes lasting for minutes) in which all of our categories (such as beautiful/ugly . . . interesting/boring . . .) fell away. Everything looked exquisite. Everything looked clear. I felt like I was seeing things as they actually are . . . It seemed like an experience of God . . . My longest and most vivid experience happened on a plane flight two years ago. My wife and I were flying from Tel Aviv to New York, on our way home after leading a pilgrimage group to Israel. About half way across the Atlantic, I became aware of the bright daylight in the cabin subtly beginning to change. *Everything began to look exquisitely beautiful and precious*; the fabric on the seatback in front of me, the faces of the passengers around me (including a man whom earlier in the flight I had thought of as the ugliest man I had ever seen—even he looked beautiful), the food that was placed before me, the sunlight and clouds outside the window.
>
> My cheeks were wet with tears. For about 45 minutes, *I experienced peace, beauty and joy; everything looked so lovely and I loved everything*. There were strong intimations of mortality, with some sadness, but no anxiety. I felt immense gratitude simply for the experience of being. I knew that I wanted to remember, forever, how the world looked in that state, and how I felt about being alive in those minutes.[18]

Here is another religious experience from the famous Trappist monk Thomas Merton:

> In Louisville, at the corner of Fourth and Walnut, in the center of the shopping district, I was suddenly overwhelmed with the

17. In the same vein, Rankin cuts to the chase when she concludes in her comprehensive survey of spiritual experience that the underlying message of all spiritual-religious experiences is "above all, [love] for each other" (Rankin, *Introduction to Religious and Spiritual Experience*, 257).

18. Borg, "When Heaven and Earth Meet," 4–5. Also Borg, *Days of Awe and Wonder*, 29–30. Emphases are mine.

> realization that I loved all those people, that they were mine and I theirs, that we could not be alien to one another even though we were total strangers. It was like *waking from a dream of separateness, of spurious self-isolation* in a special world, the world of renunciation and supposed holiness . . . This sense of liberation from an illusory difference was such a relief and such a joy to me that I almost laughed out loud . . . I have the immense joy of being man, a member of a race in which God Himself became incarnate. As if the sorrows and stupidities of the human condition could overwhelm me, now I realize what we all are. And if only everybody could realize this! But it cannot be explained. There is no way of telling people that they are all walking around *shining like the sun*."[19]

I doubt if we could ever formulate a meta-theory of religious experience from a measly sampling of a few concrete religious experiences. Elaborate discussions about the very nature of religious and/or mystical experience have been going on in the academy and the wider public for a long time now and that should be examined more thoroughly for one to get a better picture. I can just note for the purposes of this study that there is no sure way to base a "big truth" such as the existence of God on the testimony of religious experience itself.[20] Let me also express my strong support for the hypothesis that when religious experiences are stripped down to their most basic and fundamental level, what we have seems to be the experience of nonduality or unity. That is, the barriers between the ego and the other are blurred, transgressed, crossed, and transcended. This is why mystics see everyone and everything as beautiful, full of light, and basically one. As a result of that, the person who has had a heightened religious experience acquires something like a pure, all-inclusive, and magnanimous love for everyone and everything, even one's enemies. This last statement is particularly important as a lens to view GU-Paul's experience. Of course, this is not a novel theory. It is routinely proposed in the area of religious studies with such names as "the common core thesis in the study of mysticism"[21] which contends that mystical experience is ultimately the experience of "an ultimate non-sensuous unity of all things."[22]

19. Merton, *Conjectures of a Guilty Bystander*, 140–42. Emphasis is mine.

20. See, for example, the extensive discussion of this in *Encyclopedia of Philosophy*, "Religious Experience."

21. Hood, "Common Core Thesis in the Study of Mysticism."

22. Stace, *Teachings of the Mystics*, 13.

THE GENERAL VAGUENESS AND UNCLARITY OF RELIGIOUS EXPERIENCES

Another crucial point I would like to suggest here is that one major understanding of religious experience is that it "in itself . . . is neither theistic nor pantheistic, Christian nor Buddhist."[23] All these distinctions are *interpretations* of the experience. By itself, "religious experience testifies to something *far less definite* but still infinitely valuable—the insufficiency of all materialisms and naturalisms."[24] In short, many (most?) religious experiences are, it seems, more general than specific (i.e., a general perception of the unity of everything in the Divine), oftentimes even vague and in need of interpretation by the subject of the experience itself.

The *Stanford Dictionary of Philosophy* cuts to the chase about this matter when it declares this about religious experience in general: "The concept is vague."[25] Of course, this remark refers to *the concept* of religious experience itself. It is still possible that the subjects of particular religious experiences (like GU-Paul) come to believe that their experiences were clear and specific and not just a general and indefinite experience of nonduality or unity.

I would nuance that claim of clarity in the following terms: In most cases, it is difficult to differentiate between the religious experience itself and the interpretation that a subject has of it. When a subject describes the given religious experience, do they describe the experience itself without embellishment? This is almost an impossible feat because religious experiences, in William James's classical description, are by nature ineffable.[26] Or is the very description itself already an interpretation, that is, the subject has already imposed upon the original experience some categories and symbolisms that they carry from their personal context? This latter idea is more likely in my opinion.

A corollary of the suggested general unclarity, indefiniteness, and vagueness of religious experience is that it necessitates interpretation on the part of the subject of the experience. I agree with the suggestion that the interpretation of the experience will depend very much on the personal contexts of the subject.[27] In practical terms, the subject will always understand and interpret what is actually a more general, vague/nonspecific, or unitive/nondual experience in terms of their accumulated experiences

23. Hepburn, "Religious Experience."

24. Hepburn, "Religious Experience." Emphasis mine.

25. Webb, "Religious Experience."

26. See also Marcus Borg, *Days of Awe and Wonder*, 31.

27. Katz, "Language, Epistemology and Mysticism," 22–74.

which are often already rooted in a given tradition or in particular historical contexts. Hence, if the subject, for example, is a Christian, they will tend to interpret their nondual-unitive religious experience in Christian terms so they might explain an experience as God showing them how everyone is united in the love of Yeshua. Here is a case in point from English mystic Caryll Houselander:

> I was in an underground train, a crowded train in which all sorts of people jostled together, sitting and strap-hanging-workers of every description going home at the end of the day. Quite suddenly I saw with my mind, but as vividly as a wonderful picture, Christ in them all. But I saw more than that: not only was Christ in every one of them, living in them, dying in them, rejoicing in them, sorrowing in them-but because He was in them, and because they were here, the whole world was here too, here in this underground train; not only the world as it was at that moment, not only all the people in all the countries of the world, but all those people who had been living in the past, and all those yet to come.
>
> I came out into the street and walked for a long time in the crowds. It was the same here, on every side, in every passer-by, everywhere-Christ.[28]

However, if the subject of the religious experience were a Buddhist, they would have probably seen, instead of Jesus Christ, the Buddha (or the Buddha-nature) that is perceived to be present in everyone and everything.[29]

WHAT THEN WAS THE NATURE OF GRANDUNCLE PAUL'S SPIRITUAL EXPERIENCE?

If we apply the above-mentioned points to GU-Paul's "Road to Damascus" experience, let me suggest that what he had was a tremendous, life-changing nondual-unitive experience analogous to the many accounts of religious experience that we know across cultures, traditions, and historical eras. Hence, this zealous young Pharisee, who was out to stamp out the new movement that, he was convinced, was a serious misinterpretation of Israel's sacred tradition, was caught up in an experience that gave him a glimpse of the fundamental nonduality and unity of all creation. As with most religious

28. Houselander, *Rocking-Horse Catholic*, 137–38.

29. See also Jensen, "Experience," 697–701.

experiences, however, I opine that the experience itself was a more generalized and nonspecific yet marvelous nondual-unitive experience (in a similar way to that which Marcus Borg or Thomas Merton described above).

However, since GU-Paul was, at this moment, deeply into a concerted effort to persecute and extinguish, what he perceived as, "rogue" Jews, his interpretation of this nondual-unitive experience immediately took on a concrete form *specifically directed towards the objects of his animosity*. In other words, GU-Paul exclusively interpreted his religious experience in light of his hate of Yeshua's followers. Hence, in the Galatians 1 passage (which, arguably, is GU-Paul's own most explicit referral to the event), he interprets the experience to be God "revealing" to him the truth about the "Son" Yeshua, the Christ, for the purpose of commissioning him to eventually preach the opening up of the covenant in Christ to those who were hitherto excluded from it. For GU-Paul then, the Damascus experience of transgressing and transcending the barrier between himself and "the others," and seeing the nonduality and unity of everyone and everything, took the concrete form of concluding that the Yeshua-followers he hated, and more so, the Yeshua whom they followed, were actually the very agents of God's plan to bring the covenant to its climax—the salvation of everyone and everything in Christ.

In short, GU-Paul's vehement animosity toward Christ and the early Christian movement acted ironically as a negative spur for him to embrace the very Being (Yeshua) and the movement that he (Paul) had detested up until this point. It may be explained in terms of GU-Paul's effort to reduce the complicated "cognitive dissonance" that he felt about Christ and the Christian movement.[30] How did this come about in a concrete way? He must have been conflicted on the dissonance between his hate for Christ and his followers on the one hand, and the totally unexpected experience of pure, unconditional love for everyone and everything, on the other hand, that he was made to feel on the road to Damascus. How, he must have wondered, could he have been gifted with a beautiful vision that everyone is practically one in the gracious God when he was so full of hatred towards Yeshua and his followers? He concluded then that he was given this glimpse, (to use his own terms) this "revelation," because God had ordained that this very Yeshua, the Christ, whom he was persecuting was actually the means, the agent for bringing everyone and everything into unity with God, and that he (Paul) had an important part to play in order to extend this means to those who did not yet fully share in the covenant.

30. See, for example, the case for explaining Paul's conversion in terms of "cognitive dissonance." Togarasei, "Conversion of Paul in the Light of the Theory of Cognitive Dissonance," i/ii.

What is significant in GU-Paul's experience, however, is that he, I opine, interpretively combined a life-changing nondual-unitive experience with a vision of the risen Christ. Thus, I propose that one of the pillars of his theology—the notion of the cosmic Christ was born. This cosmic Christ is the "Lord" to whom "the name above every other name is given" (Phil 2:9). This is the one who reconciles everything in heaven and on earth (Rom 5:10; Col 1:20). This is the one through whom our sins are forgiven (Eph 1:7; Col 1:14), a figure that becomes God's special agent of salvation, a figure as omnipresent and powerful as YaHWeH.

EVERYTHING IS ONE "IN CHRIST"

We see this nondual-unitive experience fleshed out and reflected upon more maturely in parts of Paul's authentic letters. Anyone who has studied Paul even in a cursory way will know that one of his signature expressions, peppered throughout his letters, is the phrase "in Christ" (*en Kristō*). The most telling passage that expresses how Paul used this phrase is his famous manifesto in Gal 3:26–29:

> For in Christ Jesus you are *all children of God* through faith.
> As many of you as were baptized into Christ
> have clothed yourselves *with Christ.*
> *There is no longer Jew or Greek,*
> *there is no longer slave or free,*
> *there is no longer male and female;*
> for all of you are one in Christ Jesus.
> And if you *belong to Christ*, . . .

If we look at the central section of the quoted passage, GU-Paul declares that all earthly distinctions, which are of supreme importance to his own Jewish tradition, to the larger Roman empire, as well as to human culture in general, are blurred, transgressed, and transcended: There are no more divisions in terms of Jew or Greek, slave or free, man or woman. How is that transgression of divisions accomplished? GU-Paul's ready answer is "in Christ." The cosmic Christ was the principle of unity and oneness among people, no matter how different they were, humanly speaking, with others. This will be later reflected in the letter to the Colossians (1:15–17) (which bears Paul's name but was probably written by someone else in the Pauline school):

> He (Christ Jesus) is the image of the invisible God, the firstborn of all creation; for in him all things in heaven and on earth were created, things visible and invisible, whether thrones or

> dominions or rulers or powers—all things have been created through him and for him. He himself is before all things, and *in him all things hold together.*

Going back to the crucial Galatians passage, GU-Paul argues that if people are subsumed into Christ ("baptized into Christ," "clothed with Christ")—in other words, by virtue of incorporation into this great cosmic mystery called "Christ"—all divisions are transgressed and transcended and simply cease to be, because everyone virtually becomes "one in Christ."[31] In this way, we can see that GU-Paul made the risen and cosmic Christ his main strategy for everyone becoming one in God through Christ.

CONCLUSION

GU-Paul is known most for his being the apostle to the gentiles. He tirelessly labored so that more people, particularly those outside Israel, might come to the knowledge of Yeshua, the Christ, because in his life-changing encounter with the risen and cosmic Christ "on the road to Damascus," he glimpsed that everyone as well as everything was "one in Christ" (Gal 3:28). This was his version of what—in the Perennial Philosophy—is often called the unitive/non-dual spiritual experience of reality. This, I argue, is the *sine qua non* for us to grasp the essence of this particular spiritual ancestor.

GU-Paul might be considered the most important figure in Christianity next to Yeshua himself because, in his lifelong effort to make the way of Christ more gentile-friendly, he in effect laid the foundations that would eventually lead to Christianity becoming a world religion. Without the vision and labors of this spiritual ancestor, Christianity might have remained an obscure Jewish sect and never have become the largest and most numerous religious tradition that we know it to be today.

31. Borg and Crossan, *First Paul*, 110–11, 178–81.

11

The Great Founding Ancestor: Yeshua

Trying to Glimpse the Flesh-and-Blood Figure Behind the Icons

Without the historical study of Jesus, we risk losing the radical social-political vision of Jesus.

—Marcus Borg[1]

Jesus is a much-underrated man. When we deprive him of his humanity, we deprive him of his greatness.

—Albert Nolan[2]

INTRODUCTION: WHY DIG DEEPER TO SEE THE HISTORICAL YESHUA?

At the conclusion of our efforts to get to know our spiritual ancestors who, we claimed, continue to live in and teach us from the New Testament village, we have come back full circle to the great founding ancestor himself, Yeshua of Nazareth, the beginning of it all. Now it is time to ask: Can we go behind the narratives of the granduncles we encountered earlier to

1. Marcus Borg Foundation, "Battle over Jesus Today," 48:30.
2. Quoted in Borg, *Days of Awe and Wonder*, 122.

catch a revealing glimpse of who Yeshua was as a flesh-and-blood, historical person, as he walked the roads of Palestine two thousand years ago? At this point in our journey, who is not hoping to meet the "real" Yeshua that is free from the personal "takes," embellishments, biases or even agendas of the storyteller-ancestors and their communities?

This is a question of utmost importance for me. Some voices (even scholarly ones) say that it is irrelevant to engage in what is called "the quest for the historical Jesus" for various reasons. One, because they claim that we will never truly get back anyway to the figure of the historical Yeshua of Nazareth from the pages of the New Testament. The only thing we can realistically access from a study of the New Testament, according to this opinion, is the early Christian proclamation (in Greek, the *kerygma*) *about* Yeshua that our spiritual ancestors did, and *not* the historical figure of Yeshua himself.[3]

Another reason put forward is that the "real Yeshua" could never be the purported historical portraits put forward by scholars. Instead, the real Yeshua is the—let's go back briefly to his Western name—Jesus of Christian experience, and he is founded on and in continuity with the "canonical" Jesus. By "canonical," we mean the figure of Jesus that we can find in the New Testament writings of our spiritual ancestors. Taken at face value, this position says that you don't have to do anything further such as dig deeper into history to search for the historical figure of Yeshua, independent of the portrayals of Yeshua that granduncles Mark, Matthew, Luke, John, and Paul have done in their writings. Just be content with those accounts that they left us and have a spiritual relationship with Yeshua. In this way, a combination of the New Testament portraits of Yeshua, as well as you and your community's faith experience of him will in fact make you encounter the *real* Yeshua.[4] And how can we define the real Yeshua according to this line of thinking, one may ask? The real Yeshua is the one who, in an act of total obedience to the will of God, gave up his life in loving service of others.

Yes, I agree that the tradition about Yeshua found particularly in the Synoptic Gospels can give us a relatively good account of the main contours of the life, teaching, death, and resurrection of Yeshua. We can call this image the "characteristic" Yeshua.[5] Nevertheless, I do not agree with the above-mentioned positions that dismiss the importance of trying to "dig deeper" to get a clearer view of the historical Yeshua. As we have seen in our earlier

3. See, for example, Bultmann, *Jesus and the Word*, 14; and Bultmann, *History of the Synoptic Tradition*, 370. See also McIver, *Memory, Jesus, and the Synoptic Gospels*, 101.

4. Johnson, *Real Jesus*, 141–66.

5. Dunn, *New Perspective on Jesus*, 57–78.

efforts to get to know our storyteller-ancestors and their communities, their portrayals of Yeshua were deeply influenced and colored by their own worldviews and contexts. Hence, if it is possible at all to go further to get a glimpse of the flesh-and-blood figure at the root of all these later portrayals, I would definitely want to do that, seeing how much ground I have already covered in this quest!

There is even a more urgent reason why we need to seek the historical figure of this Yeshua, the great founding ancestor. This is wonderfully expressed by Marcus Borg in a talk he gave entitled "[The] Battles over Jesus Today."[6] There, Borg affirms the fact that when we carefully read and study the New Testament, we definitely get the message that Yeshua was the One who, in obedience to God, gave up his life in loving-service for others. That core message is certainly very important. However, *only a deeper probe into the historical Yeshua* will make so much clearer the fact that this first-century Jewish rabbi-healer had a passion for social justice, and it was that vision and action on his part that got him nailed to a Roman cross in the end! One major aim of digging deeper into the surface soil of our gospels would be to strike at the figure of a Yeshua who took a stand for the "reign of God" that was a scathing critique of the domination and oppressive systems of his day, even as it offered a vision of a state of wholeness (*shalom*) for everyone, especially those who were underprivileged and marginalized in that world. Only such a figure could rile the religious and political authorities to the extent of making them decide to put him away violently. Moreover, it is only such a figure of Yeshua that can resist being "domesticated" by the powers-that-be of every age, forces that would otherwise use his image to support agendas that are usually diametrically opposed to Yeshua's original vision. Thus, Yeshua should forever remain a "dangerous memory,"[7] one that makes every generation uncomfortable whenever we settle into the conventional, cozy standards of the status quo and forget the poor and oppressed ones that were so dear to the original Yeshua's heart.[8]

Having engaged in historical Jesus studies practically all my life as a scholar of the Bible and religion, I affirm that it is indeed possible to catch a glimpse, nay, actually a fairly good portrait of the historical figure behind the contextualized accounts of him by the storyteller-ancestors. Here are the modest fruits of my efforts.

6. Borg's response to Luke Timothy Johnson's position: Marcus Borg Foundation, "Battle over Jesus Today," 48:40.

7. This is a phrase made famous by the theologian Johann Baptist Metz. See, for example, Metz, *Faith in History and Society*, 3.

8. Confer Marcus Borg Foundation, "Battle over Jesus Today," 1:18:10, 47:30–54:00.

A SUGGESTED APPROACH TO STUDY YESHUA OF NAZARETH

To get a glimpse of Yeshua as a historical figure, I frequently suggest a method called, in fancy terms, a "Christology from below." Note that Christology is the logical and disciplined study of the person of Yeshua, the one who has been acclaimed as the "Christ" in Christianity. Concretely, the method I suggest consists of the following things (at least, at the beginning of the process): The first step is forgetting for a while the question of Yeshua's divinity (especially if one was raised a Christian) and instead focusing first on a demonstrable historical fact—that Yeshua was a first-century Jewish peasant. Relying on historical and social science research and sometimes even employing educated guesses (i.e., probable hypotheses informed by research), one tries first to reconstruct probable reasons how and why he emerged as a public teacher—a rabbi[9] and prophet-like figure from a very unlikely peasant background. Note well that Yeshua becoming a public healer-teacher was something that surprised even his own family members (cf. Mark 3:21).

We then continue to study Yeshua's public career: what he did and taught, how he acted, who he gathered around himself, who debated with and opposed him, etc. Most importantly, one will also eventually have to account for why Yeshua's public ministry ended in his being crucified on a Roman cross around 30 CE. After his death, one examines what happened to his disciples: How they were changed from fearful people to courageous witnesses, proclaiming that Yeshua had been raised (by God) from the dead. This proclamation is called "the resurrection" in Christianity.

Based on this resurrection faith, we will then study how faith in Yeshua developed and grew in various Christian communities as they slowly spread in different places. Finally, we will survey how these Christian communities gradually became more organized institutions and how they established some parameters for how Christians ought to regard Yeshua, the Christ, as the central truth of the budding religion that increasingly claimed that it was separate from Yeshua's own Judaism and what repercussions that had on Christianity itself. What I have just described is precisely the outline of this chapter's contents below.

9. As an official reference "rabbi" seems to be anachronistic because it was only widely used later on in history after Jesus' life. See, for example, Lapin, "Rabbi"; and Zacharias, "Rabbi as a Title."

YESHUA: HOW HE FIRST CAME ACROSS TO HIS CONTEMPORARIES

Yeshua of Nazareth was a member of the peasant class in his world. By "peasant class" I mean the people who were *not* part of the elite, rich, and power-wielding classes. He lived most of his life as a craftsperson (often expressed in English as "carpenter") in the early first century CE, in Nazareth, a small town not far though from a major cosmopolitan center—Sepphoris—in the Galilee region of Roman-occupied Palestine. Although there are two accounts of how Yeshua was born (in Matthew and Luke), it is very hard to tell which elements of those two stories are historical.[10] Instead, many things in those so-called "infancy narratives" seem to be non-historical. Take for example a moving guiding star (Matt 2:9–10) or angels lighting up the dark, night sky (Luke 2:13–14) as cases in point. Moreover, the time period between Yeshua's birth (around 5 BCE) and his appearance as a public figure (around 26–29 CE) is practically a kind of black hole in that we know almost nothing about the circumstances and forces that shaped him and made him who he was when he did appear as a charismatic public teacher-healer.

Since there is so much that we don't know, how do we even go about trying to glimpse the flesh-and-blood figure of the founding ancestor then? I would go about this quest in the following way. First, I would ask: When he does appear on the stage of history as a public figure, how did he come across to his contemporaries? What were the dominant impressions he gave them? What would the people who encountered him have associated him with?

The two descriptive categories that Yeshua's contemporaries would have associated the Galilean preacher-healer with were most probably "prophet" and "wisdom teacher" (sage). These were categories that had a venerable history in the tradition of Israel. To be recalled is that some prophetic figures in ancient Israel such as Elijah and Elisha were also healers. In fact, in Mark 8:37, when Yeshua asks his disciples who do people think that he is, they report that people associate him, among others, with "Elijah or one of the prophets." In line with Yeshua being considered a wisdom-teacher, noteworthy also is the incident in Mark 6:2 which recounts that when Yeshua is back home in his hometown of Nazareth after having become a public teacher-healer, his fellow Nazareans wonder, "Where did this man get all this? What is this *wisdom* that has been given to him? What deeds of power are being done by his hands?"

Therefore, it is fair to say that Yeshua came across to his contemporaries as a prophet-like rabbi who taught wisdom and performed deeds of

10. A good reference work on this topic is Miller, *Born Divine*.

power that were meant to restore wholeness in the people he encountered, especially those described as having "faith" (in Greek, *pistis*). That would have been the dominant impression that Yeshua gave his compatriots as he burst upon the scene in Galilee at the beginning of his public life around the late 20s of the first century CE. We can consider that the "surface impression" we can glean from the gospel-accounts of our storyteller-ancestors. In order to understand Yeshua better though, it is necessary that we go deeper below the surface and ask, "What forces (behind the text) made Yeshua into this kind of person?"

Marcus Borg defined the prophets of Israel as "*God-intoxicated* people"[11] who spoke for God. In the case of Yeshua, there are strong indications that, by the time he had a public ministry, he was, in his core, a deeply spiritual person who had an experiential and intimate relationship with the divine, the being known as YaHWeH in the Jewish tradition. Yeshua in fact called this august Being *Abba* (an intimate Jewish way to call one's father). That is an indication that Yeshua had an extraordinarily close relationship with God.[12] We can also deduce this conclusion, among other things, from the "authority" to speak and act in the name of God that people perceived in him when he was engaged in public ministry (cf. Mark 1:22) and from accounts in the Gospels of him spending time in prayer and intimate communion with God (e.g., Luke 6:12).

Because of all those things, I propose that we consider Yeshua a "spiritual master." To use a title of great respect from my Japanese culture, Yeshua could very well be considered a spiritual *sensei* (Japanese, "teacher"). But not just any *sensei*. In Japan, when we want to give the title of ultimate respect to a particularly special teacher, we call them *dai-sensei*, the "*dai*" here coming from the Chinese-Japanese character 大 meaning "great." Hence, Yeshua was a *dai-sensei* who acted to bring about a new order in his immediate world, an order that he called "the reign of God" (also commonly rendered as "the kingdom of God"; in Greek, *besileia tou theou*). And this reign of God was characterized by, what I shall express here as, *shalom*, a common Hebrew word-concept (often translated as "peace") that, I strongly think, can be one of the best ways to express well the main characteristics of Yeshua's vision of God's reign.

11. Borg, *Reading the Bible Again*, 128.

12. Taussig, *Jesus Before God*, 67–74.

YESHUA AS A SPIRITUAL DAI-SENSEI WHO ACTED TO CHANGE THE WORLD

Yeshua (believed in as "the Christ"/the anointed one), has predominantly been portrayed as divine in Christianity's two-thousand-year history. That, unfortunately, has a downside: It obscures the fact that before he was worshipped as God, Yeshua as a historical figure and a flesh-and-blood Jewish person who lived in the first century CE, was arguably a charismatic person who powerfully impacted many people around him. The South African theologian Albert Nolan declared, "Jesus is a much-underrated man. When we deprive him of his humanity, we deprive him of his greatness."[13] I attribute this powerful personality to his being, as stated above, a profound mystical-contemplative "Spirit-filled Person,"[14] a spiritual *dai-sensei* who let his deep spirituality overflow into determined and courageous action to realize, what he called, "the reign of God" in his own concrete place and time.

Let me elaborate. I agree with scholars such as Marcus Borg,[15] Bruce Chilton,[16] and Geza Vermes[17] that a crucial first step in drawing a historical portrait of Yeshua should be to highlight his being a Jewish mystic; in other words, to highlight his depth dimension as a person. This is the best starting point for me because it is obvious that the character and actions of any human being come from what motivates them *from within*. This principle applies to spiritual giants in history from the Buddha, Lao Tzu, the Prophet Muhammad, Yeshua (of course), Hildegard of Bingen, Julian of Norwich, Teresa of Avila, all the way down to our times with figures such as Dietrich Bonhoeffer, Mahatma Gandhi, Thomas Merton, Dorothy Day, Thich Nhat Hanh, the Dalai Lama, Pema Chödrön, and so forth. Their remarkable teachings and actions obviously stem from a deep, inner wellspring that we can properly call their inner life, their spirituality.

Let me use here an expression that is common in my Catholic tradition to describe how I consider the teacher-healer from Nazareth to have been as a charismatic, historical figure: Yeshua, I propose, could also be appropriately considered "a contemplative-in-action." He was a person who seemed to be rooted in a deep and constant experiential spiritual-knowledge that gave him a vision that everyone and everything are one in YaHWeH, the One whom he called *Abba*. That is the "contemplative" part. But he did not

13. Quoted in Borg, *Days of Awe and Wonder*, 122.
14. Cf. Borg, *Jesus*, 39–51.
15. Borg, *Days of Awe and Wonder*, 45–73.
16. Chilton, *Rabbi Jesus*, chapter 5.
17. See particularly Vermes, *Jesus, the Jew*, chapter 3.

stop at contemplation. Yeshua's deep spirituality, I'd like to emphasize, overflowed outward and moved him to act (this is tantamount to the "in action" part) in order to transform his world into a better place where his *Abba*, in whom he deeply believed that everyone and everything were united, reigned more fully; a place where, to use a common Jewish concept, *shalom* (wholeness, the totality of all good things) was present. And Yeshua summed up his program of action as—what virtually all scholars agree was his foremost priority—acting to let the *reign of God* come in the here and now.

Seen through these lenses, Yeshua of Nazareth thus stands among great sages and spirit-masters in human history (again, such as the Buddha, Lao-Tzu, the Prophet Muhammad, Confucius, etc.) who were experientially connected to, what they trusted was, the Great Reality/God that encompassed everything and drew from there the strength to transform the world in which they lived. Unfortunately, we do not have first-hand records of Yeshua's deep spirituality that was at the root of his very person and his actions. What can we do then? One way is to examine other spiritual masters in history with a view to comparing their spiritual experiences and getting possible hints about what Yeshua himself as a spirit-person could have gone through. Of course, the closest possible "contemplative-in-action" we can cite for comparative purposes is someone in the New Testament itself—the apostle Paul! I have already explained the nature of GU-Paul's mystical/spiritual experience in the last chapter so there is no need to belabor it here.

THE NON-DUAL OR UNITIVE EXPERIENCE APPLIED TO YESHUA

In order to better understand how Yeshua might have been a *dai-sensei*, a great spiritual master who sought to change the world, recall that we already saw how many accounts of religious experience seem to suggest one common denominator running through different so-called religious or mystical experiences across different historical epochs and traditions: It is the overcoming of the duality between self and others (i.e., *nonduality*) and a more heightened *unitive* awareness of the universe.[18] Hence, I repeat: I strongly support the hypothesis that when religious experiences are stripped down to their most basic and fundamental level, *what we have is essentially an experience of nonduality or unity* in which the barriers between the ego and

18. In the same vein, Marianne Rankin cuts to the chase when she concludes in her comprehensive survey of spiritual experience that the underlying message of all spiritual-religious experiences is "above all, [love] for each other" (Rankin, *Introduction to Religious and Spiritual Experience*, 257).

the other are blurred, transgressed, crossed, and transcended. This is why mystics and contemplatives can see everyone and everything as beautiful, full of light, and basically a unity with the ground of all reality known in the Western religious traditions as "God." Conversely, it is also the very reason why authentically spiritual people do not tolerate the oppression of others and are strongly moved to action in order to continue the struggle for peace and justice: oppression and injustice radically disrupt the fundamental harmony and unity of the universe.

As a result of that, the person who has had heightened religious-spiritual experiences catches a glimpse of a pure, all-inclusive, and magnanimous love for everyone and everything, even one's enemies. Is it any wonder that Yeshua charged his disciples to "love [even] your enemies" (Matt 5:44; Luke 6:27)? I already mentioned that this proposed characteristic of religious-spiritual experience is known in the area of religious-spirituality studies, among others, as "the common core thesis in the study of mysticism." It "contends that mystical experience is an ultimate non-sensuous experience of the unity of all things."[19] We mentioned that this was an important way to view GU-Paul's experience. Now, let me also say that it is very clearly for me the best way to view even Yeshua's own inner core which, as we affirmed earlier, was the source of all his actions.

THE REIGN OF GOD: A VISION OF A WORLD WHERE SHALOM REIGNS

From that experiential spiritual relationship with the divine as well as from critically drawing key insights from what he understood as the best and most wholesome parts of his Jewish tradition, Yeshua had a vision of God's ideal order for this world, an order he called "the reign of God." However, the expression "the reign" (or "the kingdom") of God that Yeshua used as the rallying cry for his ministry is actually a difficult thing to explain. Philosopher of religion John Caputo insightfully comments that when we press Yeshua about God, he prefers to talk instead about the "kingdom of God." And when we press him to talk about the nature of that kingdom, Yeshua deflects us to discussions on things such as treasures in fields, mustard seeds, dinner parties, etc.[20] At the end of the day, it is not rare that one is left scratching one's head and still asking Yeshua: So, what precisely is this "kingdom of God" and who precisely is this God you're trying to describe?

19. Hood, "Common Core Thesis in the Study of Mysticism."

20 John Caputo at the Hank Center for the Catholic Intellectual Heritage, "The Challenge of God—Plenary Address by John D. Caputo," 40:54.

I've found the following description of the reign of God to be very helpful for myself and hope that it might be so for others as well. Among other possible explanations, I will say that the expression "God's reign" which Yeshua often used was a vision of a world that would be more perfectly characterized by God finally being able to establish a state here and now where true *shalom* would be present. Note though that this will be done collaboratively with God's human cooperators. The word-concept *shalom* is surprisingly not often associated with the historical Yeshua and his announcement of the coming kingdom of God. I propose that it should be in a more explicit way. There are instances in the Gospels when the Greek equivalent of *shalom*, namely, *eiréné* (peace) is used, such as when Yeshua instructs his disciples to wish peace upon the houses they enter (Luke 10:5), or when the risen Yeshua greets his disciples with "Peace be with you" (cf. John 20:21).

I assume that when Yeshua and his earliest disciples wished "peace" upon people, they were using the greeting within the conceptual framework of their Hebrew-Aramaic language. Therefore, they were wishing *shalom* on people. *Shalom* is frequently translated in English as "peace." But *shalom as* a word-symbol is broader and more all-encompassing in the sense that it is not just peace taken as "the absence of war or conflict" (This is what the common translation in English implies). Defined better and in a fuller way, *shalom* fundamentally refers to "wholeness." It refers to a state of being complete and integral, of having all the necessary physical and spiritual resources that a person or place needs to be whole.[21] My own way of describing *shalom* applied to the ideal state called the "reign of God" envisioned by Yeshua would be: *the totality of all good and wholesome things*; particularly, health, abundance, benevolence, justice (social, distributive, and restorative, *not* retributive), peace, inclusivity, compassion, forgiveness, harmony, among many other things. Paul's list of the fruits of the spirit in Gal 5:22–23 might even be used profitably in discussing a state of shalom which is nothing else but the order that the presence of God (or of the Spirit) brings about.

THE HARSH REALITY, THEN AND NOW

Of course, the reality of Yeshua's world was vastly different from his ideal of the reign of God where *shalom* was envisioned to be available to everyone. He lived in a harsh context of a society ruled oppressively by empire (Rome and its Jewish allies) and by the various religious authorities (of Yeshua's own religious tradition). These political and religious powers-that-be

21. See Healey, "Peace: Old Testament." See also Greever, "Peace."

interpreted the covenant in ways that, for Yeshua, did not truly favor the realization of the state of *shalom*. Indeed, the clashes between Yeshua and other teachers of his day, such as the Pharisees and the scribes described in the Gospels, point most probably to Yeshua's critical opposition to some key aspects of the conventional religiosity of his day, factors that in some ways favored some groups at the expense of others. These structures also maintained oppression, marginalization, exclusion, and other forms of suffering (often in the name of religion-married-to-empire) particularly for the underprivileged and more expendable groups of society.[22]

Note that I *do not say this* in order to paint the Judaism of the time monolithically in a negative way. We will discuss this aspect more in detail below. Instead, I say this because, in my own study and personal experience of religion and religious institutions, I have to say that almost all forms of conventional religion and religious institutions have the strong tendency to fall back into a default position of having a system dominated by the principle *quid pro quo* in which the major way of viewing God and life is under the condition or rubric of trying to "fulfill requirements" in order to be deemed worthy of divine favor. Moreover, many forms of conventional religion create a small class of religious elites who usually feel religiously superior to the majority because they are convinced that they meet divine requirements better than the rest. An illustration of this can be found in Yeshua's parable of the Pharisee and the Tax Collector (Luke 18:9–14). Needless to say, Yeshua's vision of God's reign ran counter to that kind of conventional religiosity.

The harsh realities of Yeshua's world can be compared to the harsh realities of our own world (and of every human context, for that matter) because violence, greed, the lust for power and wealth, injustice and corruption, retributive justice (the logic of empire) unfortunately form—to use biblical scholar John Dominic Crossan's expression—the "normalcy of human civilization."[23] In other words, these shadow-elements comprise the normal order of human reality rather than Yeshua's vision of *shalom* (especially its distributive and restorative justice component).

22. I still think that one of the best expositions of this theme is Borg, *Conflict, Holiness and Politics*, particularly chapters 3–5. One must note however the critiques suggesting that Borg misunderstands purity in important ways. See, for example, Fredriksen, "Compassion-Is-to-Purity-as-Fish-Is-to-Bicycle," 55–67.

23. Crossan, *God and Empire*, 29–48.

WHAT WAS YESHUA TRYING TO DO IN HIS WORLD?

At a certain point in his life, Yeshua must have felt called to enact his vision of God's reign in his world through a public ministry. Thus, he left his hometown, Nazareth. The gospels record him as being baptized by John the Baptist at the Jordan river. Yeshua's baptism can be understood as symbolic of, one, the deep spirituality and union with God that Yeshua already possessed as he began his ministry and, two, an important point in his ongoing quest to respond to, what he perceived as, the will of God for him. The Gospels agree that sometime after his baptism, Yeshua began a ministry that brought him to the public eye.[24] This ministry consisted of teaching, healing (I understand this as "restoring wholeness" or the "state of *shalom*" to people), gathering followers (to follow him and form a movement-community), and enacting the reign of God through symbolic actions, such as open-table fellowship and the generous welcoming of everyone (regardless of whether they were deemed respectful or not, pure or impure) who was willing to come to him and his fellowship. It is fair to say that Yeshua had a predilection for those who were considered marginalized or unacceptable ("sinners," "the impure," etc.) by the religiously respectable people of the time.

I think that New Testament scholar Marcus Borg has done one of the most comprehensive and helpful portraits of the historical Yeshua's public career. Let me basically adopt his portrait with a few tweaks of my own. Borg sometimes referred to his sketch as having "five strokes."[25] In many of his works, he begins insightfully with a first stroke that proclaims unambiguously that (1) Yeshua was, first and foremost, a Jewish mystic or—in Borg's own expression—a "Spirit Person."[26] Recall that a mystic is a person who has an *experiential knowledge* of God due to significant (even intense and esoteric) spiritual experiences while, at the same time (I want to add), is informed by one's wrestling with one's own religious-spiritual tradition. Borg was convinced that Yeshua was one who had such experiential acquaintance with the Being Israel calls YHWH, clearly indicated by the way he addressed God—"*Abba*," an Aramaic term that shows intimacy with one's father and which was not, as far as we know, usually used at the time to call God probably because it was considered "too familiar." What impresses me, furthermore, with Borg's portrait is that he thinks that this deep spirituality (Borg uses "mysticism") was the very foundation of everything else that made up

24. See, for example, the account of Jesus' baptism in Mark 1:9–12.

25. Borg, *Heart of Christianity*, 89–91.

26. Borg, *Meeting Jesus Again*, 31–36.

who Yeshua was, including the foundation of the other four strokes used by Borg himself.[27] This is the inspiration behind my own proposal to declare above that Yeshua's spirituality should be given priority in our efforts to try to understand him as a historical figure.

Borg continues with other strokes to portray the great founding ancestor. Stroke two, (2) Yeshua was a remarkable healer and an exorcist. It is significant to note that Yeshua is probably the figure who has the greatest number of healing and exorcism acts attributed to him among all Jewish figures of the first century CE! In addition to that, stroke three states that (3) Yeshua was also a wisdom teacher, who imparted an alternative wisdom grounded in his ongoing spiritual experience of God. In stroke four, Borg locates Yeshua in the prophetic line of ancient Israel's long history. Hence, (4) Yeshua should also be considered a social prophet like the great social prophets of the Jewish scriptures and history. And prophets, it must be remembered, were people who were passionate about, what we now know as, social justice in the name of God. As mentioned, Borg calls these ancient prophets "God intoxicated voices of religious social protest."[28] In fact, they proclaimed this to the point of speaking extremely uncomfortable truths to power. This is why many of them suffered from the various authority figures and systems of their day.

Finally, Borg's fifth stroke points out that (5) Yeshua was a movement founder, namely, he set in motion a movement whose purpose was the revitalization of Judaism in his day.[29] For our purposes in this book, it is good to recall that we recognize Yeshua here as the great ancestor-founder of the New Testament village because all of the major and minor spiritual ancestors who we encounter there were crucially impacted by the life and ministry of this rabbi from Nazareth.

YESHUA'S PRIORITY—GOD'S REIGN, NOT HIMSELF

In his public ministry, Yeshua prioritized, above all, the actualizing of the reign of God in the here and the now. As an important corollary of that, we should also note that Yeshua was *not* primarily concerned with proclaiming his own identity. This is contrary to the impression that the Gospel of

27. As Borg himself has stated in a public lecture; see Marcus Borg Foundation, "Battle over Jesus Today," 32:28.

28. Again, see Borg's lecture: Marcus Borg Foundation, "Battle over Jesus Today," 33:32.

29. Marcus Borg Foundation, "Battle over Jesus Today," 33:45.

John gives us. There, Yeshua continually talks about who he is. Thus, we must say that John's portrait of Yeshua is more a reflection of what GU-John and his community believed about Yeshua sixty to seventy years after the historical Yeshua's life.

Nevertheless, Yeshua did seem to be convinced that his ministry and teaching would play a crucial role in establishing God's reign definitively in the world. Despite that, he showed an amazing non-attachment to "franchising" (or monopolizing) the work of establishing the reign of God only to those of his immediate circle of followers. This is clearly illustrated in Luke 9:49–50 where we find the curious incident in which a disciple informs Yeshua that they tried to stop a man who was driving demons in Yeshua's name because he was not "one of them." Yeshua's surprising answer to that was: "Do not stop him; for whoever is not against you is for you."

My own conclusion from the aforementioned points is this: as long as authentic spirituality and the active effort to realize God's all-encompassing *shalom* (compassion, benevolence, distributive justice, etc.) are in progress wherever we are located, we can consider all other things *as of secondary importance*. In short, the inclusive reign of God (the establishing of a state of *shalom* in the here and now), and *not* the narrow-minded and even narcissistic prioritizing of establishing and enhancing a religious organization such as a church, was the priority of Yeshua and should continue to be the priority of all people (regardless of their personal religious beliefs) who consider Yeshua as a guide and inspiration. We should add, however, that the reign of God should be the priority especially of those who explicitly bear the name "Christian" in any sense. The neglect of this priority will make Christians and the different Christian churches unfaithful to the intentions of the founding ancestor, Yeshua himself.

SHOWDOWN: YESHUA'S PASSION AND DEATH

Eventually, Yeshua ran into more and more problems with other different interpretations (and their authoritative interpreters) about how best to live Israel's covenant with God because his vision of God's reign and his active effort to realize it conflicted with and even subverted other teaching authorities' ideas about what God's reign (the ideal "order" of the world) was all about. Hence, some of his opponents began to plot against him (see, e.g., Mark 3:6 or Luke 6:11). Moreover, Yeshua's ministry, directed especially to people who were considered undesirable and expendable by many political and religious authorities, disrupted the social and religious status quo that those in authority sought to maintain.

It is not easy to pinpoint in a rigorously historical way who was clearly responsible for the arrest and death of Yeshua. However, it is fair to say that, in the end, different opponents of Yeshua who had political clout succeeded in having him arrested, charged, and ultimately crucified officially as an enemy of the Roman empire in Jerusalem around 30 CE. Before his violent death, Yeshua was certainly already aware of the danger he faced, but by intentionally going to Jerusalem and not escaping from the city when he probably could have done so without much difficulty,[30] he seemed to have accepted this death. Why? We can only speculate (in an educated way) that he probably trusted that his death would mysteriously act as a catalyst that would better bring about the realization of the reign of God that he worked for during his ministry. This was not fully understood, however, by his disciples until sometime after his death.

There are hints in the Jewish scriptures of a messiah-figure "saving" the people through his suffering (e.g., Isaiah 53). Early Christians later on used these Old Testament passages to tease out, suggest, and explain the redemptive meaning of the suffering and death of Yeshua: that is, the formula that Yeshua "saved us through suffering (the cross)" became in time a standard way to make sense of Yeshua' suffering and death. When did that interpretation begin precisely? Did it start with Yeshua himself as the gospels seem to suggest? That is a proposal that, this author thinks, is possible and not unreasonable.[31]

What we can demonstrably claim in a historical way though is that Yeshua had a passionate vision of God establishing an order ("God's reign") in the here and now for the people, especially the underprivileged and oppressed ones. That vision met with a vehement opposition. Hence, Yeshua's historical teaching and actions were deemed rogue and dangerous enough to warrant his elimination. In the face of all that, he stood firmly by his vision to the very end and gave his life for it and for the ones that this vision sought to embrace.

At Yeshua's arrest, most of his closest male disciples feared for their lives and abandoned Yeshua to his fate. Many of them escaped from Jerusalem and headed back to their native Galilee. To be noted though is that many female disciples stayed on (see, for example, Mark 15:40–41). Yeshua was crucified under the authority of Pontius Pilate, the local Roman governor at the time. Yeshua's death on the cross was initially understood by most people (including his followers) as a tragic end to the life and ministry of

30. Mentioned by Jerome Murphy O'Connor in Religious Studies, "Search for Jesus," 1:10:14.

31. See, for example, N. T. Wright's opinion expressed in Borg and Wright, *Meaning of Jesus*, 104.

a promising and charismatic Galilean rabbi's life. His followers were particularly devastated at how such a tragedy (which could even be interpreted from a Jewish perspective as a curse from God, cf. Deut 21:23) could happen to their teacher, who only wanted to establish God's reign, do good, and struggled on behalf of the underprivileged.

EXCURSUS: IT'S NEVER EVER A MATTER OF "JESUS AGAINST JUDAISM"

Before I continue, let me firmly lay down here a crucially important principle for interpreting and evaluating Yeshua both historically and theologically. Yeshua, or shall we say "Jesus" (to make him again more familiarly "Christian" and "Western") has been owned and coopted by Christianity as its own throughout its two-thousand-year history. It has completely possessed Jesus to the extent that as recent as a generation ago, when one claimed that Jesus was "Jewish," that still perturbed quite a lot of Christian sensitivities because many thought that Jesus was first and foremost "a Christian." Thanks to the historical work of scholars, it has now become normal and proper to claim Jesus' Jewishness as a foundational principle for evaluating him historically as well as theologically.

Old habits die hard, however. In many cases, claiming what Jesus was trying to do in his world still often means (or at least is understood as) contrasting Jesus' (and hence, Christianity's) supposedly noble, forward-looking, and liberating attitudes against a supposedly legalistic, backward, and even insidious "Judaism" *tout court*. Hence, discourse about Jesus all too often descends into an unfair Christian rhetoric about something along the lines of "our Christian" Jesus versus "their" outdated, "*Old* Testament" "Judaism" which should be abandoned for the "new," liberating covenant (or testament) in God's scheme of things. Let me state it unambiguously here: This is a very wrong way to think about the person and ministry of Jesus and about the nature of first-century Judaism because it is—and let this statement sink into our consciousness firmly like a mantra—*never ever* about "Jesus versus Judaism."

As a historical figure, Jesus was a first-century Palestinian Jew. He was certainly *not* a Christian. And first-century Judaism was *not* a monolithic structure that Jesus, the Christian, was supposedly trying to overturn for the purpose of letting a new, more enlightened Christian religion be born and take over. Jesus, or rather (to switch back to his less familiar but decidedly Jewish name) Yeshua was in fact trying to make a case through his life, teaching, and ministry, for how he thought that his beloved Israel was to be renewed, for how best to live Israel's covenant with YHWH. And, if he engaged in debate and even arguments with other Jewish groups (as the gospels frequently portray), it was because all of the debating parties in question, as first-century Jews, *were passionate about how to renew Israel, about how best to live the covenant* between YHWH and Israel. Hence, these debates and conflicts were *intra-Jewish discussions* about different opinions on how best to be a covenant people. They were *not* a matter of Jesus, the Christian, seeking to subvert or even overthrow a supposedly outdated and legalistic Judaism.

I am thankful to the work of scholars (some of whom are Jewish New Testament scholars) such as Amy-Jill Levine, Paula Fredriksen, and Adele Reinhartz who remind us that Yeshua has to be firmly and correctly embedded in his first-century Jewish context in order for Christianity to stop bearing a kind of "false witness" against Jews and Judaism. In the stark words of Levine, "Judaism does not have to be made to look bad for Christianity to look good."[32] In fact, even some aspects of the work of Christian historical Jesus scholars (even Marcus Borg who, by now you surely know, is one of my main influences) have been criticized for making caricatures of or misunderstanding aspects of first-century Judaism in order to portray what Yeshua was supposedly trying to accomplish in his world at the cost of giving a negative impression of the Judaism and the Jews of the time.[33] These important critiques have to be kept carefully in mind when we try to understand what Yeshua was trying to do in his first-century Jewish world.

My modest contribution to this discussion would be to point out something that is deeply rooted in my identity as a minoritized BIPOC scholar (Asian-North American) here in the West.[34] On the one hand, yes, Yeshua was involved as a first-century Jew in intra-Jewish discussions about how he thought was the best way to live God's plan and to enable the reign of God to be realized in some way in his world. However, on the other hand, these debates and arguments, especially with respected, even authority-wielding groups (either juridical or moral authority) such as the scribes, Sadducees, Pharisees, Herodians, etc., were—let me use a term that is pivotal in minoritized scholarship and has to be unpacked—"asymmetrical" affairs. In other words, the playing field was *not level*. It was most of the time

32. Amy-Jill Levine in an interview: Religion and Ethics NewsWeekly, "Jewish Jesus," 11:41.

33. See, for example, the general argument of Levine in Levine, *Misunderstood Jew*.

34. Some of the works where I develop my points more fully are the following: Kato, *How Immigrant Christians Living in Mixed Cultures Interpret Their Religion*; Kato, "Interpretation," 63–75; and Kato, *Religious Language and Asian American Hybridity*. Confer also this important work: Bailey et al., *They Were All Together in One Place?*, 3–43.

a lopsided argument with Yeshua as the disadvantaged party who was often given short shrift. Yeshua's position was not mainstream or mainline in his day. Rather, it had little support from; better yet, it was often opposed by the more respected and authoritative groups of the day. Hence, from the point of view of these more powerful and influential groups, Yeshua's message was considered marginal and therefore marginalized; it was contradicted and ridiculed; at times it was branded as rogue and even thought of as something tantamount to "heresy" vis-à-vis more authoritative, established, and respected opinions such as the interpretations of the Pharisees, scribes, and priests, among others.

The late British New Testament scholar Maurice Casey even used the word "orthodoxy" to describe these more dominant and respected interpretations of the covenant in Yeshua's historical context (with the critical proviso that this was *not* at all how "orthodoxy" is usually understood in a Christian context).[35] If Casey's claim is true (as I think so), Yeshua in effect was often going against (some kind of respected) "orthodoxy" (better: authoritative or influential positions) in his day and when one does that, one also suffers the consequences. In short, this aspect would have been one of the major factors why Yeshua's opponents thought that he had to be put away. As I said above, from a strictly historical point of view, it is difficult to determine exactly who caused the arrest and death of Yeshua, but it is safe to say that some prominent opponents of Yeshua most probably played a crucial role in his being crucified on a Roman cross after just a relatively short period of public ministry.

Let me say clearly though: It goes without saying that this fact *does not mean* that all Jews (or Judaism as a whole) at the time were inimical to Yeshua. With those thoughts clearly expressed, let us go back to completing our portrait of what became of the movement after Yeshua's untimely death on the cross.

RENEWED FAITH AFTER YESHUA'S DEATH: THE RESURRECTION

Sometime after Yeshua's death, the very same disciples, who were terrified at the time of his arrest and fearfully abandoned him to his cruel fate, mysteriously regrouped and rebooted the movement and community that Yeshua had begun during his ministry. The fact of the reorganization of the movement after Yeshua's death is undoubtedly historical. The conclusion I draw from that then is that these disciples must have undergone some

35. Casey, *Jesus*, 319–38.

kind of experience that transformed them from fearful people to bold witnesses who, it is recorded, proclaimed that Yeshua had been raised by God from the dead and that he had been glorified as messiah (in Greek "Christ," meaning "the anointed one") and as "Lord" at the right hand of God (e.g., Phil 2).

This transformation of those early disciples and their proclamation of Yeshua as the "Christ" (Hebrew *mashiach*, "the anointed one") and as "Lord" (Gk. *kyrios*) suggest that some of them had a life-changing experience after Yeshua's death on the cross. More precisely, the New Testament says that they mysteriously "encountered" the crucified one as risen from the dead. Thus, they came to believe that God had raised him from the dead.[36] This is arguably what changed them from fearful, defeated people into courageous witnesses. This is what the Christian tradition eventually came to call "the resurrection" event. Notice though that *we do not have direct access* to the resurrection itself of Yeshua. We depend on the spiritual ancestors who proclaimed it. Here we see again their importance. The resurrection event's original proclaimed form was "Jesus has been raised from the dead (this implies that the action was done by God)" (1 Cor 15:14). This also became the rallying faith and cry of the rebooted Jesus movement after Yeshua's death on a Roman cross.

THE HEART OF THE DISCIPLES' PROCLAMATION: THE PASCHAL MYSTERY

When the disciples of Yeshua restarted the movement as a result of a reawakened faith that Yeshua had been raised from the dead, they made Yeshua himself the central factor in their message: They proclaimed his life, teaching, actions, and how those led to his death. But they did not stop at that. They courageously affirmed that everything Yeshua stood for was powerfully vindicated by God through the resurrection despite Yeshua's tragic death on the cross. Hence, they urged people to follow the way of Yeshua because, although the *sequela Christi* (Latin, [the process of] "following Christ") may mean suffering, opposition, and perhaps even death, this way would also be ultimately vindicated by God just as was done in the case of Yeshua. This is, in standard Christian terms, known as "the Paschal Mystery"; one follows the way of Yeshua, a way that leads through the cross

36. A recent insightful approach to the resurrection that puts the crux of the matter not on "what happened" but "how the disciples believed" in the resurrection is found in Chilton, *Resurrection Logic*, 203–10. I think this might be one of the best critical approaches to the resurrection that could still speak to a secular age.

but, ultimately, to the glory of the resurrection. Let me also add that this is an archetypal pattern found in many spiritual-wisdom traditions of the world (e.g., from ignorance to an awakening-enlightenment in Buddhism) and even in the natural order (from the seeming death of nature in winter to the new life brought about by spring).

The disciples were also convinced that Yeshua was present within the community through, what they referred to as, "the Holy Spirit" to guide and strengthen it until the day when God's order would definitely be established on earth through God's messiah Yeshua.

THE ORIGINS OF THE COMMUNITY OF YESHUA'S FOLLOWERS

Yeshua's disciples formed communities first in Palestine and gradually in other places throughout the Roman empire (and also outside it). These communities would eventually become a religious tradition separate from Yeshua's native Judaism. It eventually developed into a religion that we now know as Christianity. These communities would also be corporately known in time as "the Christian Church." The church is also called "the body of Christ" (1 Cor 12:27) because its main mission is to keep alive the presence and the cause of Yeshua, "the Christ," in history. Christianity would eventually put the emphasis on believing certain notions enshrined in "creed" (e.g., the Apostles' Creed and the Nicene Creed) as the touchstone for being a Christian. The most important and distinctive of these articles of faith was the idea that Yeshua, besides being human, is also "same in essence" as God, the Father (YHWH in the Jewish Scriptures). Simply put, that means that Yeshua is also divine.

What I have presented above is the fruit of many years of trying to outline for my students the main contours of an approach that would hopefully enable them to catch a glimpse of the flesh-and-blood first-century Jewish rabbi-healer who is the founding ancestor of the New Testament village, Yeshua of Nazareth.

PART III

Back Home

Embracing and Wrestling with Our Spiritual Tradition

12

Back Home to Embrace and Wrestle with Our Spiritual Tradition

The Secularized West: Source of Immorality or (Deeply Flawed) Embodiment of "the Reign of God"?

We remain what Christianity has made us, and in many respects the postmodern West is more Christian than ever.

—Don Cupitt[1]

BACK TO OUR WORLD, THE SECULARIZED WEST

We have journeyed to—what we have called throughout this work—the (textual) village of the New Testament. It is there that some of our spiritual ancestors continue to live. Besides, they continue to be able to converse with us if we make dialogue with them possible by acquiring good reading and interpretation skills. In our journey to and back from there, we have encountered and gotten to know a little better the most important ancestors: granduncles Mark, Matthew, Luke, John, Paul and, of course, the great

1. Cupitt, *Meaning of the West*, 36.

ancestor-founder of the village, Yeshua of Nazareth himself. Let us not forget the multitudes of grand-aunts that form part of the whole picture but are unfortunately not explicitly credited in the patriarchal worlds and texts of the past.

Thus, we have also gotten a good picture of the most important figures, ideas, and forces that were at the heart of a movement in the first century of the common era, a movement that, at a later time, would become Christianity.[2] This religion in turn is the tradition that shaped our Western civilization in such a crucial and irrevocable way that neglecting or forgetting it would result in us not knowing a vital part of our collective identities, yes, even in this secular world we live in.

The stark truth though is this: We do not live anymore in the world of those spiritual ancestors. We live in *this*, our contemporary world, a place so different from the New Testament textual and historical world that it is a formidable challenge to see how that world is still connected with ours. The people in that world were thoroughly imbued with—what we now call—spiritual and religious "realities." This word is used because, even if some of us now think that they are "not real," they were in fact "very real" for our ancestors. To name a few: God, the unseen order, good and evil spirits, supernatural power, miracles, among many others. In short, it was a—to use Charles Taylor's expression—"enchanted world."[3] On the other hand, our secular world, particularly for those of us who live in the so-called West (or in the so-called "global north"), grows more and more "disenchanted" in that we are, by default, deeply skeptical of "enchanted" (spiritual) realities; we are naturally doubtful of what our senses cannot connect with, what our supposedly advanced science cannot verify.

The burning question we posed at the beginning of this work and to which we will respond more completely in this chapter as a way of concluding our reflections remains: Why do we still need to read the Bible in this secular world? To rephrase that using the metaphor of our visit to the village: Why do we still need to visit the New Testament village and return to it time and again? Well, the answer to that question is equally blunt and surprising: I suggest that, despite the apparently unbridgeable differences between that world and ours, our contemporary so-called secular Western world is in fact the grown-up child of the New Testament biblical world! To make it clearer: We actually share spiritual DNA with the spiritual ancestors we met in the New Testament village. And because that is so, we have to go visit the village

2. A noteworthy recent work on the earliest development of Jesus movements is Vearncombe et al., *After Jesus Before Christianity*.

3. See, for example, Taylor, *Secular Age*, 29–43.

and get to know them. Only thus would we understand better where we ourselves come from and where the spiritual roots of our civilization lie. It is as simple as that but I will unpack it more extensively below.

It would be a good thing at this point to review what was discussed in chapter 2 about our secular world and the need for roots. I'm sure that, by now, you'll be able to appreciate more what was stated there. To reiterate briefly, reading as well as engaging with the Bible thoughtfully is an important way by which we can re-connect with our spiritual roots in this our secular world. And having roots—as we learned from philosopher Simone Weil—is an essential, nonnegotiable human need.

Following the metaphor of a crime scene investigation (discussed in chapter 4), we examined the stories and messages that our New Testament granduncles have told us and tried to peer behind the texts in order to understand better the different circumstances that made them who they were. Now that we're back in our world, it is time to ask: What have we learned about these ancestors from our journey? What is it that we can take away from our encounters with them?

REFLECTING ON THE LEGACIES OF OUR SPIRITUAL ANCESTORS

I mentioned earlier that the purpose of our visiting the New Testament textual village and encountering important spiritual ancestors there was to make as it were a first acquaintance and grasp some key characteristics without which (*sine qua non*) we would not begin to understand them, their world, and what they left as a lasting legacy to the spiritual tradition that came to be known in time as Christianity. Let us now recap the most important points of the legacy each spiritual ancestor has given us.

We learned that granduncle Mark and his clan were probably located in a context of great suffering, a circumstance often identified as persecution by biblical scholars. From that painful context was born his dominant portrayal of Yeshua as a suffering Messiah: the chosen one of God who was nonetheless misunderstood, opposed, plotted against, betrayed, abandoned, sorrowful and even in despair at the very end of his life on the cross. In this way, GU-Mark, it seems, wanted to impart the lesson to his community that to "follow Yeshua on the way" of life and discipleship (see Mark 10:52) boils down to facing life's inevitable suffering with courage while not losing hope and compassion, as the way still leads to a tomb that is empty and a promise of encountering the Risen One (Mark 16:6–7). Indeed, the dominant image of Yeshua in Mark as a suffering Messiah invites the Yeshua-follower to contemplate this figure full of pathos with compassion. Hopefully, that same compassion becomes for each one the dominant way to view all human suffering and even the whole of existence.

GU-Matthew, on the one hand, was struggling to find a balance between his attachment and devotion to the sacred tradition inherited by his people Israel, and, on the other hand, his faith and trust that Yeshua was indeed the promised Messiah sent to Israel to fulfill God's covenant with them. This was a claim though that was ultimately rejected by the majority of his Jewish contemporaries. Nevertheless, Yeshua is considered to be so important that GU-Matthew dares to identify him as an embodiment of God, applying to him the epitaph mentioned in Isaiah 7:14, "Emmanuel," "God-with-us." Thus, GU-Matthew bequeathed forever to Christianity the foundational principle that Yeshua's nation and people, both referred to as "Israel," was always going to be a fundamentally important part and parcel of the developing spiritual tradition among Yeshua's followers. This is clearly shown in how the Christian church later on embraced and affirmed the Jewish Scriptures (often referred to as "the Old Testament") with its stories and teachings, as an integral part of its own spiritual legacy. We shall see below how one key concept from Israel's heritage, the idea that humans are made in the image of God (in Latin, *Imago Dei*) played a crucial role in the development of the secular West.

Moreover, GU-Matthew's message is particularly important and insightful for us who ourselves struggle to figure out how, on the one hand, we can continue to valorize our spiritual traditions from the past while, on the other hand, find ways to make them relevant to a very different and difficult contemporary situation in which we find ourselves.

GU-Luke went out of his way to write not only an account of Yeshua's life but also a second work that dealt with what happened to Yeshua's followers and their communities in the aftermath of Yeshua having gone back to the One who had sent him. In this, GU-Luke was trying to tell us that the covenant that God made with Israel was now, through God's anointed One—Yeshua, being offered beyond Israel to the wide-world of the gentiles, the ones who were hitherto perhaps considered as marginal and second-class citizens of the covenant. We can feel the passion of GU-Luke for the inclusion of the gentiles as full-fledged members of God's people.

It is fair to say that GU-Luke's lasting legacy to us then is his message about (God and Yeshua's) inclusivity. He brings this to the fore in the gospel where he spotlights the predilection of Yeshua for those who were outside the mainstream, the marginalized, the oppressed, and the downtrodden. He arguably brings his narrative to its high point in the Acts of the Apostles where he focuses on how the message of Yeshua is, in stages, brought to, realized, and accepted joyfully by the gentiles, mainly through the work of Yeshua's intrepid apostle Paul and his collaborators.

GU-John, writing toward the end the first century, was the one who profoundly grasped, perhaps more than others through his deep spirituality and mysticism that Yeshua was a unique embodiment of the One God and thus was to be identified as closely as possible with the divine being Israel knew as YHWH. Of course, Yeshua, the Christ, being an embodiment of Israel's God is a strand of thought found elsewhere in the New Testament. We have mentioned GU-Matthew calling him "Emmanuel" ("God-with-us"). GU-Paul also describes Yeshua as the "image of God" in several places in letters he wrote or in those attributed to him. However, we can say that it was GU-John who arguably identified Yeshua most closely with Yahweh to the point that he could be acknowledged in his gospel by lofty statements such as: "the Word was God" (John 1:1), "one with the Father" (10:30), and even "My Lord and my God!" (20:28). Thus, in his story, GU-John sought to present the Yeshua walking the dusty roads of Palestine and living on this earth as, although human, also something like an exalted divine being-come to "dwell among us" (1:14); an exalted Messiah who knew everything that was going to happen to him (18:4) and as one who freely lay down his life (10:17) to "draw all things" to himself (12:32).

It is GU-John's narrative that can act as the most direct springboard for us to see how Christianity later on came to consider Yeshua or (to revert to his more familiar Western name) Jesus as God-incarnate (the noun is "incarnation") and make this teaching the very centerpiece of its institutional creed. This in turn accounts for the fact that Jesus becomes the hero-archetype, the savior-archetype par excellence in Western culture and even in contemporary popular culture as can be seen in Harry Potter, Frodo Baggins, even Superman (among many others) who are all arguably Christ-figures.

GU-Paul is known most for his being the apostle to the gentiles. He tirelessly labored so that more people outside (the nation and people of) Israel might come to the knowledge of Yeshua, the Christ, because in his life-changing encounter with Christ "on the road to Damascus," he glimpsed that everyone and everything was "one in Christ" (Gal 3:28). This was his version of what—in the Perennial Philosophy—is often called the unitive/non-dual spiritual experience of reality. GU-Paul might be considered the most important figure in Christianity next to Yeshua himself because, in his lifelong effort to make the way of Christ more gentile-friendly, he in effect laid the foundations that would eventually lead to Christianity becoming a world religion. Without the vision and labors of this spiritual ancestor, Christianity might have remained an obscure Jewish sect and might never have become the largest religious tradition with the most number of believers that we know it to be today.

In reviewing the legacies of granduncles Luke and Paul, I'm reminded of an insightful observation that the great scholar of world religions Huston Smith made. He said that the Jews had risen to such a spiritual level that it was as if God thought: "The achievement of the Jews is too important to be kept to themselves. It needs to break out of its shell and be made available to the world at large. I will see to it that that is done."[4] Smith likened Christianity's split with Judaism to Buddhism's split with Hinduism and views those events as the case of an ethnic religion developing into a more universal faith. Thus, Buddhism and Christianity go on to become world religions from their matrices of origin, Hinduism and Judaism, which continue to be largely ethnic religions.[5] We've learned here that, in the case of Christianity, we can trace the beginnings of a world religion from an obscure "Way" that involved a small band of Jewish followers of a certain Yeshua because of the visions put forth by two spiritual ancestors, granduncles Luke and Paul, whom we've encountered in the New Testament village.

Finally, we also got a glimpse of how Yeshua himself probably was as a historical figure, particularly, how he sought to proclaim and realize the new order he called "the reign of God" (*basileia tou theou*). This was a reality (even a social order) that—he was convinced—God was already establishing in *the here and now* through his own ministry. In God's new order of things, the abundant blessings of wholeness (peace, justice, compassion, inclusivity, prosperity, abundance, etc.), of God's *shalom* would be present especially for those who in this world were underprivileged, excluded, poor, oppressed and marginalized. Enough has been said in the last chapter and there is no need to belabor those points again here.

THE SEEDS SOWN BY THE ANCESTORS

Look closely at all those key characteristics, those *sine-qua-non*'s that we more clearly identified as we engaged with each of our spiritual ancestors in the New Testament village because they are like seeds that—to use one of Yeshua's parables[6]—when eventually sown in the soil of the West would in time bear fruit. To name the most salient: compassion, the link with Israel's heritage, inclusivity; the human Yeshua as God's embodiment ("incarnation"

4. Smith, *Soul of Christianity*, 35.

5. Smith, *Soul of Christianity*, 35.

6. See Matt 13:1–23; Mark 4:1–20; Luke 8:4–15. Also saying #9 in the Gospel of Thomas.

in technical terms) and, because of that, the idea that the human could indeed be God's very embodiment; mysticism and spirituality, everything as one in God through Christ (the source of inclusivity), the reign of God's holistic *shalom* being realized in the here and now; justice, healing, and wholeness particularly for the underprivileged and oppressed, and many others.

Consider those values carefully, take away the explicit references to God and translate them into more "secular" terms: compassion, acceptance, inclusivity, the human as the expression of the finest qualities of reality, the sense of transcendence, interconnectivity, solidarity, harmony, healing, wholeness, social justice and peace, concern for the underprivileged. Aren't those values so familiar to us who live in the so-called secular West? Where did they come from? Did they magically emerge, as a popular iteration often claims, from the so-called "Enlightenment" as people abandoned the supposedly dark abyss of an unenlightened Christian past? I beg to disagree! Let the experience of the New Testament village you've just had inform your assessment this time. If you do so, you would know by now that those seeds were planted long ago by the ancient spiritual ancestors that you encountered in the New Testament village. That is why we in the West have to embrace and wrestle with our spiritual tradition found in the New Testament. Only by doing that could we come to know our spiritual ancestry.

EMBRACING AND WRESTLING WITH A SPIRITUAL TRADITION IN A SECULAR AGE

You probably noticed that all of the spiritual ancestors we encountered in the village were themselves heirs of a (Jewish) spiritual tradition that, even at that time, was already considered ancient and venerable. In the midst of that, they embraced the tradition as well as wrestled with it, trying to adapt it to new and vastly changed circumstances and make it continually relevant for their communities. Our encounters and conversations with them move us to do something similar in our time. What relevance does their inspiring example set for us today?

We ourselves in the West live in vastly changed circumstances vis-à-vis our Christian spiritual tradition. We can say that the biggest difference lies in the fact that we now are in an increasingly secularized age and world. It is beneficial then at this juncture to review some important points about this present reality.

The word "secular" comes from the Late Latin word *saeculāris* (meaning "temporal") which, in turn, comes from the Latin word *saeculum* ("an age").[7] Those nuances hint at the shift in focus from the "eternal" of a past age to the "temporal," the "here and now" in our time. Defined more precisely, "secular" refers to a public order where ideally there is no one who has hegemony or control over others. Hence, it includes the separation of church and state so that each would not interfere with the affairs of the other. Instead, there is the existence and acceptance of a plurality of opinions (including religious ones). The secular order is envisioned then to be an open-ended, polymorphic, polyvocal order of diverse sorts of people saying all sorts of things. In principle, anyone in a secular society has the right to ask any question.[8]

When we say though that the West is largely "secularized," we mean that it (that is, a great number of people living in it) is largely focused on *this* world, *this* life and how humans and their habitat could exist and flourish *in the here and now*. The flip side of this secularization is that Western societies pay less and less attention nowadays to God, religion, the supernatural or the next life (particularly, heaven or hell). What is more, even many self-professed religious believers in Western(ized) societies, although nominally "religious," live their daily lives by and large without really being much aware of God and the supernatural realm.

The more seriously religious people who live in this secularized realm, however, bemoan this secularized environment and frequently see it as the source of godlessness, immorality and of the many present-day evils that beset us. It is thought that this secularized world spawns a godless and hedonistic milieu, as well as a loss of traditional "godly" values. It is common to encounter voices saying that the West is lost in a crisis of meaning because of the loss of the authority of religion (read "Christianity") which supposedly held everything together once upon a time.[9]

WHERE I CURRENTLY STAND ON "THE WEST"

For a very long time, I (especially my younger, more conservative Catholic-Christian self) also thought of secularization in those above-mentioned negative ways. That drastically changed when I was introduced to alternative ways of looking at the situation by very creative thinkers. One such is the philosopher of religion and radical philosopher-theologian Don Cupitt who, I think, is one of the most creative and insightful philosophical-theological

7. See "Secular, adj. and n.," *Oxford English Dictionary*.

8. This is from philosopher John Caputo's helpful description from The Wheatley Institution, "John D. Caputo," 18:05.

9. Carroll, *Ego and Soul*, 1.

minds today and deserves to be read and studied more widely. He has a startlingly different take on this phenomenon of secularization. Cupitt has argued in many of his writings (particularly, in *The Meaning of the West*) that this so-called secularized West is actually something like the logical and evolved form or grown-up, more mature version of Christianity.[10] In fact, I think it is fair to say that he suggests that the postmodern, humanistic West (which many traditional Christians consider as the evil antithesis of Christianity) should actually be considered Christianity as it was meant to be.[11] In short, it is the realized (and necessary to add) "yet very flawed" "Reign of God." How about that alternative and surprising assessment for a change?

I think I have some say in this because I am an immigrant here in the West who originally came from a staunchly Catholic-Christian developing country (the Philippines, which happens to be Westernized in many ways), and who also lived for a long time in a non-Western country (Japan). Moreover, for six years, I stayed in Western Europe (indeed, in Rome, arguably the heart of "the West" in many ways), sent there to do graduate studies on the New Testament. Later in life, I freely chose to leave my homelands in Asia to resettle and live in the West (now in Ontario, Canada). That life-journey has made me see in an up, close, and personal way the differences between the West and some non-Western countries.

Based on my personal experience and study of the matter then, let me affirm first of all that there are so many genuinely good and wholesome things in Western societies. This is why so many of us have decided to uproot ourselves, migrate, and settle here. In a blog post published in Australia's *Sea of Faith* website years ago, I came upon this statement which largely reflects my own personal immigrant sentiments as well as those of many immigrants I know personally:

> There are plenty from elsewhere . . . who desperately want to live in the West. And for good reason. They may not be perfect, but Western societies look after their own like no-one else does, including their weaker members and even those who dissent from prevailing political or social views. (Would you rather be gay in Abuja, Riyadh, Beijing or Sydney?) Western technology is the envy of the rest of the world, even of people like Osama bin Laden who use it to attack the West. Western medicine gives us an ever-longer, healthier lifespan. Western governments actively seek the moral, physical and intellectual improvement of their

10. Cupitt, *Meaning of the West*, chapters 1 and 3.

11. Cupitt, *Meaning of the West*, chapters 1–3.

> people and contribute to the well-being of the world's poorest through (relatively) string-free aid budgets. (That's not to mention the work of Western NGOs such as Oxfam, Red Cross, Amnesty International and *Médecins sans Frontieres.*) The West is innovative, constantly on the move, and—most important of all—it loves life wholeheartedly (Spearritt, 2008).[12]

Lest that sound smug and triumphalist, let me say unambiguously before anything else that *it is definitely not my intention here to glorify the West uncritically* because, goodness (!), there is absolutely no shortage of serious dysfunctions, even horrendously evil things to be found in the West today. We are all disgusted at its unbridled capitalism and consumerism, the staggering gap between rich and poor, a superiority complex (white privilege in most cases), racism, its active agency in the widespread destruction of nature in the West itself but also in the global south, and so forth. In fact, I originally wrote this essay in the wake of the death of George Floyd Jr. at the hands of police officers in Minneapolis in June 2020. This event led to widescale demonstrations and public unrest in the US and other places around the world to highlight the evil of racial discrimination against black people. It is heartbreaking to see such a damning instance of social dysfunction in the 2020s in the West! Therefore, I want to say unambiguously: *Yes, I am well aware of the many serious dysfunctions of Western societies.*

Despite that and in the face of all that, I still think that it is important to be mindful that so many good and wholesome things in life that we do widely enjoy here in the West can only be dreamed of by many people in many non-Western countries. Let me reiterate: Please take these statements from someone who has left his original countries in Asia, decided to live here in the West, and is very happy to have done so. That's my personal context.

THE WEST AND THE DECLINE OF MANY OF ITS CHRISTIAN INSTITUTIONS

In this chapter, as a way of responding better to the above-mentioned question "Why do we still need to read the Bible in a secular world?" I would like to ask and respond first of all to a more foundational question about the West which, I will later show, is related intimately to our main topic: Is the secularized West really all that evil as traditional religious believers think it to be? Let me get ahead of myself and answer with (a cautious and qualified)

12. Spearritt, review of *The Meaning of the West*.

"No." As hinted to above, a more careful examination of the matter will surprisingly show that the secularized West actually shares as it were the very DNA of Christianity in striking ways and we have to say instead that the much maligned secularized, irreverent, and irreligious West is—surprise, surprise!—actually Christianity's child . . . but all grown-up now! If that is true, then, as I have argued more extensively in chapter two, we have to go back to the very roots of Christianity, the roots of which lie most directly in the New Testament of the Christian Bible. And when we do so (as we have modestly tried to do in this book), we can then ask: What can we cherish and treasure? What should we resist and reject? What should we pass on to posterity?

It seems ironical to emphasize the importance of seeking out the West's Christian roots because it is plain to see that many forms of institutional Christianity in the West are in rapid decline. This is a difficult thing to witness for many "card-carrying" Christians. That includes me because, despite my general disappointment with institutional Christianity, I do consider myself a Christian from the Catholic tradition but, at the same time, also ecumenical, that is, radically open to other forms of Christianity. And, yes, I still make it a point to attend church regularly.

The alternative paradigm I present here suggests that this fast-declining situation of institutional Christianity in the West is not necessarily a bad thing. The first and biggest reason for that is the following: The founding and maintenance of a "church" was arguably never the goal of Yeshua, the founding ancestor, in the first place. The church (in Greek, *ekklēsia*) that resulted as a development of the movement started by our New Testament spiritual ancestors was only a kind of "stop-gap" measure and was always meant to cede its place eventually to a greater reality beyond itself—a reality that Yeshua and the Gospels call "the reign of God." God's new order was always and still is supposed to come more perfectly *on earth* and, when it does, the Christian church has to bow out and enable this greater reality to take over, even if that means its disappearance. Of course, it is necessary here to recall a foundational truth that is frequently forgotten by the Christian church itself: the "reign of God" *is not equal* to the church! There is a curious story in John 3 where the disciples of John the Baptist report to him that Yeshua himself is now baptizing and everyone is going to him. In response, John says:

> He who has the bride is the bridegroom. The friend of the bridegroom, who stands and hears him, rejoices greatly at the bridegroom's voice. For this reason, my joy has been fulfilled. He must increase, but I must decrease. (John 3: 27–30)

This powerfully symbolizes what the Christian church (which is tantamount to being just the friend of the bridegroom) is in deference to God's reign (which is the groom). It is also helpful to remember that when Christians say in the Lord's prayer, "May your kingdom come on earth as it is in heaven," they are actually praying for the "decreasing" of the church and the "increasing" of the reign of God.[13]

A STATE OF SHALOM NOW VERSUS A LATER HEAVEN

In connection with this theme, there is a common misunderstanding that we have to set right: the vision of a more perfect state of *shalom* which includes of course a holistically good life *here on earth first* (and *not* primarily in an afterlife called "heaven") was the original vision, firstly, of Judaism in general in the first century common era. And since first-century Palestinian Judaism was—it should be kept firmly in mind—Yeshua's own matrix of location, historically speaking then, it is accurate to say that Yeshua himself was first of all a kind of prophet-rabbi-healer who concerned himself primarily with the alleviation of the oppression and suffering of people in the "here and now" of his world and taught people primarily how to live and act so as to make *this world* a compassionate place—to use Cupitt's succinct summary—"without resentment and rancor."[14] This is clearly illustrated in a teaching that many New Testament scholars firmly believe to have come from the very lips of the historical Yeshua himself, "Love your enemies!" (Matt 5:44; Luke 6:27).

For many Christians (and Westerners in general) that is startling news because they have been taught wrongly that (the Westernized) Jesus concerned himself with showing us how to live in this passing present world in such a way as to be saved from eternal damnation and gain eternal salvation in a future life in heaven. Going back to the New Testament village and doing a more accurate study of the world of our spiritual ancestors will show that the usual "received" form of Christianity focused on eternal salvation was definitely *not* the focus of Judaism in the first century, nor was it the original emphasis of Yeshua's own historical teaching, life, and ministry.

After Yeshua's death though, his followers soon elevated him to a lofty divine status.[15] Thus, he came to be understood and portrayed in time and

13. For more on this theme, see Cupitt, *Meaning of the West*, 120.

14. Cupitt, *Meaning of the West*, 140–41.

15. For more on this, confer Hurtado, *Lord Jesus*. See also Ehrman, *How Jesus Became God*.

throughout most of the history of Western Christianity thereafter as the divine Savior who lived, taught, suffered, died, and rose from the dead *primarily* to procure an other-worldly kind of salvation in a state/place known as "heaven."

Now when we shift paradigms and begin to underscore the "this-world" emphasis of Yeshua within his original Jewish matrix, we are startled to see that this prioritizing of the here and now is a remarkable common trait between him and his time on the one hand, and *us today in the secular West*, on the other. It would be hard to deny that many of us in our day-to-day living are now primarily concerned with having a wholesome existence here and now, for ourselves and for others, and not preoccupied so much with securing, as it were, an admission ticket to heaven. In that sense, we have become quite "secular" or "secularized," compared to our immediate ancestors of a few generations in our immediate past. It might come as a surprise then that our spiritual ancestors' first-century Jewish world as well as Yeshua himself was, in this sense, quite "secular" (this term is used here anachronistically of course). We have to qualify that declaration though by adding that Yeshua and his disciples were in possession of *a bigger, transcendent worldview* in which God was understood to be actively working to establish a truly good and just order, yes, in the here and now. This is a major difference from the radically immanent worldview of today's secular age.

IS CHRISTIANITY STILL WORTH KEEPING THEN? THE SHADOW OF EMPIRE

As mentioned, it is clear that Christianity (i.e., many of its institutional forms in the West) is in a sorry state of deterioration. It has already become quite irrelevant and abandoned in many pockets of Western societies, especially among young and middle-aged people. How do we evaluate that situation after having come to know our New Testament ancestors better? Is Christianity as we know it now still worth saving? Or is it perhaps high time to go beyond institutional Christianity as it is now to a "next stage" in spirituality, whatever that may be?

I vividly remember an incident that happened in a colloquium on sexual abuse in the Catholic Church which I attended a few years ago. At a certain moment, a survivor of clerical sexual abuse took it upon herself to tell the audience: (words to the effect of) "Here we are talking of rebirthing the church. Why? The church in the form it is now *should die*! We should think about what has to come out after that death."[16] I think about that

16. See my blogpost, Kato, "Wounded Body of Christ."

remark often when I survey what the Christian church has become today after two millennia of existence. And I do agree that the church in the form it is now should probably be let go. It is just the inordinate attachment to the past that prevents us from changing what really needs to be changed. That is an emerging conclusion that I personally have come to accept (quite reluctantly, I should add!) while wrestling with the tradition that our New Testament ancestors have left us. I say that for many reasons, some of which I'll explain further below.

One major reason is the dark reality of empire that continues to live insidiously within much of institutional Christianity. I also have to add that "empire" also continues to live in much of Christian thinking and theology. Hence, decolonization of thinking and institutional structures is a particularly urgent need for our times. The Christian church became the Roman empire's bedfellow early on in its history when it became an integral part of the *imperium* beginning with the emperor Constantine's policy of favoring it in many ways. In time, imperial ways and an imperial mindset became so much a part and parcel of Christianity's structure that it became too attached to the exalted role, influence, power, prestige, and privilege that it continued to receive through the centuries. This inordinate imperial hubris with its lustful attachment to the many perks of empire make it difficult for the Christian church to let go of outdated notions and ways of doing things long after its real, physical empire has shriveled up and died. Moreover, the church continues to believe firmly that many of its doctrines, principles, and traditions are eternally valid and unchanging. A lot of that is simply not true because many so-called "sacrosanct" elements in Christianity, when analyzed critically, can be considered merely historically conditioned and not applicable anymore in the present. Many Westerners have intuitively grasped that and abandoned traditional Christianity in droves. Sadly, there does not seem to be a future that would reverse that trend except in small pockets of conservative, traditionalist, and (even) reactionary Christians.

A poignant illustration of the Christian church's misplaced orientation and disordered attachment to its self-serving ways is found in Russian novelist Fyodor Dostoyevsky's novel *The Brothers Karamazov* which contains a famous poem about "The Grand Inquisitor." There we see Christ himself returning to earth in Seville (Spain) sometime when the Spanish Inquisition was most active.[17] Christ ministers to people as Yeshua did long ago in Palestine only to be arrested by the Spanish inquisition and told by the Grand Inquisitor that, irony of ironies(!), he is no longer needed by the church. In fact, it is pointed out that his ministry actually interferes with

17. Dostoyevsky, *Brothers Karamazov*, 288–311.

what the church is trying to do. What on earth is the church trying to do that even Christ himself disturbs it, one might ask? It is to put people under the control of the church itself whereas (again sadly ironically) Christ was trying to give them genuine freedom, even from the church itself.

Although Dostoyevsky wrote in the late 1800s, the church mentality he portrayed is still prevalent in many forms of organized Christianity today. We can say that many dimensions of this mentality are definitely quite obsolete for our age. It is sad to observe how institutional Christianity seems to be trapped in many ways in a kind of navel-gazing and still largely insists on many mythological and outdated beliefs and teachings that many Westerners can *no longer* assent to with integrity. I would even add, many Westerners reject institutional Christianity (or at least major aspects of it) *in good conscience*. At least, I know I do so on many counts!

I would have to say, therefore, that the traditional "churchy" Christianity in the West is definitely on the way out *whether we like it or not*. I certainly would like a more robust Christianity to continue in the West in a form that could truly help contemporary Westerners in their quests for greater depth and transcendence. The burning question though is: Does Christianity as a whole have the will to transform itself radically to move in that direction? Of that, I am not sure. Truth be told: I don't think it will happen. Nevertheless, the radical theologian Don Cupitt thinks that, despite institutional Christianity's decline in the West, Westerners should definitely continue to cherish and preserve the valid ethical and spiritual insights and principles of the West's Christian heritage because they are genuinely significant achievements.[18] Needless to say, I strongly agree with this suggestion.

THE SURPRISING SOURCE OF THE WEST'S SECULARIZATION

Let me add another surprising aspect of the new paradigm to view the West vis-à-vis its Christian heritage. If we search for the deep source of why the West became secularized and concerned more with the here and now, we might have to look in an unlikely place. The "culprit" might very well be the Bible, particularly, the New Testament village we have just visited! One can make a good case that the following biblical notions, first, of *God's creation of the world as good*; and, second, the more characteristically Christian teaching on the *Incarnation* (the idea that God became human in the person of Yeshua of Nazareth) might actually be the theoretical wellsprings of the

18. Cupitt, *Meaning of the West*, vii–viii, x, and 10.

West's secularization in the first place.[19] I was really startled when I first encountered this idea. It just never occurred to me to look at the matter in this way before. But upon more reflection, this suggestion has gradually made quite a lot of sense to me through the years. If indeed true, this idea makes it even clearer how intimately linked the West is with its biblical and Christian heritage because that spiritual heritage actually propelled it towards becoming the secularized place we know it to be now.

Let me make a slight digression here. If the term "secular" or "secular milieu" might seem negative to some readers, I actually think that sometimes it is better to exchange the term "humanism" or "humanistic age" instead because they sound more positive. I continue to use "secular" because of convention and in order to contrast the term with a bygone "religious age."

To go back to the biblical accounts, when the whole work of creation was done, God looks at the grand work just completed and is delighted that everything is "very good" (*tov meod* in the intensive form in Hebrew). That story comes of course from the book of Genesis (1:31) in the Jewish scriptures (the Christian Old Testament). This idea of the world and everything in it as good undergirds the whole mentality of the New Testament village including the spiritual ancestors we encountered there because, as we saw, they were located and steeped in a thoroughly Jewish worldview. Moreover, GU-Matthew particularly insisted in his legacy that Christians should always treasure their foundational link with the heritage of Israel and, if there's one deep and fundamental link between Christianity and its Jewish parent, it is precisely this life-affirming clear declaration that everything that God created is fundamentally good. This would be proven later on in Christian history when mainline Christianity strongly affirmed against Marcion and his followers that everything God created (yes, even the material realm!) is good, contrary to what the Marcionites claimed.

The second principle of the Incarnation is suggested by GU-John in his Gospel (John 1:14). We saw that it may have been so radical a teaching at the time that it probably put his community outside the acceptable parameters of standard Jewish monotheistic belief and resulted in the Johannine community's being cut off from the local Jewish synagogue.[20] Reflecting further on this, what is the teaching of "divine incarnation" anyway but the "dangerous" idea of God becoming human—dangerous because it contains the potential of collapsing the widely-held assumption that there is an unbridgeable gap between the wholly transcendent Divine Being (YHWH in

19. Confer also Cupitt, *Meaning of the West*, 40–48.

20. Brown, *Community of the Beloved Disciple*; Lincoln, *Gospel according to St. John*, 82–89.

the Hebrew Bible) and immanent human beings and things? When you posit the idea that in Yeshua, the Christ, *divinity and humanity*—is believed to have—*met and fused*, the (perhaps unintended) consequence of that notion is some kind of bridging; better even, an obliteration of *the distance between the divine and the human.* Thus, in the person of Yeshua, the human-divine Messiah, the divine and the human meet. But that is not all: the divine and the human even fuse in perfect union. In technical terms that fusing of the divine and the human came to be called the "hypostatic union" in the history of Christian teaching.

But how are those core Christian doctrines with deep roots in the Bible the source of "secularization"? The first teaching on creation-as-very-good obviously urges us to affirm the value of everything we know in this realm of time and space, including all material and bodily realities. But wait! Isn't that a core tenet of the secularized milieu in which we are located now? It can even be the wonderful foundation of a contemporary ecological-humanism.

With regard to the second teaching, we can say that after the idea of the incarnation became established Christian doctrine, it was but logical to go *from* "union between divine and human in Jesus" *to*, as mentioned above, applying this principle to the common notion that there is a vast chasm between the divine and the human realms. Therefore, by virtue of the human and divine realms meeting and fusing with each other through the incarnation of Yeshua whom the New Testament calls "the firstborn of all creation" (Col 1:15), the distance between the divine realm and this material world was, in a sense, collapsed; the gulf between the "sacred" and the "profane" was lost and the focus of human religiosity shifted from God "out there" to God-divinity in "the here and now," "in carne" (in the flesh); in other words, in the secular.[21]

Now try to add to that the other insights we have learned from our New Testament ancestors during our visit to the village: Since the created world is so fundamentally good to the extent that even God through the incarnation could be thought of as being able to embrace human nature and live in this natural world, it is reasonable and in keeping with the tradition then to bear deep respect and compassion for one's fellow humans, particularly in the face of human suffering (as suggested by GU-Mark); to include everyone without exception, particularly, the poor, the oppressed, and the marginalized (as suggested by GU-Luke); and to have a grand vision of everyone and everything united in God through the Messiah Yeshua (as suggested by GU-Paul).

21. See Cupitt, *Meaning of the West*, 6–7, 15–25.

Despite all the twists and turns that Western history has taken after Christianity became an integral part of it, those above-mentioned biblical seeds were planted deeply in its soul-soil. They started growing, sprouting, and bearing fruit time and again in history when the conditions were right.[22] Applied to our times, we can ask: How have those seeds grown and borne fruit in this contemporary world?

PARADIGM SHIFT: THE WEST AS AN EVOLVED FORM OF CHRISTIANITY

As mentioned earlier, a common narrative is that from the European Enlightenment onward, many people in the West were able to achieve a break from religion in general and Christianity in particular and embrace a vision of humanity, of human life, and of the world itself as being in itself good without needing to have recourse anymore to the Christian God and the Christian supernatural scheme of things. Let's call this understanding a "paradigm of rupture" implying that, for the West to become "enlightened," it needed to have a rupture with its "unenlightened" Christian parent. I am proposing (together with other thinkers) a different picture, a paradigm shift in understanding the matter.[23] Let's call it a paradigm of continuity and development. According to this view I subscribe to here, there *has not been* a "break" between the West and its Christian religious roots. Rather, Christian society has naturally evolved and developed from an explicitly religious entity to a secular one precisely because of some fundamental Christian notions rooted in the Bible that were sown deep in its core. In Don Cupitt's surprising words, "we remain what Christianity has made us, and in many respects the postmodern West is more Christian than ever."[24]

True, the central piece of the New Testament ancestors' worldview—God—has been left out of the picture in the secular West. Why? If considered more soberly, there are reasonable factors that explain this phenomenon. One major cause is that, as the general consciousness of people in the West evolved, the almost idolatrous, anthropomorphic, and childishly mythological images of God that our spiritual ancestors believed in, and which religious institutions like the Christian church generally continue to uphold, does not seem to be credible anymore in the face of a scientifically

22. See for example, Stark, *For the Glory of God*.

23. Once again, I direct the reader to the following works for more elaboration on this matter: see Holland, *Dominion*; Stark, *For the Glory of God*; Stark, *Victory of Reason*; Ehrman, *Triumph of Christianity*.

24. Cupitt, *Meaning of the West*, 36.

advanced, more diverse and interconnected globalized world. What we need is a deeper, more inclusive, more spiritually robust, and sophisticated image of God (or the Ultimate) that could resonate better with people who have transcended an earlier ethnocentric and mythological stage of belief. This is a project that I am engaged in now together with many other theologians and thinkers, but it is beyond the scope of this present work.

Still, one can make—I think at least—a strong case that, despite everything, the secular West has somehow "remained Christian" in profound ways. Cupitt argues that proof of this can be clearly seen in various ways, such as in the many wholesome values that Westerners live by; or the belief in, indeed even the systematic social institutionalization of ideals such as charity, fairness, poverty-relief, protection of a society's most vulnerable members, and the greater empowering of women and other minoritized/marginalized groups, among many other typically "Western" values. Again, it is profitable to inquire: where do all these typical Western characteristics come from? According to the paradigm I offer here, there is one logical and major source—it is Christianity itself.[25]

In summary, I deem it quite reasonable to claim that the contemporary, secularized West is, in a deep sense, the direct heir of some of the finest traits of Christian ethics and spirituality. I would even rephrase that to the following: The West, I think it fair to say, is practically the grown-up child of Christianity. True, it is a child who has, in a sense, forgotten its parent and the many things its parent passed down to it. That does not take away the fact that the West bears Christianity's DNA. As my own mother used to say to me, "Blood is thicker than water." The values that Western societies accept as common-sensical, treasure, and fiercely defend; the values that are enshrined in some remarkable documents such as the UN charter of human rights, the declaration of human responsibilities,[26] the declaration towards a Global Ethic,[27] the Charter for Compassion,[28] among many others, seem to suggest that, at their root, these values come originally from the West's Christian parent. At the end of the day, we can even say that these values find their ultimate source in the deeply humanitarian ethics of—what we can argue is the historical, pre-mythological—Yeshua of Nazareth himself. Yeshua's ethic lives on in our contemporary humanitarianism and (Cupitt even claims) in the modern Western welfare state.

25. Cupitt, *Meaning of the West*, vii–viii; see also Murray, "Losing Their Religion."

26. See InterAction Council, "Universal Declaration of Human Rights." See also Küng and Schmidt, *Global Ethic and Global Responsibilities*, 6–30.

27. Küng and Kuschel, *Global Ethic*. See also Parliament of the World's Religions. "Towards a Global Ethic."

28. Armstrong, *Twelve Steps to a Compassionate Life*, 6–8.

THE WEST AS THE (VERY FLAWED YET SOMEHOW) REALIZED REIGN OF GOD

We have seen thus far that the main aim of the life and ministry of the historical Yeshua of Nazareth lay in trying to establish a utopian kind of society here on earth (he called "the Reign of God"), in which God would be sovereign and true humanity would be enhanced. Therefore, when those ("Yeshuan"/Christian) values that enhance true humanity have become the "common sense" of a given society, is it not fair to say that this situation is a very positive achievement? That holds true even when the society in question has become rather detached from its earlier attachment to an explicitly acknowledged divine being and realm. It is also fair to say that this has happened (very modestly) to some extent in the West. We can say, therefore, that, *in a very limited and flawed way*, the West can be considered the realized reign of God that Yeshua worked to achieve. That is one way of looking at the secularized West and I think it is true in profound ways. In short, the state of things (in which major elements originally coming from Christianity have taken root to a certain extent in society) means that the spirit of genuine Christianity has—I reiterate, in a very flawed way—been fulfilled in the here and now; it is the state that Christianity was always meant to achieve. In Cupitt's insightful words:

> Nobody in the West can be wholly non-Christian. You may call yourself non-Christian, but the dreams you dream are still Christian dreams, and you continue to be part of the history of Christianity. That's your fate. You may consider yourself secular, but the modern Western secular world is itself a Christian creation.[29]

I may not be able to assent a hundred percent to Cupitt there (I treat that statement as hyperbole-for-emphasis) but I do largely agree that, to be located in Western societies and to embrace, benefit from, and live according to the wholesome humanistic values of the West means, to a certain extent, to participate "in spirit" in what genuine Christianity always sought to achieve, a Christianity that is, in a profound way, the cultural parent of the West. And where do we find the roots of Christianity? Of course, in the New Testament village. This is why it is necessary to visit that village (as we have done in this book) from time to time and to continually ruminate on the lessons it can teach us with every new visit.

29. Cupitt, *Meaning of the West*, 67.

CRITICAL DEMURRERS: TROUBLING SHADOWS IN THE WEST

Having said all those positive things about the West, I strongly insist again that it is *not* my intention to glorify the West in a one-sided triumphalist way. We are all too familiar with the very troubling shadows that are present in Western societies. The West is where many terrible things continue to happen: rampant consumerism; cancerous economic growth; exploitation of poorer sub-groups within our societies and the effort to extend that exploitation to countries through unfair terms; abuse of the earth resulting in environmental and ecological destruction; neo-colonialism and neo-imperialism; and so on and so forth. The list can be endless. These are all well-known pathologies and dysfunctions of the West.

Nevertheless, it must be remembered, that these negative factors are at the same time being constantly pointed out, critically reflected upon, resisted, and struggled against by the finest souls among us. And *that* is precisely the point. No matter how many shadows are found in our Western societies, there seems to exist a built-in apparatus to critically self-reflect, resist, and provide solutions to it. I have not elaborated on this aspect in this work but the possibility for that self-examination and self-correction (the application of reason and critical thinking) is arguably also among the greatest gifts that has been given to us in a major way by the Christian heritage.[30] I say this because, yes, I'm basically a hopeless romantic and optimist.

The history of the West, when viewed from a more optimistic "glass is half-full" (instead of a pessimistic "glass is half-empty") perspective, does show that there has been progress made on so many counts in upholding human rights and dignity. We can complain all we want about present-day evils and dysfunctions but a perspective that also takes into account all the progress we've made in the West should be a necessary part of a more balanced evaluation of the matter. And to be included with that, I strongly maintain here, are the fine traits that we've inherited from our Christian legacy while also being cognizant of its very deep shadows.[31] At the end of the day, *that is the grown-up thing to do about one's ancestry.*

I would also like to state clearly for the record that I'm a person of color, a proud member of the group commonly referred to now as BIPOC (Black, Indigenous, People of Color). As a person of color, I claim unapologetically that I *am* also an integral part of Western society. We sometimes

30. Cupitt, *Meaning of the West*, chapters 10 and 11.

31. A useful book that points out the dysfunctional aspects of the Bible while affirming a God of love is Spong, *Sins of Scripture*.

hear anti-Western discourse by BIPOC people that gives the impression that they are not part of Western society. I think that this is not a good strategy. We have to claim our place in this Western world and forever ditch the idea that only white people can be "Westerners." Let us stand tall and proud and claim this Western identity as part of ourselves (although we may be hybrid and have other non-Western legacies as well). Let us not consent to be marginalized here anymore. After all, this is our home now and we do not need to apologize for being here. Let us do our part in "browning the West" so that non-whites can also rightfully and proudly claim their place in this world.

I would also like to apologize if I've sounded so far as if I'm trying to forcefully include people here as "anonymous Christians." That term is from Catholic theologian Karl Rahner.[32] It was meant to "include" non-Christians as potential Christians and thus also include them in the plan of salvation provided by God. Although Rahner's idea was revolutionary in Catholic theological circles in the 1960s and 1970s when originally proposed, it sounds incredibly condescending to us now and it was also squarely refuted by one of my theological heroes, Hans Küng, because of that.[33] I'd like to clarify that my intention here is *not* theological but *cultural and humanistic.* I'm trying to culturally trace the West's spiritual ancestry and my quest has made me conclude that it is virtually undeniable that this ancestry lies in the Christian tradition with its deepest roots in the New Testament.

WHY WE STILL NEED TO READ THE BIBLE IN A SECULAR AGE

And with that we come to the ultimate reason I can offer for why we still need to read the Bible, particularly, the New Testament, in this our secular age. It is only by visiting the New Testament village that we can be put in touch once again with the original impetus that gave rise to the Christian tradition, a legacy that still impacts us as Westerners (or hybrids with some Western component in us) in so many profound ways today. It is only by meeting those ancestors in the New Testament village, conversing with them, learning, agreeing, disagreeing, adding some critical perspectives to their views[34] can we root ourselves in the tradition and pass on what

32. Rahner, "Christianity and the Non-Christian Religions," 5:115–34.

33. Küng, *On Being a Christian*, 98.

34. One particularly urgent task today in interpreting our traditions (such as the Bible) is the effort to think intersectionally about them. That means to reflect on how these traditions are impacted by various interacting systems of oppression and privilege. For more on this, confer Yee, "Thinking Intersectionally."

needs to be passed on to the next generation. It is this creative embracing of and wrestling with the tradition I have advocated here that will fulfill our deep need for roots.

Postscript

Is There a Place for God and the Christian Church in All This?

This question deserves another sustained critical reflection not possible in this work. Let me limit myself to a few brief remarks. I think that a Christianity (that wants to maintain its form exactly as it is now) does not seem to have a future in the West. Although this "old time" Christianity seems to be flourishing in many parts of the non-Western world and in some pockets of the West itself, when (or if) these areas undergo a development in the direction in which Western societies have taken since the Enlightenment, institutional Christianity will suffer the same grim fate. It goes without saying that institutionalized Christianity has to undergo a complete overhaul if it is to continue being a relevant entity in the West.

"God" is an even bigger issue than institutional Christianity. Personally, I believe that there is a place for God in the secularized life of Christianity's grown-up child (the West) but, like institutional Christianity, this notion will also have to undergo a complete revision and overhaul. Let us remember though that humans are beings that fundamentally seek depth and transcendence. Because of that they will always seek to find ways to address the "bigger-than-life" questions, questions of which "God" has been the standard symbol and answer in the West for most of its history. How the idea of God will evolve in the West should be the fruit, I suggest, of embracing and wrestling with our spiritual tradition in the light of new data and experience.

However, that is not the task that we proposed for this work. Our goal here has been more modest. It was merely to go back to the New Testament village where we could encounter and converse with some of our important spiritual ancestors because doing so would make us more aware of our roots, our spiritual ancestry. What we do with that awareness henceforward would have to be the topic for another work. I hope you, dear readers, will also eventually be able to read that sometime in the future.

Bibliography

Aland, Barbara, et. al., eds. *The Greek New Testament*. 4th rev. ed. Stuttgart: German Bible Society, 1993.

Anderson, Paul N. *The Riddles of the Fourth Gospel: An Introduction to John*. Minneapolis: Fortress, 2011.

Arendt, Hannah. *The Origins of Totalitarianism*. New York: Harcourt, 2018.

Armstrong, Karen. *The Lost Art of Scripture: Rescuing Sacred Texts*. London: The Bodley Head, 2019.

———. *Twelve Steps to a Compassionate Life*. New York: Knopf, 2010.

Aslan, Reza. *God: A Human History*. New York: Random, 2017.

Bailey, Randall C., et al. *They Were All Together in One Place? Toward Minority Biblical Criticism*. Atlanta: Society of Biblical Literature, 2009.

Beavis, Mary Ann, and Michael J. Gilmour, eds. *Dictionary of the Bible and Western Culture*. Sheffield: Sheffield Phoenix, 2012.

Berkowitz, Roger. "Why Arendt Matters: Revisiting *The Origins of Totalitarianism*." *Los Angeles Review of Books*, March 18, 2017. https://lareviewofbooks.org/article/arendt-matters-revisiting-origins-totalitarianism/#!.

Bhullar, Amrita. "The Growth of Spiritual Intelligence." *Indian Journal of Educational Studies: An Interdisciplinary Journal* 2 (2015) 122–31.

Bock, Darrell L. *A Theology of Luke and Acts: God's Promised Program, Realized for All Nations*. Grand Rapids: Zondervan, 2012.

Borg, Marcus. *Conflict, Holiness and Politics in the Teachings of Jesus*. Harrisburg, PA: Trinity, 1998.

———. *Days of Awe and Wonder: How to Be a Christian in the 21st Century*. New York: HarperOne, 2017.

———. *The Heart of Christianity: Rediscovering a Life of Faith*. New York: Harper, 2003.

———. *Jesus, a New Vision: Spirit, Culture, and the Life of Discipleship*. New York: Harper, 1987.

———. *Meeting Jesus Again for the First Time: The Historical Jesus and the Heart of Contemporary Faith*. New York: HarperOne, 1996.

———. *Reading the Bible Again for the First Time: Taking the Bible Seriously but Not Literally*. New York: Harper, 2001.

———. "When Heaven and Earth Meet." *Living Pulpit* 5 (1996) 4–5. http://www.richardmburgess.com/yahoo_site_admin/assets/docs/lk_2_Borg_-When_Heaven_and_earth_Meet.352182841.pdf.

Borg, Marcus, and John Dominic Crossan. *The First Paul: Reclaiming the Radical Visionary Behind the Church's Conservative Icon*. New York: HarperOne, 2009.

Borg, Marcus, and N. T. Wright. *The Meaning of Jesus: Two Visions*. New York: HarperOne, 1999.

Brown, Raymond E. *The Community of the Beloved Disciple: The Life, Loves, and Hates of an Individual Church in New Testament Times*. New York, Mahwah: Paulist, 1979.

———. *Introduction to the New Testament*. New York: Doubleday, 1997.

———. *An Introduction to the New Testament: The Abridged Edition*. Edited and abridged by Marion L. Soards. New Haven, CT: Yale University Press, 2016.

Bultmann, Rudolf. *The History of the Synoptic Tradition*. Translated by John Marsh. Oxford: Blackwell, 1968.

———. *Jesus and the Word*. London: Fontana, 1958.

Carroll, James. *Constantine's Sword: The Church and the Jews*. Boston: Houghton Mifflin, 2001.

Carroll, John. *Ego and Soul: The Modern West in Search of Meaning*. Sydney: HarperCollins, 1998.

Carvalho, Corrine L. *Primer on Biblical Methods*. Winona, MN: Anselm Academic, 2009.

Casey, Maurice. *From Jewish Prophet to Gentile God: The Origins and Development of New Testament Christology*. Louisville: Westminster John Knox, 1991.

———. *Is John's Gospel True?* London: Routledge, 1996.

———. *Jesus: An Independent Historian's Account of His Life and Teaching*. London: T. & T. Clark, 2010.

Charlesworth, James. *The Historical Jesus*. Nashville: Abingdon, 2008.

Chilton, Bruce. *Rabbi Jesus: An Intimate Biography*. New York: Doubleday, 2000.

———. *Resurrection Logic: How Jesus' Disciples Believed that God Had Raised Him from the Dead*. Waco, TX: Baylor University Press, 2019.

Chilton, Bruce, and Jacob Neusner. *Judaism in the New Testament: Practices and Beliefs*. London: Routledge, 1995.

Crossan, John Dominic. *God and Empire: Jesus Against Rome, Then and Now*. New York: Harper, 2007.

———. *Jesus: A Revolutionary Biography*. New York: Harper, 1994.

Crossan, John Dominic, and Jonathan Reed. *In Search of Paul: How Jesus's Apostle Opposed Rome's Empire with God's Kingdom*. New York: HarperOne, 2004.

Cupitt, Don. *The Meaning of the West: An Apologia for Secular Christianity*. London: SCM, 2008.

———. *The New Religion of Life in Everyday Speech*. London, SCM, 1999.

———. *The Old Creed and the New*. London: SCM, 2006.

Dalai Lama. "18 Rules for Living." https://www.huffpost.com/entry/dalai-lama-18-rules-of-li_b_2572518. See this website that claims that the 18 rules are not from the Dalai Lama: https://buddhism-controversy-blog.com/2014/03/01/dalai-lama-fake-quotes/.

Dong, Lan. *Reading Amy Tan*. Santa Barbara, CA: ABC Clio, 2009.

Dostoyevsky, Fyodor. *The Brothers Karamazov*. Middlesex: Penguin, 1958.

Drescher, Elizabeth. *Choosing Our Religion: The Spiritual Lives of America's Nones*. New York: Oxford University Press, 2016.

Dunn, James D. G. *A New Perspective on Jesus: What the Quest for the Historical Jesus Missed*. Grand Rapids: Baker, 2005.

———. *Unity and Diversity in the New Testament: An Inquiry into the Character of Earliest Christianity*. 3rd ed. London: SCM, 2006.

Dyas, Dee, and Esther Hughes. *The Bible in Western Culture: The Student's Guide*. London: Routledge, 2005.

Dyer, Wayne. *You'll See It When You Believe It: The Way to Your Personal Transformation*. New York: William Morrow, 1989.

Ehrman, Bart. *How Jesus Became God: The Exaltation of a Jewish Preacher from Galilee*. New York: HarperOne, 2015.

———. *The Triumph of Christianity: How a Forbidden Religion Swept the World*. New York: Simon and Schuster, 2018.

Feldman, Louis H. *Jew and Gentile in the Ancient World*. Princeton: Princeton University, 1993.

Fortna, Robert T. "The Gospel of John and the Historical Jesus." In *Profiles of Jesus*, edited by Roy W. Hoover, 223–30. Santa Rosa, CA: Polebridge, 2002.

Fox, Matthew. *The A.W.E. (Ancestral Wisdom Education) Project: Reinventing Education. Reinventing the Human*. Kelowna, BC: CopperHouse, 2006.

———. *Original Blessing*. New York: Tercher, 2000.

Frankl, Viktor. *Man's Search for Meaning*. 4th ed. Boston: Beacon, 1992.

Fredriksen, Paula. "Compassion-Is-to-Purity-as-Fish-Is-to-Bicycle and Other Reflections on Constructions of 'Judaism' in Current Work on the Historical Jesus." In *Apocalypticism, Anti-Semitism and the Historical Jesus*, edited by John Kloppenborg and John Marshall, 55–67. London: T. & T. Clark, 2005.

———. "Paul, the Perfectly Righteous Pharisee." In *The Pharisees*, edited by Joseph Sievers and Amy-Jill Levine, 112–35. Grand Rapids: Eerdmans, 2021.

Garroway, Joshua D. "Ioudaios." In *The Jewish Annotated New Testament*, edited by Amy-Jill Levine and Marc Zvi Brettler, 596–99. 2nd ed. New York: Oxford University Press, 2011, 2017.

Gelpi, Donald. *The Firstborn of Many: A Christology for Converting Christians*. Vol. 3. Milwaukee: Marquette University Press, 2001.

Gorman, Michael. *Reading Revelation Responsibly: Uncivil Worship and Witness: Following the Lamb into the New Creation*. Eugene, OR: Cascade, 2011.

Green, Joel, ed. *Hearing the New Testament: Strategies for Interpretation*. Grand Rapids: Eerdmans, 1995.

Greever, Joshua M. "Peace." In *The Lexham Bible Dictionary*, edited by John D. Barry et al. Bellingham, WA: Lexham, 2016.

Gregg, Carl. "Do We Need a Moratorium on the Word 'God'?"*Patheos*, October 8, 2012. https://www.patheos.com/blogs/carlgregg/2012/10/do-we-need-a-moratorium-on-the-word-god/.

Griffith-Jones, Robin. *The Four Witnesses: The Rebel, the Rabbi, the Chronicler and the Mystic*. New York: HarperSanFrancisco, 2000.

Hagner, Donald A. *Matthew 1–13*. Word Biblical Commentary 33A. Dallas: Word, 1998.

Hamm, M. Dennis, SJ. "Luke." In *The Paulist Biblical Commentary*, edited by Jose Enrique Aguilar Chiu et al., 1076–77. Mahwah, NJ: Paulist, 2018.

Hank Center for the Catholic Intellectual Heritage. "The Challenge of God—Plenary Address by John D. Caputo." YouTube video, 40:54. June 29, 2016. https://www.

youtube.com/watch?v=BRSkOUJ1b9w&list=PLV7Diz4DTv4lbiEzoKoaJwu4hEiFcQMml&index=3&t=1895s.

Harris, Stephen L. "The Diverse World of First-Century Judaism." In *The New Testament: A Student's Introduction*, 42–67. 7th ed. New York: McGraw Hill, 2012.

———. *Exploring the Bible*. New York: McGraw Hill, 2010.

Hartley, L. P. *The Go-Between*. London: Penguin, 2015.

Healey, Joseph P. "Peace: Old Testament." In *The Anchor Yale Bible Dictionary*, edited by David Noel Freedman, 5:206–12. New York: Doubleday, 1992.

Hepburn, Ronald. "Religious Experience, Argument for the Existence of God." In *Encyclopedia of Philosophy*. https://www.encyclopedia.com/humanities/encyclopedias-almanacs-transcripts-and-maps/religious-experience-argument-existence-god.

Hertzel, David. *Ancestors: Who We Are and Where We Come From*. Lanham, MD: Rowman & Littlefield, 2017.

Holland, Tom. *Dominion: The Making of the Western Mind*. London: Little, Brown, 2019.

Hood, Ralph W., Jr. "The Common Core Thesis in the Study of Mysticism." *Oxford Research Encyclopaedia of Religion*. https://oxfordre.com/religion/display/10.1093/acrefore/9780199340378.001.0001/acrefore-9780199340378-e-241.

Houselander, Caryll. *A Rocking-Horse Catholic*. Charleston, SC: Nabu, 2011.

Hurtado, Larry. *The Lord Jesus: Devotion to Jesus in Earliest Christianity*. Grand Rapids: Eerdmans, 2003.

InterAction Council. "A Universal Declaration of Human Responsibilities." InterAction Council, September 1, 1997. https://www.interactioncouncil.org/publications/universal-declaration-human-responsibilities.

Janicki, Toby. *God-fearers: Gentles and the God of Israel*. Marshfield, MO: First Fruits of Zion, 2012.

Johnson, Luke Timothy. "Literary Criticism of Luke-Acts: Is Reception-History Pertinent?" *JSNT* 28 (2005) 159–62.

———. "Luke-Acts, Book of." In *The Anchor Bible Dictionary*, edited by David Noel Freedman, 4:403–20. New York: Doubleday, 1992.

———. *The Real Jesus: The Misguided Quest for the Historical Jesus and the Truth of the Traditional Gospels*. New York: Harper, 1996.

Just, Felix, SJ. "The Gospel according to Matthew: Five Major Discourses of Jesus." https://catholic-resources.org/Bible/Matthew-Discourses.htm.

———. "The Gospel according to Matthew: Quotations from the Old Testament." https://catholic-resources.org/Bible/Matthew-OTQuotations.htm.

———. "Symbols of the Four Evangelists." https://catholic-resources.org/Art/Evangelists_Symbols.htm.

———. "Various Outlines of the Fourth Gospel." https://catholic-resources.org/John/Outlines-Gospel.htm.

Kaltner, John, and Steven L. McKenzie. *Sleuthing the Bible: Clues that Unlock the Mysteries of the Text*. Grand Rapids: Eerdmans, 2019.

Kato, Julius-Kei. *How Immigrant Christians Living in Mixed Cultures Interpret Their Religion: Asian-American Diasporic Hybridity and Its Implications for Hermeneutics*. Lewiston, NY: Edwin Mellen, 2012.

———. "Interpretation." In *Asian American Religious Cultures*, edited by Jonathan H. X. Lee et al., 1: 63–75. Santa Barbara, CA: ABC-CLIO, 2015.

———. *Religious Language and Asian American Hybridity*. New York: Palgrave Macmillan, 2016.

———. "Why Read the Bible in a Secular Age? An Unapologetic Apologia for the Importance of Biblical Studies Today." *The Fourth R: A Journal for Religious Literacy* 33 (2020) 17–20.

———. "The Wounded Body of Christ: Toronto Theological Colloquium on the Catholic Sexual Abuse Crisis (Part 2)." http://spiritual-notandyet-religious-jkk.blogspot.com/2019/03/the-wounded-body-of-christ-toronto_19.html.

Katz, Stephen. "Language, Epistemology and Mysticism." In *Mysticism and Philosophical Analysis*, edited by Stephen Katz, 22–74. Oxford: Oxford University Press, 1978.

Kaye, Sharon. "William of Ockham (Occam, c. 1280—c. 1349)." In *Internet Encyclopedia of Philosophy*. https://iep.utm.edu/ockham/.

Keener, Craig S., and John H. Walton, eds. *The NIV Cultural Backgrounds Study Bible*. Grand Rapids: Zondervan, 2016.

Kim, Uriah, and Seung Ai Yang, eds. *T&T Clark Handbook of Asian American Hermeneutics*. London: T. & T. Clark, 2019.

Knight, Douglas A., and Amy-Hill Levine. *The Meaning of the Bible: What the Jewish Scriptures and Christian Old Testament Can Teach Us*. New York: HarperOne, 2011.

Küng, Hans. *On Being a Christian*. Translated by Edward Quinn. New York: Doubleday, 1976.

———. *Does God Exist? An Answer for Today*. New York: Vintage, 1981.

Küng, Hans, and Karl-Josef Kuschel, eds. *A Global Ethic: The Declaration of the Parliament of the World's Religions*. New York: Continuum, 1993.

Küng, Hans, and Helmut Schmidt. *A Global Ethic and Global Responsibilities: Two Declarations*. London: SCM, 1998.

Lapin, Hayim. "Rabbi." In *Anchor Yale Bible Dictionary*, edited by David Noel Freedman, 5:600–602. New York: Doubleday, 1992.

Levine, Amy-Jill. *The Misunderstood Jew: The Church and the Scandal of the Jewish Jesus*. New York: HarperOne, 2007.

Lincoln, Andrew. *The Gospel according to St. John: Black's New Testament Commentaries*. New York: Continuum, 2005.

Longenecker, Richard, ed. *The Road from Damascus: The Impact of Paul's Conversation on His Life, Thought, and Ministry*. Grand Rapids: Eerdmans, 1997.

Lopez, Davina C. "The New Perspective on Paul." https://www.bibleodyssey.org/en/people/related-articles/new-perspective-on-paul.

Maddox, Robert. *The Purpose of Luke-Acts*. Edinburgh: T. & T. Clark, 1982.

Malina, Bruce. "Clean and Unclean: Understanding Rules of Purity." In *The New Testament World: Insights from Cultural Anthropology*. Rev. ed. Louisville: Westminster John Knox, 1996.

Malina, Bruce J., and Richard L. Rohrbaugh. *Social-Science Commentary on the Gospel of John*. Minneapolis: Fortress, 1998.

Marcus Borg Foundation. "The Battle over Jesus Today." YouTube video, 48:30. April 5 2018. https://www.youtube.com/watch?v=_X5ejSr9S3A.

Marcus, Joel. "The Jewish War and the Sitz im Leben of Mark." *Journal of Biblical Literature* 111 (1992) 441–62.

Marguerat, Daniel. *The First Christian Historian: Writing the Acts of the Apostles*. Cambridge: Cambridge University, 2002.

McGrath, James. *What Jesus Learned from Women*. Eugene, OR: Cascade, 2021.

McIver, Robert K. *Memory, Jesus, and the Synoptic Gospels*. Atlanta: SBL, 2011.

McKnight, Scott. "Proselytism and Godfearers." In *Dictionary of New Testament Background*, edited by Craig A. Evans and Stanley E. Porter, 835–47. Downers Grove, IL: InterVarsity, 2000.

Mellows, Marilyn, writer and producer. Show no. 1612W, "From Jesus to Christ: The First Christians—Part II." *Frontline*. Directed by William Cran. Aired April 7, 1998, PBS. https://www.pbs.org/wgbh/pages/frontline/shows/religion/etc/script2.html.

Mercadante, Linda. *Belief without Borders: Inside the Minds of the Spiritual but Not Religious*. New York: Oxford University Press, 2014.

Merton, Thomas. *Conjectures of a Guilty Bystander*. New York: Doubleday, 1968.

Metz, Johann-Baptist. *Faith in History and Society: Toward a Practical Fundamental Theology*. Translated by J. Matthew Ashley. New York: Herder & Herder, 2007.

Miller, Robert J. *Born Divine: The Births of Jesus and Other Sons of God*. Santa Rosa, CA: Polebridge, 2003.

———, ed. *The Complete Gospels*. 4th ed. Sonoma, CA: Polebridge, 2010.

Moss, Candida. "Everyone's Favorite Gospel Is a Forgery." *Daily Beast*, March 14, 2020. https://www.thedailybeast.com/everyones-favorite-gospel-the-gospel-of-john-is-a-forgery-according-to-new-research?ref=home.

Mullins, Terrence. "Jesus, the 'Son of David.'" *Andrew University Seminary Studies* (AUSS) 29 (1991) 117–26. https://digitalcommons.andrews.edu/auss/vol29/iss2/17/.

Murray, Douglas. "Losing Their Religion: The Priests Who Turned from God." *UnHerd*, May 25, 2018. https://unherd.com/2018/05/losing-religion-priests-turned-god/.

Oden, Robert A., Jr. "Cosmogony, Cosmology." In *The Anchor Bible Dictionary*, edited by David Noel Freedman, 1:1162–71. New York: Doubleday, 1992.

Ophir, Adi, and Ishay Rosen-Zyi. *Goy: Israel's Multiple Others and the Birth of the Gentile*. Oxford: Oxford University Press, 2018.

Pagels, Elaine. *The Origin of Satan*. New York: Vintage, 1996.

Parliament of the World's Religions. "Towards a Global Ethic." https://parliamentofreligions.org/wp-content/uploads/2022/03/global_ethic_pdf_-_2020_update.pdf.

"Pathos." *American Heritage Dictionary of the English Language Online*. The Free Dictionary, 2016. https://www.thefreedictionary.com/pathos.

Patrick, Dale. "Election-Old Testament." In *The Anchor Bible Dictionary*, edited by David Noel Freedman, 2:434–41. New York: Doubleday, 1992.

Pervo, Richard I. *The Mystery of Acts*. Santa Rosa, CA: Polebridge, 2008.

Pittman, Frank. *Grow Up! How Taking Responsibility Can Make You a Happy Adult*. New York: St. Martin's Griffin, 1998.

Plevnik, Joseph. "Honor/Shame." In *Handbook of Biblical Social Values*, edited by John Pilch and Bruce Malina, 106–15. Peabody, MA: Hendrickson, 1998.

Plum Village. "How to Love and Understand Your Ancestors When You Don't Know Them? | Thich Nhat Hanh." YouTube video, 2:58. January 17, 2015. https://www.youtube.com/watch?v=pdodGeRNjto&list=PLV7Diz4DTv4nv-RTpS-oQuDNHUhob1OLP&index=3&t=130s.

Quote Investigator. "You Are Not a Human Being Having a Spiritual Experience. You Are a Spiritual Being Having a Human Experience." https://quoteinvestigator.com/2019/06/20/spiritual/.

Rahner, Karl. "Christianity and the Non-Christian Religions." In *Theological Investigations*, 5:115–34. Baltimore: Helicon, 1966.

Rankin, Marianne. *An Introduction to Religious and Spiritual Experience*. London: Continuum, 2008.

Religion and Ethics NewsWeekly. "Jewish Jesus: Amy-Jill Levine Extended Interview." YouTube video, 11:41. March 22, 2013. https://www.youtube.com/watch?v=1PDyISl7TGc&list=PLV7Diz4DTv4mov974p3xFPHXrGgmJkNUk&index=11.

Religious Studies. "The Search for Jesus (FULL)." YouTube video, 1:10:14. January 18, 2014. https://www.youtube.com/watch?v=-aFZxIn2OxY&t=3173s.

Richards, E. Randolph, and Brandon J. O-Brien. *Misreading Scripture with Western Eyes: Removing Cultural Blinders to Better Understand the Bible*. Downers Grove, IL: InterVarsity, 2012.

Ricœur, Paul. *Interpretation Theory: Discourse and the Surplus of Meaning*. Fort Worth: Texas Christian University, 1976.

Ruether, Rosemary Radford. *Faith and Fratricide: The Theological Roots of Anti-Semitism*. New York: Seabury, 1974.

Ruprecht, Louis, Jr. *The Tragic Gospel: How John Corrupted the Heart of Christianity*. San Francisco: Jossey-Bass, 2008.

Saint Exupéry, Antoine de. *The Little Prince*. London: Farshore, 2017.

Sanders, E. P. *Jesus and Judaism*. Philadelphia: Fortress, 1985.

Schippe, Cullen, and Chuck Stetson, eds. *The Bible and Its Influences*. Fairfax, VA: BLP, 2006.

Scott, Bernard Brandon, et al. "If Not Christians, What?" The Fourth R 34 (2021) 13–18.

"Secular, adj. and n." *Oxford English Dictionary Online*. https://www-oed-com.proxy1.lib.uwo.ca/view/Entry/174620?redirectedFrom=secular&.

Shanks, Hershel, ed. *Christianity and Rabbinic Judaism: A Parallel History of Their Origins and Early Development*. Washington, DC: Biblical and Archeological Society, 1992.

Silberman, Isabella. "Religion as a Meaning System: Implications for the New Millennium." *Journal of Social Issues* 61 (2005) 641–63. https://spssi-onlinelibrary-wiley-com.proxy1.lib.uwo.ca/doi/pdfdirect/10.1111/j.1540-4560.2005.00425.x.

Smith, Huston. *The Soul of Christianity: Restoring the Great Tradition*. New York: HarperSanFrancisco, 2005.

Smith, James K. A. *How (Not) to Be Secular: Reading Charles Taylor*. Grand Rapids: Eerdmans, 2014.

Soards, Marion. "The Historical and Cultural Setting of Luke-Acts." In *New Views on Luke and Acts*, edited by Earl Richard, 33–47. Collegeville, MN: Liturgical, 1990.

Spearritt, Greg. Review of *The Meaning of the West: An Apologia for Secular Christianity*, by Don Cupitt. April 2009. https://sof-in-australia.org/article/cupitt-don-the-meaning-of-the-west/.

Spong, John Shelby. *The Fourth Gospel: Tales of a Jewish Mystic*. New York: HarperOne, 2013.

———. *The Sins of Scripture: Exposing the Bible's Texts of Hate to Reveal the God of Love*. New York: HarperOne, 2005.

Stace, W. T. *The Teachings of the Mystics*. New York: New American Library, 1960.

Stark, Rodney. *For the Glory of God: How Monotheism Led to Reformations, Science, Witch-Hunts, and the End of Slavery*. Princeton, NJ: Princeton University Press, 2003.

———. *The Triumph of Christianity: How the Jesus Movement Became the World's Largest Religion*. New York: HarperOne, 2011.

———. *The Triumph of Faith: Why the World Is More Religious Than Ever*. Wilmington, DE: Intercollegiate Studies Institute, 2015.

———. *The Victory of Reason: How Christianity Led to Freedom, Capitalism, and Western Success*. New York: Random, 2005.

Takaki, Ronald. *Strangers from a Different Shore: A History of Asian Americans*. New York: Penguin, 1989.

Tan, Amy. *The Bonesetter's Daughter*. New York: Ballantine, 2001.

———. *The Joy Luck Club*. New York: Penguin, 1989.

———. *The Kitchen God's Wife*. New York: Ballantine, 1991.

Taussig, Hal. *Jesus Before God: The Prayer Life of the Historical Jesus*. Santa Rosa, CA: Polebridge, 1999.

Taylor, Charles. *A Secular Age*. Cambridge, MA: Harvard University Press, 2007.

Tenpel. "Dalai Lama Fake Quotes." https://buddhism-controversy-blog.com/2014/03/01/dalai-lama-fake-quotes/.

Thiessen, Matthew. *Jesus and the Forces of Death: The Gospels' Portrayal of Ritual Impurity within First-Century Judaism*. Grand Rapids: Baker, 2020.

Togarasei, Lovemore. "The Conversion of Paul in the Light of the Theory of Cognitive Dissonance." *Zambezia* 31 (2004). http://ir.uz.ac.zw/jspui/bitstream/10646/519/1/07-Togarasei.pdf.

Tracy, David. *Plurality and Ambiguity: Hermeneutics, Religion, Hope*. Chicago: University of Chicago Press, 1987.

Tuan, Mia. *Forever Foreigners or Honorary Whites? The Asian Ethnic Experience Today*. Piscataway, NJ: Rutgers University Press, 1999.

Valliere, Paul. "Tradition." In vol. 13 of *The Encyclopedia of Religion*, edited by Lindsay Jones et al., 13:9267–81. 2nd ed. Detroit: Macmillan, 2005.

Van Voorst, Robert E. "The Gospel of Mark: Following Jesus, the Suffering Messiah." In *Reading the New Testament Today*, 148–84. Belmont, CA: Thomson-Wadsworth, 2005.

Vearncombe, Erin, et al., eds. *After Jesus Before Christianity: A Historical Exploration of the First Two Centuries of Jesus Movements*. New York: HarperOne, 2021.

Vermes, Geza. *Jesus, the Jew: A Historian's Reading of the Gospels*. Philadelphia: Fortress, 1981.

Webb, Mark. "Religious Experience." In *The Stanford Encyclopedia of Philosophy*, edited by Edward N. Zalta. https://plato.stanford.edu/archives/win2017/entries/religious-experience/.

Weil, Simone. *The Need for Roots: A Prelude to a Declaration of Duties towards Mankind*. London: Routledge, 2020.

The Wheatley Institution. "John D. Caputo: Post Modern, Post Secular, Post Religious." YouTube video, 18:05. November 21, 2016. https://www.youtube.com/watch?v=1ABEuQXQbso&list=WL&index=14.

Woods, Thomas E., Jr. *How the Catholic Church Built Western Civilization*. Washington, DC: Regnery, 2005.

Wright, David P. "Unclean and Clean (OT)." In *The Anchor Bible Dictionary*, edited by David Noel Freedman, 6:738–41. New York: Doubleday, 1992.

Wright, N. T., and Michael Bird. *The New Testament in Its World: An Introduction to the History, Literature, and Theology of the First Christians*. Grand Rapids: Zondervan Academic, 2019.

Yee, Gale. "Thinking Intersectionally: Gender, Race, Class, and the Etceteras of Our Discipline." *JBL* 139 (2020) 7–26.
Zacharias, H. Daniel. "Rabbi as a Title." In *The Lexham Bible Dictionary*, edited by John D. Barry et al. Belling, WA: Lexham, 2016.
Zohar, Danah, and Ian Marshall. *Spiritual Intelligence: The Ultimate Intelligence*. London: Bloomsbury, 2000.

BIBLICAL RESOURCES (WITH A FOCUS ON THE NEW TESTAMENT)

Recommended for Reference & Further Study

Anselm Academic. *Understanding the Bible: A Guide to Reading the Scriptures*. Winona, MN: Anselm Academic, 2008.
Barr, David L. *New Testament Story: An Introduction*. Belmont, CA: Wadsworth, 2009.
Beavis, Mary Ann, and Michael J. Gilmour. *Dictionary of the Bible and Western Culture*. Sheffield: University of Sheffield Press, 2012, 2017.
Borg, Marcus J. *Reading the Bible Again for the First Time: Taking the Bible Seriously but Not Literally*. San Francisco: HarperOne, 2001, 2015.
Brettler, Marc Zvi, et al. *The Bible and the Believer: How to Read the Bible Critically and Religiously*. New York: Oxford University Press, 2012.
Brown, Jeannine K. *Scripture as Communication: Introducing Biblical Studies*. Grand Rapids: Baker Academic, 2007.
Brown, Raymond. *Introduction to the New Testament*. New York: Doubleday, 1997.
———. *An Introduction to the New Testament*. Edited and abridged by Marion L. Soards. New Haven, CT: Yale University Press, 2016.
Carmody, Timothy R. *Reading the Bible: A Study Guide*. Mahwah, NJ: Paulist, 2004.
Carter, Warren, and Amy-Jill Levine. *The New Testament: Methods and Meanings*. Nashville: Abingdon, 2013.
Carvalho, Corrine L., ed. *Anselm Companion to the Bible*. Winona, MN: Anselm Academic, 2014.
———. *Primer on Biblical Methods*. Winona, MN: Anselm Academic, 2009.
Chiu, José Enrique Aguilar et al., eds. *The Paulist Biblical Commentary*. Mahwah, NJ: Paulist, 2018.
Collins, John, et al. *The Jerome Biblical Commentary for the Twenty-First Century*. 3rd rev. ed. London: T. & T. Clark, 2022.
Davies, Stevan L. *The New Testament: An Analytical Approach*. Salem, OR: Polebridge, 2011.
Dyas, Dee, and Esther Hughes. *The Bible in Western Culture: The Student's Guide*. London: Routledge, 2005.
Ehrman, Bart. *The Bible: A Historical and Literary Introduction*. 2nd ed. New York: Oxford, 2017.
———. *A Brief Introduction to the New Testament*. 5th ed. New York: Oxford, 2020.
———. *The New Testament: A Historical Introduction to the Early Christian Writings*. 7th ed. New York: Oxford, 2019.
Frigge Marielle. *Beginning Biblical Studies*. Rev. ed. Winona, MN: Anselm Academic, 2013.

Green, Joel B., ed. *Hearing the New Testament: Strategies for Interpretation*. Grand Rapids: Eerdmans, 1995.

Griffith-Jones, Robin. *The Four Witnesses: The Rebel, the Rabbi, the Chronicler and the Mystic*. New York: HarperSanFrancisco, 2000.

Harris, Stephen L. *Exploring the Bible*. New York: McGraw Hill, 2010.

———. *The New Testament: A Student's Introduction*. 9th ed. New York: McGraw Hill, 2020.

———. *Understanding the Bible*. New York: McGraw Hill, 2007.

Johnson, Luke Timothy. *The Writings of the New Testament*. Minneapolis: Fortress, 2010.

Keener, Craig S., and John H. Walton, eds. *The NIV Cultural Backgrounds Study Bible*. Grand Rapids: Zondervan, 2016.

Knight, Douglas A., and Amy-Jill Levine. *The Meaning of the Bible: What the Jewish Scriptures and Christian Old Testament Can Teach Us*. New York: HarperOne, 2011.

Landry, David, and John Martens. *Inquiry into the New Testament: Ancient Context to Contemporary Significance*. Winona, MN: Anselm Academic, 2018.

Levine, Amy-Jill, and Marc Zvi Brettler, eds. *The Jewish Annotated New Testament*. 2nd ed. New Revised Standard Version Bible Translation. New York: Oxford University Press, 2017.

McGinn, Sheila E. *The Jesus Movement and the World of the Early Church*. Winona, MN: Anselm Academic, 2014.

McMahon, Christopher. *Reading the Gospels: Biblical Interpretation in the Catholic Tradition*. Winona, MN: Anselm Academic, 2012.

Patte, Daniel, gen. ed. *Global Bible Commentary*. Nashville: Abingdon, 2004.

Perkins, Pheme. *Reading the New Testament: An Introduction*. 3rd ed. Mahwah, NJ: Paulist, 2012.

Powell, Mark Allan. *Introducing the New Testament: A Historical, Literary, and Theological Survey*. Grand Rapids: Baker, 2009.

Scholz, Daniel J. *Jesus in the Gospels and Acts: Introducing the New Testament*. Winona, MN: Anselm Academic, 2013.

Schippe, Cullen, and Chuck Stetson. *The Bible and Its Influence*. Front Royal, VA: BLP, 2006.

Senior, Donald. *Jesus: A Gospel Portrait*. New rev. ed. Mahwah NJ: Paulist, 1992.

Smith, Mitzi, and Yung Suk Kim. *Toward Decentering the New Testament: A Reintroduction*. Eugene, OR: Cascade, 2018.

Sugirtharajah, R. S. *Voices from the Margin: Interpreting the Bible in the Third World*. 3rd ed. Maryknoll, NY: Orbis, 2015.

Van Voorst, Robert E. *Reading the New Testament Today*. Belmont, CA: Thomas Wadsworth, 2005.

Witherington, Ben, III. *Invitation to the New Testament: First Things*. New York: Oxford, 2017.

Wright, N. T., and Michael F. Bird. *The New Testament in Its World: An Introduction to the History, Literature, and Theology of the First Christians*. Grand Rapids: Zondervan Academic, 2019.

Zanzig, Thomas. *Jesus the Christ: A New Testament Portrait*. Winona, MN: Saint Mary's Press, 2000.

Index

Printed in Great Britain
by Amazon